THE SACRED CALL:
A Tribute to Donald Hollowell
— Civil Rights Champion —

by
Louise Hollowell and Martin C. Lehfeldt

FOUR-G Publishers, Inc.
1997

THE SACRED CALL:
A Tribute to Donald Hollowell
—Civil Rights Champion—

*We of the younger generation especially
must feel a sacred call
to that which lies before us.
I go out to do my little part
in helping my untutored brother.
We of this less-favored race
realize that our future
lies chiefly in our own hands.
On ourselves alone will depend
the preservation of our liberties
and the transmission of them in their integrity
to those who will come after us.*

        — from "The New Idealism,"
          Paul L. Robeson's valedictory
          speech at Rutgers College
          graduation exercise in June, 1919

THE SACRED CALL:
A Tribute to Donald Hollowell
— Civil Rights Champion —

by
Louise Hollowell and Martin C. Lehfeldt

FOUR-G Publishers, Inc.
1997

Copyright © 1997
by Donald and Louise Hollowell

All rights reserved. No part of this volume may be reproduced in any form or by any means without the written permission, in advance, of the author.

FOUR-G Publishers Cataloging-in-Publication

Hollowell, Louise
   The sacred call: a tribute to Donald Hollowell — civil rights champion, / by Louise Hollowell and Martin C. Lehfeldt -- Winter Park, FL. FOUR-G Pubs, 1997.
   305 pages ; 23 cm.

   1. Hollowell, Donald L. -- Biography . 2. Afro-American Lawyers -- United States -- Biography. 3. Afro-American Civil Rights Workers -- United States -- Biography. 4. Civil Rights Movement -- United States -- History -- 20th Century. I. Lehfeldt, Martin C. II. Title.

   KF299.A35 H34 1997
   ISBN: 1885066-19-8

Copies of this book are available from:

VANLEE Associates, Inc.
P. O. Box 92423
Morris Brown Station
Atlanta, GA 30314

Or, from the publisher:
FOUR-G Publishers, Inc.
P. O. Box 2249,
Winter Park, FL 32790
(407) 679-9331

Printed in the UNITED STATES OF AMERICA

TABLE OF CONTENTS

ACKNOWLEDGEMENTS vii
FOREWORD ix
INTRODUCTION xi
PROLOGUE 1
  1 On the Twelfth Day of Christmas… 3
  2 From Boyhood to Manhood 27
  3 Alma Mater 40
  4 Fighting For Freedom 49
PHOTOGRAPHS P1-P48
  5 The Way Becomes Clear 83
  6 A New Battlefield 92
  7 On the Cusp of Change 107
  8 The Movement's New Attorney 128
  9 "Mr. Civil Rights" 143
  10 "I Never Thought I Would Live That Long" 155
  11 The Coming of Change 180
  12 A Political Detour 202
  13 Closing the Docket 209
EPILOGUE 229
LIST OF CASES CITED 233
CREDITS AND PERMISSIONS 236
AWARDS AND RECOGNITIONS 237
ABOUT THE CO-AUTHORS 242

DEDICATIONS

First, I dedicate this book to my devoted mother, Mrs. Lillie Scott Thornton, and to the dear and caring parents of my husband, Don — Mr. & Mrs. Harrison Hollowell.

Moreover, I dedicate it to the Inc. Fund and to all those Civil Rights and other organizations that helped to stir the conscience of the people of the State of Georgia and across the nation, and further promoted the cause of equality and justice for all people.

Finally, I dedicate it to those who lost their lives and to those who endured atrocities, brutality, and intimidation in the struggle to acquire full freedom.

Above all, I thank Lane College and the Loyola University Law School of Chicago for giving Don a chance.

I also thank Marvin Arrington and the firm of Arrington and Hollowell for their encouragement and for providing some of the funds to get this project started.

Louise Hollowell

While Vivian W. Henderson was President of Clark College and I served as his Vice President for Development, this gifted leader was my mentor, colleague and friend. From 1969 until his death in 1976, that personal and professional association constituted the most important educational experience in my life. He generously shared his insights and made sure that I was regularly included in his circle of friends and colleagues. From those years I gained a perspective without which I could not have properly assisted with the telling of the Hollowell story, and I therefore gratefully dedicate my contributions to this volume to his memory.

Martin C. Lehfeldt

ACKNOWLEDGMENTS

Many people contributed to this book in ways both great and small. First, of course, the book draws heavily upon the personal recollections and the experiences that affected its principal subject, Donald Hollowell and his wife, Louise, most powerfully. Helping to breathe additional life into their stories are the reminiscences of many other people. Their names and the names of others who helped bring this book to completion are:

William H. Alexander; William Anderson; Joseph Arrington, Jr.; Iris Baker; Julian Bond; Benjamin Brown; Thomas Chatmon; Preston Cobb; Samuel DuBois Cook; Mel L. Davis; Jesse Douglas; Cama Duke; Eugene H. Gadsden; Jack Greenberg; E. D. Hamilton; Bill Hollins; Harry H. Hollowell; Thelma Hollowell; Hamilton Holmes; Julie V. Hunter; Mary Jackson; Margaret D. Jackson; Thomas Jackson; William Jackson; Leroy R. Johnson; Vernon E. Jordan, Jr.; C. B. (Chevene) King, Sr.; Lonnie C. King;

Alice Lewis; Elridge W. McMillan; Merlissie Middleton; Howard Moore, Jr.; Michael Morgan; Constance Baker Motley; Murlean Murray; Vickie Norman; William Outlaw; Corinne Patterson; Eddye W. Peacock; John H. Ruffin; A. C. Searls; Charles Sherrod; P. Randolph Shy; Leahnora Simmons; Joseph H. Stevens, Sr.; Calvin Turner; Loretta Y. Turman; Elbert P. Tuttle; Horace T. Ward; John Watkins; Charles E. Wells; and Charles L. Weltner.

The book is not intended to be a scholarly work and therefore does not cite every bibliographic or legal reference. Nonetheless, even a highly personalized account of this kind depends heavily upon other sources. Among those publications that helped to provide the historical backdrop against which the story of Donald Hollowell unfolds are Atlanta's newspapers — the *Constitution, Fulton Daily Report, Daily World, Inquirer, Journal* and *Voice* — and the *Pittsburgh Courier* and *Southwest Georgian.* Other principal works upon which we have drawn are:

Atlanta Rising: The Invention of an International City, 1946-1996, Frederick Allen, Longstreet Press, Inc., 1996.

Bearing the Cross: Martin Luther King, Jr. and the Southern Christian Leadership Conference, David J. Garrow, Vintage Books, 1988.

Before the Mayflower: A History of Black America, Lerone Bennett, Jr., Penguin Books (5th edition), 1982.

In My Place, Charlayne Hunter-Gault, Farrar Straus Giroux, 1992.

My Soul is Rested: The Story of the Civil Rights Movement in the Deep South, Howell Raines, Penguin Books, 1983.

Parting the Waters: America in the King Years, 1954-63, Taylor Branch, Simon and Schuster, 1988.

Race and the Shaping of Twentieth Century Atlanta, Ronald H. Baylor, The University of North Carolina Press, 1996.

Where Peachtree Meets Sweet Auburn: The Saga of Two Families and the Making of Atlanta, Gary M. Pomerantz, Scribner, 1996.

Several friends and relatives performed the valued service of reviewing the manuscript as it moved through various drafts. They include: Julian Bond, Elizabeth Lehfeldt, Linda Graham Lehfeldt, Elridge W. McMillan, Michael Morgan and Mel L. Davis.

FOREWORD

It is a long way from 1939 Indiana Street, Wichita, Kansas to the making of a soldier, devoted husband, civil rights lawyer, community leader, and public servant, who now in retirement is receiving reverence, honor and deep appreciation from a cross section of the community. This book is about that journey made with great dignity and unparalled achievement. Herein described, with simple eloquence and elegance, is Donald L. Hollowell's life as a servant of the law and a drum major for justice. It is also about his life with and love for his wife, Louise Hollowell — his soulmate, confidante and true partner for over fifty-four years.

This book is a documentary about the journey of one member of an exclusive, small, unheralded, unsung, and, at times, unappreciated, heroic group of black lawyers in the South who put their lives on the line in the fight for equal opportunity and racial equality. They travelled the dark and lonely roads of the South to segregated court rooms with all white juries and Jim Crow judges, advocating and pleading that justice run down like water and righteousness like a mighty stream.

The untold story of this book is the enormous influence Hollowell exerted on the lives and experience of young black lawyers. They include senior federal district judge, Horace T. Ward, Jr.; Howard Moore, Jr., now practicing in California; Atlanta circuit judge, William H. Alexander; Marvin Arrington, senior partner at Arrington & Hollowell and President of the Atlanta City Council; and myself.

At the Gate City Bar Association dinner on February 20, 1997, which honored Hollowell and its founders, I tried to speak for all of us blessed with an association with Hollowell:

> *We went to work for Hollowell thinking we knew more than we did. We got a post-graduate education in the law and life that can never be duplicated.*
>
> *More than the years of law school classes and lectures, it was Don Hollowell's patience and understanding, his sharing and teaching, that turned us into lawyers. And*

more than simply lawyers, for as we watched and participated in his valiant battles with an uncaring, unresponsive system, we came to understand that good lawyering has to include a passion for truth, a reverence for justice, and a respect for process.

We learned from Don Hollowell that battles lost today can be won tomorrow, and that the law that was used against us could be turned to protect us. And we learned from Don Hollowell that our strength came not from our law degrees but from the community that nurtured us.

This book is a fitting and proper recitation of the life and work of a good and great man.

> Vernon E. Jordan, Jr.
> Washington, D.C.
> April, 1997

INTRODUCTION

During World War II black men heard and answered the trumpet call to arms that sounded across America. After all, did they not belong to this so-called democracy "of the people, by the people, and for the people?" Thousands of them served with devotion and distinction both at home and in far-off lands. Many of them fought valiantly and many died to make things better for their homeland and their allies. Yet throughout the war they also had to fight another battle against the inequalities and injustices perpetrated upon them by the segregated military system and its white soldiers.

Out of the Midwest came Donald Hollowell, a young man of twenty-three, already a veteran of military service, who was recalled to duty, thereby interrupting his college education to fight for freedom. From the first day that he reported for duty in Georgia he encountered officially sanctioned rank discrimination and abuse. The experience instilled in him a passion for justice that never disappeared.

Don and I first met in 1941 during his service at Fort Benning, Georgia. Over the next several months, as we visited each other and attended football games, church services, dances and other social events together, we fell in love and married. He was intelligent and handsome, but one of his most attractive features was his resistance to any form of discrimination against black people. I shall never forget the thrill and admiration I felt as he would regularly remove "For Colored Only" signs from the public conveyances on which we were forced to ride as second-class citizens.

A few years after the war, on a trip to Leavenworth, Kansas, we visited Professor Earl M. Lawson, a highly respected elementary school principal who had been one of Don's early coaches and mentors. Professor Lawson, who had been an officer in World War I, was delighted when Don presented him with the gift of a sign that he had "liberated" from a bus he rode one weekend from Atlanta to Columbus. Lawson, who proudly displayed the memento of attempted intimidation in his den for many years, was most pleased that one of his former students who had grown to manhood in a climate of oppressive racial discrimination had refused to accept it. No matter who tried to pin a badge of inferiority on him, Don Hollowell refused to be labeled in this insulting way.

These early examples of relatively passive protest were the embryo of passionate activism that sprang to full growth when Don determined to become a lawyer. After much reflection and some vacillation, he rejected the tempting option of selecting a career that would have kept him on the sidelines of the struggle for justice and instead opted to prepare himself for a life of active involvement.

Even after he earned a law degree from Loyola University, the highly-regarded Jesuit institution in Chicago, there were temptations to stay away from the thick of the battle. Friends encouraged him to remain in the Midwest, and his father made him a splendid offer to move to California. However, since I had established my business and residence in Atlanta and was pursuing my academic career there, he decided to explore his chances of succeeding in that city. Encouraged by what he learned from both black and white lawyers in the city, he made the decision to adopt the South as his home.

Within only two years, drawing upon his own initiative and the support of good friends and family members, he established himself as an attorney who was ready to champion the rights of underprivileged black clients and to lend his leadership to the ongoing struggle for social progress and racial integration. I am proud that he counts my love and support and the strong encouragement of my mother as major factors that contributed to his perseverance during often difficult times.

Don has received many honors and awards, but the full story of his development as a man and an attorney has never been told. It has been my dream for many years to see his biography in print. Now, at last, drawing upon his and my recollections and interviews with people who know him well, we will relate to you the story of this extraordinary man.

Louise Hollowell

PROLOGUE

On May 17, 1954, the U.S. Supreme Court ruled unanimously that racially segregated education in public schools was unconstitutional.

However, the initial shouts of rejoicing by those who had fought for this historic victory soon stilled to a murmur. It quickly became clear that their national government had little desire to enforce this new law of the land. The dream seemed once again to be deferred.

But then protest began to bubble up, especially through the hard, resistant soil of the Southern way of life. Courageous black families pushed for and, with the reluctant intervention of the federal government, succeeded in desegregating Central High School in Little Rock, Arkansas. Several years later a small group of ministers and other community leaders in Montgomery, Alabama, organized a successful city-wide boycott of the segregated public transportation system.

Finally, as the decade of the 1960s began and a new generation of men and women, both black and white, began to grasp for the reins of leadership, years of smoldering, pent-up frustration came to a head. The student-led Civil Rights Movement burst into being, and the medium of television made it almost impossible for anyone to ignore what was happening.

As the Movement swept across the old Confederacy, the battle lines steadily shifted from the streets to the courts. Thousands of men, women and children could march and demonstrate and dramatize their case before television audiences around the world. Yet, after the cameras were turned off and the protestors were led to jail, the disposition of their cases was in the hands of the lawyers.

But which lawyers? Very few Southern white attorneys would challenge the status quo by accepting clients whose goal was to overturn it. There was a limit to the number of lawyers the overworked and slimly staffed NAACP Legal Defense and Educational Fund, Incorporated (Inc. Fund) could dispatch from New York. Furthermore, plaintiffs had to be represented by local counsel with certification from the states in which the cases were being heard. The burden of legal representation thus fell upon a handful of Southern black attorneys who had the training, talent and temperament to handle these difficult cases. They were isolated warriors. Like knights errant of a more ancient age, they roamed a hostile region, seeking to defend the weak and powerless. The grail they sought was justice.

One of those champions was Donald Hollowell. During the better part of a decade — between the 1954 Supreme Court decision and passage of the 1964 Civil Rights Act — he emerged as the principal civil rights attorney in the State of Georgia.

The white newspapers of the day sometimes described him simply as the "Negro lawyer for the plaintiffs." In most of the later histories of that era, his name appears only in passing references and footnotes. Yet the arrival of this "field lawyer," as he sometimes modestly described himself, in courthouses throughout Georgia was a powerful statement. For his clients, long suppressed by the very judicial system that was supposed to protect them, his presence as their legal representative emboldened them to seek the rights that belonged to them. For his opponents, like local sheriffs and judges whose behavior had for years escaped surveillance, his appearance signaled that those days were coming to an end.

This book tells the story of some of the forces that shaped him and some of the battles he fought. As such, it is a long overdue tribute to him, his colleagues and his clients for the dues they paid to advance the cause of equal treatment under the law.

1

ON THE TWELFTH DAY OF CHRISTMAS...

It was January 6, 1961, the 12th day of Christmas. The holidays had come and gone, and Donald Hollowell was waiting with escalating nervousness for a present that still hadn't arrived. What the well known Atlanta civil rights attorney longed to see was a ruling from U. S. District Judge William A. Bootle.[1]

Three weeks earlier, Bootle had concluded five days of hearings in Athens, eighty miles east of the capital city. At issue was the question of whether the racially segregated University of Georgia would admit Hollowell's clients, Hamilton Holmes and Charlayne Hunter, as its first Negro students. They had been trying to matriculate for a year and a half. It had taken until now to overcome a jumble of bureaucratic obstacles and to pursue all available administrative remedies before a federal judge would consider the case that was listed on the docket as *Holmes v. Danner*. (Danner was the University's Registrar.) In the meantime, Miss Hunter had enrolled at Detroit's Wayne State University and Holmes had started his undergraduate work at Morehouse College in Atlanta.

Bootle had offered no clue about when he might render a decision, and no one had an inkling of what it might be. Nevertheless, the judge, like everyone else close to the case, knew only too well that the deadline for second semester registration was fast approaching.

Hollowell was tired. Even before the student sit-ins and demonstrations bubbled up in early 1960, the NAACP Legal Defense and Education Fund (known colloquially as the Inc. Fund) had been preparing to launch a new legal barrage on the University of Georgia. It tapped him to be the chief counsel for its team of lawyers.

The State of Georgia readied itself to return fire. By the time Holmes and Hunter applied for admission during the summer of 1959 before what they hoped would be their freshman year, the University's guns were primed. It smugly responded that it required first-year students to live in dormitories and that it had completely allotted all housing space. As Holmes would later recall, "By that time, the dormitories probably were full," to which he added, "It may have been the only honest answer we were to get."

Through a complex series of administrative maneuvers and delays, the university had successfully managed to block the students' attempts at admission for more than a year despite their clearly impressive credentials. Miss Hunter had been president of the Turner High School honor society, editor-in-chief of the newspaper and a member of the student council. She was the daughter of Major Charles Hunter, an African Methodist Episcopal chaplain with the U.S. Army stationed in Texas, and Althea Hunter, manager of the Wilson Realty Company in Atlanta.

Her classmate, Holmes, was the oldest child of another middle-class family. In 1946, his father, Alfred F. Holmes, a businessman who then owned a tombstone company, had moved the family to Detroit for five years, but they were Atlantans. They were not strangers to the movement for equal opportunity for Negroes. The young man's father and his physician grandfather, H. M. Holmes, Sr., had already successfully challenged the segregation of Atlanta's public golf courses. It was a subject especially dear to Alfred Holmes' heart. In 1958 he had been the national Negro amateur golfer of the year.

The son's athletic ability came from both sides of the family. His mother had won tennis championships. Holmes himself played halfback on and co-captained the football team at Turner. He was also co-captain of the basketball team on which he played guard. He was president of the class his junior and senior years and graduated as valedictorian with a 3.83 average.

In a foreshadowing of things to come, on the evening of their graduation ceremonies in Atlanta's Municipal Auditorium, the program included a series of readings by Miss Hunter and other members of the class narrated by Holmes. The collection of selections bore the title, "Moments of Decision."

Hollowell and the other Negro leaders who conferred with the young man and his family were not naive about the opposition he might encounter. Initially, therefore, they had proposed that he seek admission to Georgia State or Georgia Tech, feeling that the racial climate within the city would be safer. Holmes, however, who already was considering a career as a physician, preferred to attend an institution that would provide the best possible foundation for medical school. He held out for the University of Georgia. Charlayne Hunter too felt that her interest in journalism would be best served by undergraduate work at the university in Athens.

While state officials continued to stonewall them, the Inc. Fund team kept hammering away on the legal front. The lawyers were determined that this case would not suffer the same fate as Horace Ward's unsuccessful attempt to enroll in the university's law school in 1950.

With fateful irony, Ward, who eventually graduated from Northwestern University's law school, had become Hollowell's first law partner in September, 1960. He brought with him a special passion to see this case achieve what his own efforts had not been able to accomplish.[2]

Working closely with Hollowell and Ward was Constance Baker Motley, the Inc. Fund's forty-year old principal trial attorney, who already was a veteran of landmark legal battles throughout the South. The two knew each other well. They had worked closely together when they represented the students who a few years earlier had sought to desegregate the Georgia State College of Business Administration.

Mrs. Motley, as Charlayne Hunter-Gault describes her, was a "no-nonsense" kind of person. There was a wonderfully warm, motherly and humorful side to this woman, who would regularly leave her attorney husband and young son in the North to conduct wide-ranging and dangerous forays through the hostile Southern terrain. In the courtroom, though, her stern face and powerful frame demanded attention and respect. That "Motley woman" as a South Carolina reporter (who chose not to honor her with the title of "Mrs.") called her was a force with which to be reckoned.[3]

The attorneys' unwavering attempts to break through the University logjam had brought them to the Macon court of Judge Bootle. Throughout the process he had scrupulously ruled that Holmes and Hunter would first have to complete all university requirements for admission before he could consider further action. By late 1960, the plaintiffs had meticulously negotiated every one of the mazes placed in their path. All that remained at that stage in the labyrinth through which the state was forcing them to maneuver were pre-registration interviews.

The two students dutifully appeared for a meeting with the Registrar, Walter Danner. After interviewing them, the physically diminutive official denied admission to Holmes and declared that Miss Hunter was ineligible to enroll for the winter quarter. It would be too difficult, he asserted, to reconcile her credits from Wayne State's quarter system with Georgia's semester system.

Their attorneys continued to press for a judicial ruling. Bootle at last agreed to schedule final hearings on the suit in Athens. For five days, from December 12 to 16, before a steadily growing crowd of spectators in the second floor courtroom of the marble post office building, the federal judge listened to testimony brought forward by both sides. Holmes would later recall with awe the powerful impression that Hollowell and the other attorneys made upon him. He had never before been in a courtroom, but watching the cool and masterful way in which "Negro lawyers were taking on the State of Georgia" became an enduring memory.

His lawyers were loaded for bear. Motley, assisted by Vernon Jordan,[4] Hollowell's law clerk, and Gerald Taylor, the Registrar of Morehouse College, had been virtually commuting from Atlanta to Athens for several weeks to research the University's own admissions files. On each trip they would pore through the records, looking for evidence to contradict the University's contention that race was not the issue in its refusal to admit Negro students.

Jordan at last discovered one of the nuggets for which they had been mining — the record of a young white transfer student from another university on the same kind of academic calendar as Wayne State who had been admitted for the winter quarter.

Drawing upon this kind of meticulous research, Hollowell and Motley intensively questioned President O. C. Aderhold and other officials of the university, continuing to catch them in an embarrassing series of contradictions. Rather than simply reading Holmes' many high school accomplishments into the record, Hollowell instead put Miss Hunter — whose credentials had not been challenged — on the stand and through an adroit series of questions elicited her account of her classmate's achievements.

In response, Danner reported that he found Holmes' answers during his interview to be "evasive" and "immoral." To substantiate his claims, he noted that Holmes, when asked about previous arrests, had failed to mention a traffic ticket. Danner also cited Holmes' frequenting of establishments on Hunter Street — where Hollowell's office was located — which he described as a red-light district. The registrar went on to insist that he had not denied admission to Charlayne Hunter; rather, he claimed, University rules permitted only junior college transfers and probationary students to enroll during the winter quarter.

Though it was a patent lie, every University official denied under oath that the two Negroes were being denied admission on the basis of their race.[5] Before Bootle adjourned the hearing, Motley employed a tactic she had used in other desegregation cases. She extracted from Danner the sworn concession that he would favor the admission of a qualified Negro to the University. Hamilton Holmes and the lawyers returned to Atlanta. Charlayne Hunter flew back to Detroit. Judge Bootle retired to Macon to ponder all that he had heard. And Don Hollowell waited with increased impatience. Now it was January 6, the Feast of the Epiphany that celebrates the arrival of the Magi bearing gifts to the manger in Bethlehem. Less liturgically minded Georgians were more concerned about the future of the University's football team. Eight-column headlines in the early edition of the *Atlanta Journal*, the city's afternoon newspaper, that Friday announced that Johnny Griffith, the freshman coach, would succeed the legendary Wallace Butts, varsity coach of the Bulldogs for the past twenty-two years. Elsewhere on the front page another report speculated that Governor Vandiver's opening speech to the state legislature the next week would focus on major budget issues.

As the day wound down, though, Hollowell was reading a different document — the holiday present for which he had been waiting. He and his colleagues pored over the twenty-eight page ruling that had just arrived from Judge Bootle's office in Macon. At last they came to the sentences for which they had been arguing since Hamilton Holmes and Charlayne Hunter graduated from high school in 1959:

...it is found by this court that the two plaintiffs are fully qualified for immediate admission and would already have been admitted had it not been for their race and color.... It is the further intent of this injunction that the defendant and other persons... are hereby enjoined from refusing to permit the plaintiffs to enroll.

The suit that Hollowell and his fellow attorneys had filed also sought five thousand dollars in damages to Holmes and Hamilton. Bootle had declined to grant that award, but Hollowell was satisfied. He had the court order he needed.

There was no time to waste. The deadline for University enrollment was Monday, only three days away. After nearly two years of steering his case through every roadblock the State could throw in his path, Hollowell had no illusions that a federal order would suddenly produce the registration materials that the two students would need. The only way to beat the deadline would be to drive to Athens and pick them up. He snatched up the telephone and began organizing the trip.

The next morning Hamilton Holmes and Hollowell climbed into the big black Chrysler of Dr. Samuel Williams, the Friendship Baptist Church pastor and head of the Atlanta NAACP. Hollowell, as always, was dressed with understated elegance, wearing a dark overcoat and gray fedora. Accompanying the three men were Holmes' father and Julian Bond, who joined the group as a reporter for the *Atlanta Inquirer*.[6]

News of Bootle's ruling had reached the campus the previous evening. When they heard the reports, some student leaders had gone so far as to call for and even to predict calm. As a result, there was some initial hope that the court-ordered desegregation of the 175-year old university might proceed without incident. After all, only four days earlier, two Negro freshmen had enrolled at the University of Tennessee without serious difficulty. However, by late that Friday night, the uneasy quiet that had pervaded the institution since word of the ruling had reached Athens vanished.

Hundreds of milling undergraduates began to burn gasoline-soaked crosses and throw firecrackers as they screamed their protests against racial integration. William Tate, the Dean of Men, single-handedly tried to enforce calm, but no sooner would he disassemble one flaming cross than another would appear to take its place. Confronting another crowd at the university arch, he tore down an effigy of Hamilton Holmes and confiscated student identification cards. The university police, meanwhile, limited their efforts to confining the disorder to the campus.

By late Saturday morning, when Hollowell and his client stepped from Williams' car and strode on to the University property, the mayhem had stopped. However, the campus still felt like enemy territory. Without hesitation, though, the attorney sedately led his party past reporters and curious onlookers to the administration building. The arrival of the Atlanta entourage caught University officials completely by surprise, as did Hollowell's almost matter-of-fact demeanor. Just before the noon closing time for the registrar's office, he laid a copy of Bootle's order on Walter Danner's desk.

Danner, who had not seen Hollowell since the attorney had last questioned him on the witness stand in December, said nothing. Surely, though, the small, slightly-built administrator must have wondered to himself about the events that had led to his new notoriety as the University's chief records keeper. He didn't bother to study the court order. He knew what it said. Instead, he quietly handed over a packet of registration materials and reminded Holmes that he would have to come back on Monday to select his courses. The young man assured Danner that he would return. Hollowell informed the reporters who had gathered to record this historic moment that Charlayne Hunter, who was still in Detroit, also would be present to register for classes. Then, calmly stepping outside the building and lighting a cigarette, he led the way back to the automobile for the return trip to Atlanta.

Even as Hollowell was escorting Hamilton Holmes to the University, the state was organizing another end run. When Judge Bootle's ruling arrived on Friday, Governor Ernest Vandiver[7] had hurriedly scheduled a session with his attorneys at the executive mansion in Ansley Park for Saturday morning.

At 10:30 a.m., while Hollowell and his party were driving eastward toward Athens, the governor was meeting with the state's top legal guns. Attorney General Eugene Cook was there. So was B. D. (Buck) Murphy, who a decade earlier had been deputized by Governor Talmadge as special counsel to fight Horace Ward's attempts to enroll at the

University. Cook and Murphy were joined by Freeman Leverett, a member of Cook's office; Griffin Bell, the governor's chief of staff, and Henry Neal, Vandiver's legal aide.

When the meeting broke up at 12:35 p.m., Cook had his orders. At Governor Vandiver's direction, he immediately drove to Macon to deliver a motion for a stay of Bootle's injunction. He also stopped by the home of the court clerk, John P. Cowart, to file the brief formal notice that the state intended to appeal the decision. The crux of the appeal was a plea to give the General Assembly a chance to act.[8] A principal issue was the 1956 measure passed by the legislature which called for a mandatory cutoff of state funds to the University if it were to admit Negro students. The effect of that action, of course, would virtually require that the institution be closed.

Without specifying whether the legislature would move to change the law, the motion Cook carried to Macon noted that a stay of the injunction could ward off "the possibility of great hurt and damage to more than 7,000 students." Although it was the weekend, Bootle agreed to set a hearing for 9:30 a.m., Monday, in his Macon courtroom, and sent a message to Hollowell and Motley to request their presence. Meanwhile, O. C. Aderhold, the University's president, informed the press that unless he received contrary instructions, his institution was prepared to admit Holmes and Hunter.

At four o'clock on Saturday afternoon, Dean of Students Joe Williams convened a group of student leaders to discuss the situation and express the hope that they would use their efforts to encourage order. Various student organizations met and began drawing up resolutions. Some went on record as favoring both open schools and segregation, without offering any suggestion about how to accomplish these contradictory goals, and sent their statement to the Georgia legislature. Smaller numbers of them called for open schools at any cost. A more vocal minority chanted slogans of defiance to all change.

On Sunday, January 8, Charlayne Hunter returned on a flight from Detroit to Atlanta. Hollowell interrupted his preparations for the appearance before Judge Bootle to join a swarm of her relatives and other friends who waited to meet her at the airport.

Meanwhile, Governor Vandiver and his advisers spent much of the day in strategy sessions with legislators, members of the Board of Regents and other education officials. Before Bootle's injunction, the governor in his State of the State address to the legislature had been preparing to recommend spending measures which would total $400,000,000, including $100,000,000 for highway maintenance. Even those whopping increases now seemed of marginal concern.

That same Sunday, the day before Holmes was scheduled to complete his registration in Athens, the *Atlanta Daily World* matter-of-factly reported in its sports section an achievement that might have been a lucky omen. According to the newspaper, the young man's grandfather, Dr. H. M. Holmes, Sr., had managed a different kind of achievement. The previous Wednesday, while playing golf, the 77-year old physician had picked up a four wood and shot the first hole-in-one of his career on the fifth hole of the Adams Park course.

The formidable Mrs. Motley also returned to Atlanta from New York. Early Monday morning she joined Hollowell as the two set out in his light-green Dodge on yet another southward trek to Macon.

On the west side of Atlanta, the two students were readying themselves for their historic trip to the University of Georgia. Miss Hunter and her mother climbed into Althea Hunter's automobile with Vernon Jordan. Horace Ward joined Holmes and his father in a second vehicle, and the two cars headed east.

The six Atlantans arrived in Athens without benefit of security. They left their vehicles and walked beneath the landmark arch that framed the main entrance to the heart of the old campus. Towering over the entourage was the six-feet, five-inch Jordan who steered the small group past waiting reporters and clusters of curious and often angry students. Accompanied by Deans Williams and Tate, they began the registration process. Their itinerary was barely underway, however, when they heard students cheering. Jordan looked back at the door behind them, where students were peering through the transom above it and heard one of them proclaim, "That big nigger lawyer's not smiling now." A few minutes later he took a telephone call that explained the reason for the jubilation. Judge Bootle had stayed his own earlier ruling.

Hollowell and Motley, standing before the judge in Macon, were as dumbfounded as the state's attorneys were quietly ecstatic. What was going on? Bootle explained that he was issuing the stay in order to give the State of Georgia the opportunity to appeal ("test the correctness of," as he put it) his ruling of the previous Friday.

Hollowell was deeply concerned. His clients already were registering for classes in Athens. Another delay at this point could defer their admission until the next school term. As soon as he and Mrs. Motley could escape from Bootle's court and find a telephone, she placed a call to Judge Elbert P. Tuttle,[9] Chief Justice of the U.S. Fifth District Court in Atlanta.

It was already after eleven o'clock in the morning. Could Judge Tuttle, asked Mrs. Motley, vacate Bootle's stay? Tuttle asked her whether they had filed a notice of appeal. She assured him that they would, and he agreed to wait in his Atlanta office for a 2:30 p.m. meeting with them. The two climbed back into Hollowell's car for the drive back to Atlanta. As they roared northward up the highway, well above the speed limit with Hollowell at the wheel, they passed Buck Murphy, the state's special counsel. Hollowell turned to his colleague and said, "If the State Patrol stops us, here's the story. We're going to tell them that we're with Murphy, and there's a federal judge waiting for us."

In Athens, Hollowell's two clients with their parents and other attorneys had left the campus and sought sanctuary in the home of Ray Ware, a local Negro businessman in whose home they had sometimes gathered during the December hearings. Jordan got on the telephone and learned that Hollowell and Motley were somewhere en route to Judge Tuttle's chambers. There was nothing to do but sit and wait. Joined by a handful of reporters, the group engaged in desultory conversation or watched television. Miss Hunter fell asleep.

Hollowell and Motley were only marginally late for their appointment with Judge Tuttle at the imposing U. S. Post Office building on Forsyth Street in Atlanta. They arrived in his chambers at 2:32 p.m. It became immediately evident that he had no patience with the latest steps in the legal minuet that seemingly refused to end. Bootle's stay, he declared, had been "improvidently granted," and he promptly overturned it. His order observed "that the quickest disposition that can be made of this case... is the best solution not only for the Negroes, but for all concerned."

Hollowell called the Ware home. He asked Hamilton Holmes, who answered the telephone, to put Jordan on the line. After informing his young law clerk of the latest news, he told him to escort the two students back to the University. Soon thereafter, they resumed their registration process and had their pictures taken for student identification cards. Their circuit of the campus concluded at the registrar's office where they filed their academic schedules. At last they were official undergraduates, and the University of Georgia had its first Negro students.

There was no question in their attorneys' minds that the state would appeal Judge Tuttle's decision. Hollowell and Motley left the federal building and returned to Hollowell's office on Hunter Street. For the rest of the afternoon they assembled all of the pertinent documentation from the judicial jitterbugging of the past several days and dictated the essential points as well as the outline of a legal motion to the Inc. Fund office in New York City. It would be up to their colleagues in the north to convert that information into a response that could counteract what was sure to be a petition from the State of Georgia to the U.S. Supreme Court.

While Charlayne Hunter and Hamilton Holmes, exhausted by the surreal stop-and-go events of the day in Athens, returned to Atlanta and tried to get some sleep, Hollowell and Motley were ready for a bit of relaxation. Mrs. Motley was staying with her cousin, Mamie Thomas, the wife of R. E. Thomas, another Negro attorney. The Hollowells joined them and other friends that evening for a party. Even as they were celebrating the historic results of the day, though, news came over the television that Governor Vandiver was preparing a statement that he would present at midnight. There seemed to be no doubt what its content would be. Invoking the state law that prohibited the public funding of integrated schools, he was going to order the closing of the University.

"Connie," Hollowell announced, as he pulled himself from a chair, "We've got some more work to do." The two attorneys left the party and returned to his office. There they went to work drafting another series of motions that enjoined the governor, the Board of Regents, and, as Mrs. Motley remembers, "anyone else we could think of," from pursuing the draconian course of action that Vandiver had in mind. Hollowell himself typed the final versions.

As they worked through the night on Hunter Street, the lights also were burning brightly at the capitol. In addition to readying his midnight message, the governor and his legal aides — as Hollowell and Motley had anticipated — were also preparing their appeal to the U.S. Supreme Court. When they finished, Vandiver then dispatched Cook, Leverett and another aide, Charles H. Allen, to Washington on a state-owned plane to seek judicial relief.

Meanwhile, news of the governor's likely action had reached Athens. More than a thousand students, anticipating the closing of the university, began marching and yelling. Some drove their cars through the campus and town, blocking traffic along Route 78. Exuberance soon escalated into disorder. A large Confederate flag appeared, and segregation chants filled the night air. Soon a marching band was leading another crowd. A group of freshmen burned crosses by the tennis courts and the track field. Firecrackers seemed to be exploding everywhere. The only attempts to impose order — since the police showed no signs of caring — came from Dean Tate. The burly administrator again and again would wade into the crowds, yelling for calm and trying to identify the leaders and disperse them. The rowdiness continued well past midnight.

Hollowell and Motley finished their work and returned home for a few hours sleep. As he laid down near dawn, he was feeling deathly ill. His wife called their physician, Clinton Warner, who threw a coat over his pajamas and quickly drove to the Hollowell home. After examining his patient, he announced that he was going to administer an injection. Warner didn't identify its contents, but he told Louise Hollowell that it was not a full-strength shot. Then he restated the message to her husband, assuring him that the medication would not prevent him from being alert for his appearance before Judge Bootle. However, he would require a driver for the trip.

Events were moving swiftly that morning, Tuesday, January 10. Georgia's legal delegation entered the imposing U.S. Supreme Court building at 10:45 a.m. In Cook's briefcase was a seven-page petition to stop the ordered integration of the university until there had been a formal appeal. In effect, it asked for the reinstatement of Judge Bootle's second order which had put the registration of the two Negro students on hold until Judge Tuttle overruled him. Cook handed the petition, whose major author was Leverett, to Edmund Cullinan, the Deputy Clerk of the Court, with instructions that it be delivered to Justice Hugo Black, the supervising judge of the Fifth Circuit.

The representatives of the State of Georgia might have felt less confident had they realized that Hollowell and Motley's dictated motion already had beaten them to the punch. Earlier that morning, Jack Greenberg, the Legal Defense Fund attorney who would later become the Inc. Fund's chief counsel and director, had arrived from New York and preceded Cook into the Supreme Court building where he filed the motion on behalf of Hollowell's clients. In effect, it opposed the State of Georgia's petition even before that motion arrived, arguing that there was nothing further to litigate.

The Deputy Clerk would deliver both documents later that morning. As chance would have it, when Cook and his companions walked down the hallway toward the exit only seventeen minutes after their arrival, they passed the seventy-four year old Justice Black who was just leaving the building's barber shop. No one spoke.

Even as the Georgia officials sought help in Washington, Mrs. Motley and Hollowell were racing back to Judge Bootle in Macon. Despite the injection administered by Dr. Warner, Hollowell still was too sick to drive. He reclined as best he could on the back seat, propped up by pillows, while his law clerk, Vernon Jordan, as Mrs. Motley tells the story, decided he "would try to get the car up to ninety miles an hour."

Judge Bootle listened to the plaintiffs' and the states' attorneys for two hours. When the session ended, Hollowell and Motley had what they wanted — a temporary injunction restraining the governor from cutting off funds to the University.

In Athens, the University's administration council had gone into session at eight o'clock that morning. In response to the governor's midnight order, it already had a mimeographed statement declaring a "holiday" which would go into effect when Holmes and Hunter appeared for their classes. Crowds of students gathered in front of the Commerce-Journalism building where Miss Hunter's noon class in journalism ethics was scheduled.

At 2:25 p.m. that same Tuesday afternoon, Miss Hunter and Holmes arrived in Athens. A crowd of several hundred white students had gathered to continue the protest. Led by Dean Williams, the two Negro students bypassed the protesters and entered the administration building from the rear. The deception didn't work for long. As soon as the crowd learned what had happened, it swept into the building and began to roar, "Two-four-six-eight, we don't want to integrate." Paul Kea, Assistant Director of Admissions, climbed on a bench in the hallway and demanded silence. When he turned his back, the chanting started again. This time Dean Tate[10] and other administrators ordered the hall cleared. It was the first time that university officials had officially ordered students to stop protesting.

By Tuesday afternoon, Attorney General Cook had received the message that the full U. S. Supreme Court had denied the state's motion. Justice Black, rather than acting unilaterally, had chosen to present the petition to all of his colleagues who were in session that day. Georgia's last-ditch effort to temporize further had failed.

In the meantime Vandiver had also learned of Bootle's latest injunction. He sent a telegram to the judge, protesting the decision but making it clear that he would not defy the order that banned the cutoff of funds.

That Tuesday evening Federal Marshal Bill Littlefield formally served the injunction notice on the Governor at the executive mansion. Vandiver, insulted by this tangible legal reproof, was furious. It was for him as if the federal authorities were rubbing his nose in their power to interfere with state government. Besides, he had already announced his intention of complying with the order. Going to a typewriter, he personally pounded out a letter of protest, concluding with "we have indeed arrived at a sad state of affairs."

While the Governor fumed and typed, an impromptu party began to come together at the Hollowells' home on Dale Creek Drive in Collier Heights. Word of the Supreme Court's decision and of Judge Bootle's ruling was spreading through town. Friends and associates, both Negro and white, gathered to celebrate and began to chant a joyful litany that summed up the events of the past forty-eight hours: "From Bootle to Tuttle to Black and Back." Vernon Jordan and his vivacious wife, Shirley, ushered the group to the Hollowell's den where they led the celebrants in dancing the "Mashed Potato."

In Athens, although there were scattered, noisy demonstrations and general rowdiness outside Myers Hall, where Miss Hunter's room was located, the campus was relatively quiet. As Miss Hunter, who had converted to Catholicism in 1959, tried to study, her eyes turned often to the small carved figure of the Virgin Mary she had carried with her through the entire ordeal. The other comfort for both her and Holmes[11] was the knowledge that they could always reach Hollowell. His deep, calm voice and fatherly manner had been marvelous antidotes to the hysteria that swirled about them since their first trip to the campus.

No crowds waited outside Charlayne Hunter's dormitory when she emerged on Wednesday morning, January 11. Dean Tate, who had driven to Holmes' residence to pick him up, discovered the young man already walking fearlessly by himself toward the campus.

By nine o'clock that morning, the two students were seated in their first classes. Miss Hunter did not have to push her way through any throngs as she joined other undergraduates for the introductory psychology course. Hamilton Holmes' appearance for a zoology class similarly generated more curiosity than active protest. Both students later met at Dunlap Memorial Library for an orientation to that facility and then continued to the rest of their classes. Reporters did besiege them outside the academic buildings and scattered clusters of students subjected them to calls of "Nigger, go home," and chants of "Dog food, dog food." Nonetheless, the day proceeded with reasonable calm. As ordered by President Aderhold, Dean Williams escorted Miss Hunter about the campus, and Dean Tate was Holmes' constant companion.

By evening there was strong evidence that the University had weathered the storm. Miss Hunter returned to her dormitory and Holmes to the Killian home. Many of the other students went to the gymnasium to watch a basketball game with Georgia Tech. To the dismay of the local fans, Tech won the game in overtime, 89-80, after tying the score in the last second of regulation play. The frustrating loss quickly became a catalyst for the release of a volatile buildup of sublimated rage.

As the crowd spilled out of Woodruff Hall, all hell broke loose. The crowd became a mob, screaming "Let's go get the niggers," and rushing toward "Ag Hill" on the south portion of the campus. Later it was possible to determine that outsiders, including members of the Klan, instigated and orchestrated some of the violence, but at the time there was too much chaos to sort out the cause. Both students and townspeople began a firecracker and rock-throwing melee along Lumpkin Street outside of Miss Hunter's dormitory. Reporters were favorite targets, and some were injured. Dean Tate dispatched members of the football team to guard the doors to Myers Hall, but elsewhere there was no control. Policemen again stood and watched.

On Thursday morning, January 12, the governor issued a proclamation written the previous night that ordered the removal of Holmes and Hunter from the campus. Citing the danger to their lives and to the lives and property of others and noting the inability of local authorities to maintain order, he directed the state patrol to transport the two students back to Atlanta. The established order had won yet another firefight. It was only salt in the wounds when Peter Zack Geer, the governor's executive secretary, praised publicly the mobs whose violence had necessitated the order.

Concerned for his clients' safety, even though they were back in Atlanta, Hollowell called Herbert Jenkins, the police chief, with whom he had a cordial relationship, and requested him to provide uniformed surveillance at their homes. No sooner had he made those arrangements than Louise Hollowell reminded him that she and he might also be at risk. It clearly had not occurred to him that they might be in personal danger, but he then requested Chief Jenkins to provide security for their home as well.

It had been almost exactly one hundred years since the shots at Fort Sumter signaled the beginning of the Civil War. On January 12, 1961, Roy Wilkins, Executive Secretary of the NAACP, issued a withering statement:

> As every Negro knows, the Civil War is still being fought and the play-acting battles of the current centennial celebration are merely historical backdrops for the continuing action downstage.
>
> [One hundred years ago] Southern men with arms fought

other men with arms according to the rules of warfare. The breed is so improved that today young white Georgians feel the odds are about right when 1,000 of them can stone a single Negro girl.

More than two-thirds of the University faculty—four hundred and five professors—signed a resolution that deplored the violence and placed them squarely on the side of law and morality. The statement concluded:

...we, the undersigned, insist that the two suspended students be returned to their classes and that all measures necessary to the protection of students and faculty and to the preservation of orderly education be taken by appropriate state authorities.

Messages of solidarity and support from the faculties of Georgia Tech, Agnes Scott College, Morehouse College and Emory University echoed and applauded the Georgia professors' statement.

Judge Bootle this time showed little patience with the delay. Observing that state authorities could have prevented the riots, he swiftly ordered the immediate readmission of Holmes and Miss Hunter. By the following Monday, January 16, they were back in class. During the remaining course of the week, as the state and university gradually withdrew its tight security measures and, at the request of the students, banned reporters, life returned to a state approaching normalcy.

Governor Vandiver went to work on a special speech to the General Assembly. That Wednesday night, January 18, in an extraordinary night session of the legislature, he proposed a new program. It called for an amendment to the state constitution that would protect any child from being required to attend an integrated school, replacing the amendment that had required segregated schools. It requested a tuition grant program for parents wishing to send their children to private schools. It offered a local referendum provision that would permit any community to vote to close its schools if ordered to integrate them. In effect, it suggested that Georgia could have its all-white cake and eat it too.

The *Atlanta Constitution* on January 21 featured heavy coverage of President Kennedy's inauguration the day before. It described

Governor and Mrs. Vandiver, sitting in a white convertible and leading the Georgia unit in the parade down Pennsylvania Avenue. An inside story of the same edition noted that James Gray of Albany, who had touted Vandiver to the President, had attacked the governor in a front-page editorial of his *Herald*. Gray charged Vandiver with "capitulating to federal power" and responding "to the bleeding heart appeal to 'save our schools.'"[12] A longer story on the same page reported that the Clarke County Grand Jury (which had already indicted five Klansmen, a supporter and two students for their role in the campus riots) had commended University officials for their leadership.

There were also, predictably, more negative responses. Roy Harris, the segregationist newspaper publisher from Augusta and member of the Board of Regents, continued to call shrilly for the firing of President Aderhold. A petition to the governor, bearing the names of 2,148 Crisp County citizens, urged him to "hold the line in the fight against mixing the races at any level in Georgia." Their state representative had already taken the floor of the House on January 16, to blame the University's integration on "ignorant city officials, renegade politicians, subversive racial agitation groups and scalawag newspaper editors."

During the week that Holmes and Hunter returned to campus, though, Georgia citizens and organizations throughout the state rallied behind the governor's reluctant decision to accept the force of federal law. Churches and their denominations were in the forefront of this wave of support. Nearly one thousand of the state's leading businessmen, including Ivan Allen, the president of Atlanta's Chamber of Commerce, signed a five-page resolution which proclaimed that "disruption of our public school system would have a calamitous effect on the economic climate of Georgia." It also was not lost on more careful observers that the Civil Rights Commission appointed by President Eisenhower was beginning to exhibit an increasingly stiffened backbone. One of its recent recommendations had been that federal funds be withheld from racially segregated institutions.

Within ten days of Vandiver's speech, the General Assembly had passed his desired measures and a mood of self-congratulation prevailed. The lawmakers had kept the schools open — clearly the desire of the majority of Georgia citizens — and preserved the "democratic principles" of free association. Never mind that elsewhere in the South the federal courts were systematically striking down similar laws. The governor became a fleeting hero in the white world.

Even though it would mean a series of wearying legal challenges for many years to challenge the new measures, Georgia Negroes could draw comfort from the fact that educational segregation no longer was the law and that the state's leaders had backed away from the policy of "massive resistance." The word "never" was starting to vanish from a great deal of political rhetoric.

As the days moved forward, other events began to compete for public attention. The newly inaugurated President of the United States was breathing fresh life into Washington. Marilyn Monroe filed for divorce from playwright Arthur Miller. Many of Georgia's citizens, resigned to the seeming inevitability of change, paid little notice to the fact that other institutions were next in line to receive the attention of Negro plaintiffs. Four more Turner High School graduates were following in the steps of Holmes and Hunter by filing applications for admission to Georgia Tech.

Hollowell still had to conduct a few more mop-up operations on behalf of his clients as the battle wound to a close. The University, pleading the need for the students' safety, was excluding Holmes and Miss Hunter from extra-curricular activities and forcing Charlayne Hunter to eat all of her meals in the dormitory. The attorney went before Judge Bootle once again, and the justice convened a special hearing in Columbus at which he ruled that the two students were entitled to all of the benefits of undergraduate life.

Both of them still had college careers to complete. Donald Hollowell — a man they revered — would attend their graduation in 1963[13] and watch as they both continued on the road to illustrious careers,[14] but his legal involvement in their lives was over. He had other battles yet to fight.

ENDNOTES

[1] William Augustus Bootle, then fifty-eight years old, was a South Carolina native. A longtime Republican and former Dean of the Mercer University Law School, he also had been a U. S. Attorney in Macon before Franklin Roosevelt's presidency. In 1954 President Eisenhower appointed him to the federal bench.

[2] Ward would go on to compile a distinguished record. He is alleged to have had the highest score ever recorded on the state bar examination until that time. After several years as a partner in the Hollowell firm, he served as a Deputy Attorney for the City of Atlanta and an Assistant Attorney for Fulton County, maintained his own law practice, was a member of the Georgia State Senate for ten years and a judge in the Fulton County Civil Court and Superior Court. In 1979 he was sworn in as a U.S. District Judge for the Northern District of Georgia, a position from which he recently retired.

[3] Constance Baker Motley has been a Senior U.S. District Court Judge in New York since 1986. From adolescence she was a highly motivated, almost driven woman. While still a teenager in New Haven, Connecticut, her involvement in community affairs came to the attention of George Blakesley, a Yale alumnus who had been responsible for the construction of Walter Camp Field. His philanthropy extended to historically Negro colleges as well as to local projects like a community center for New Haven's Negro community. Blakesley was so impressed by Connie Baker's work as chairperson of a youth council that he offered to pay for her higher education. When she told him of her intention to become a lawyer, his reply was, "Well, I don't know much about women and the law, but if that's what you want to do, I'm ready to pay for it." His faith was not misplaced. She completed her undergraduate education (beginning at Fisk University in Nashville and finishing at New York University in 1943) and then earned her L.L.B. from Columbia University Law School in 1946. In 1945 Thurgood Marshall hired her as a member of the still very small staff of the Legal Defense Fund. She passed the New York bar in 1948. After twenty years with the Inc Fund, she served one term as a member of the New York State Senate and as President of the New York City's Borough of Manhattan. She was appointed to the U.S. District Court (Southern District, New York) in 1966 and became its Chief Judge in 1982.

[4] Jordan had been Hollowell's law clerk for some six months since graduating from the Howard University School of Law. A native of Atlanta, where his mother owned and operated a highly regarded catering service, he had completed Howard High School and then done his undergraduate work at DePauw University in Greencastle, Indiana.

As Jordan tells the story, Kenneth Days, a fraternity brother, first introduced him to Hollowell while Jordan was still in law school. After completing Howard he made plans to return to Atlanta where he had two offers of employment, one from Hollowell and one from another established Negro attorney. The other lawyer was prepared to pay him seventy-five dollars a week, while Hollowell could guarantee only the excruciatingly modest figure of thirty-five dollars. Nontheless, Jordan liked the "classy" way in which Hollowell took him and his wife, Shirley, to dinner to discuss the job offer as well as the decorum and dignity of the Hollowell home. He opted for an association with Donald Hollowell.

Jordan went on to a distinguished career that included service as the Field Secretary for the Georgia NAACP, the directorship of the Voter Education Project, the presidency of the United Negro College Fund and the National Urban League, partnership in the prestigious Washington law firm of Akin, Gump, Strauss, Hauer and Feld, the chairmanship of the transition team for newly-elected Mayor Sharon Pratt Kelly of Washington, D. C., and the chairmanship of President-elect Clinton's transition team. He continues to serve on a wide variety of prestigious corporate and nonprofit boards and remains a close personal friend of and adviser to the President as Mr. Clinton begins his second term.

[5] Newell Edenfield, while President of the Georgia Bar Association and long before he became a federal judge, had called for the repeal of all segregation laws. Far from being a liberal on the subject, Edenfield was simply a crusty pragmatist. He reasoned that these laws furnished Negro plaintiffs with all the evidence needed to prove discrimination on the basis of race. Edenfield was an astute man.

[6] The *Atlanta Inquirer* was a feisty Negro publication that had come into existence soon after the Civil Rights Movement took root in Atlanta, primarily as a reaction to the conservative stance of the much older *Atlanta Daily World*, whose editorial policy at the start was to urge caution and patience on the part of the students and other demonstrators.

[7] Vandiver was an avid segregationist, but his well-known views had not stopped his consideration for a post in the new administration of John F. Kennedy. James Gray, publisher of the *Albany Herald* and chairman of the State Democratic Party's Executive Committee, who was a personal friend of the President-elect, allegedly had pushed Vandiver's candidacy for Secretary of the Army while swimming with Kennedy during a social weekend at the family's Palm Beach estate. There also were reports that the Governor had cut a deal with the Presidential candidate, promising to support the national ticket in return for Kennedy's pledge not to federalize troops in Georgia, as had happened in Little Rock. The NAACP, unaware that Vandiver had withdrawn his name from consideration on January 5, formally protested his possible appointment on the basis that his segregationist philosophy stood in contradiction to the racial integration of the armed forces that was underway.

[8] Bootle had timed his original order in anticipation of the beginning of the university's winter quarter. However, it also managed to coincide with the opening of the annual forty-day session of the Georgia General Assembly.

[9] Like Bootle, Tuttle became a federal judge in 1954 when he was named to the 5th U. S. Circuit Court of Appeals. He too was a Republican, who had served as chairman of the state party when Dwight Eisenhower became President. He and his brother-in-law, William Sutherland, formed their own law firm in 1923, and Tuttle had been president of the Atlanta Bar Association. He had served briefly in the Army Air Force at the end of World War I, was in combat in the South Pacific where he commanded a field artillery battalion and later rose to the rank of Brigadier General in the Army reserves. As a judge, he was known for his ability to compose opinions in a clear, sparse style—a skill that derived in part from his two-year experience as a newspaper reporter after the First World War.

He was a not a Southerner. Yet, although born in Southern California, raised in Hawaii where he attended a multi-racial school and educated at Cornell University and its law school, he had achieved a high degree of acceptance in his adopted Atlanta. Evidence of that respect was his election to the presidency of the Atlanta Chamber of Commerce. The white community that had embraced him seemingly paid scant attention to his service on the boards of Atlanta University and Morehouse and Spelman Colleges. Most people were also unaware or had forgotten that Tuttle once commanded a National Guard unit that rescued a Negro prisoner from a Georgia lynch mob and that he later defended the civil rights of two Negro clients in successful appeals to the U.S. Supreme Court.

Elbert Tuttle served as Chief Judge of the 5th U.S. Circuit Court of Appeals from 1960 until his retirement at the age of 70 in 1967, after which he became a senior judge. After the creation of the 11th U. S. Circuit Court of Appeals in 1981, he continued to serve regularly on its appeals panels until his death on June 23, 1996, a month before his 99th birthday.

[10] "He's big. He's aggressive. He looks mean, and he can act mean. But he's really a sentimental fellow, with a heart of gold and an abiding, consuming love for the University of Georgia and the students who attend it." Those were some of the words used by one of his associates to describe Dean Tate to Douglas Kiker, who covered the events in Athens for the *Atlanta Journal*. "Wild Bill" Tate, a graduate of the University and former English professor, emerged as one of the few symbols of moderation. His ability to charge into crowds with abandon attracted attention. Mentioned less often but equally telling were his courtesy and friendliness to Holmes during their days together.

[11] Holmes, actually, was somewhat removed from the fray, since he was to be living off-campus with the Killian family. He later told a *Pittsburgh Courier* reporter that a small group of whites, presumably townspeople, had found the

Killian home in which he was living and showed up one night to cause trouble. When they discovered that his hosts and their neighbors were more than ready to resist, the troublemakers left and never returned. It probably did not hurt that one of the Killian sons, still living at home, was one of the first Negro officers on the Athens police force.

The Killians, in addition to providing a home for the young man from Atlanta, served the cause in another way. They had recently opened a restaurant in the Negro community, and that eating establishment served as a place where the students could discuss strategy with Hollowell and his team.

[12] Some analysts later offered the pragmatic observation that neither social philosophy nor concern for education carried the day. Rather, Hollowell and his colleagues were successful because they suspected from the start that Georgians could never live without the Bulldogs, their beloved football team.

[13] The first Negro to receive a degree from the University of Georgia actually was Mary Frances Early, who enrolled after the court-ordered desegregation. She completed a master's degree in music education, graduating on August 21, 1962, and went on to a distinguished career as a music educator and administrator in the Atlanta public school system.

Although she never received the public attention that came to Charlayne Hunter and Hamilton Holmes, Ms. Early and her quiet courage would merit a chapter of their own in any book about heroes of that period. She was the valedictorian of the first class to graduate from Turner High School (for which she wrote the school song) and of her senior class at Clark College in 1957. While enrolled in graduate courses at Michigan State University, she watched the television accounts of the University of Georgia's desegregation and felt herself moved by "the desolation on the faces of Char and Hamp." She resolved to do something "for the cause." With the assistance of Jesse Hill, an executive with the Atlanta Life Insurance Company, whom Hollowell advised behind the scenes, she too wound her way around the obstacles that Walter Danner and other officials sought to place in her path and finally was accepted for the summer quarter on April 25, 1961. The University assigned her to be Ms. Hunter's roommate in a sorority room of the building that was converted into a suite for the two of them.

She too had to withstand both the abuse and the ostracism of many students. Football players threw lemon slices at her as she stood in the dining hall line. On her way to the library one evening, another group of young men barred her way. One said, "I smell a dog," and another jeeringly yelled, "That's not a dog, that's a nigger." Coeds in their dormitory whispered to her that they couldn't associate with her for fear of jeopardizing their candidacy for the sororities they hoped to join, and she became accustomed to people getting up and leaving tables at which she took a seat. As she remembers, "whenever we returned to Atlanta, the state patrol would follow us to the county line." Ms. Early also recalls with appreciation the kindnesses of a few individual faculty members and of the Rev. "Corky" King, the chaplain at the Presbyterian Westminster House, all of whom "caught some flak" because of their friendliness to her.

One of her cherished keepsakes from those difficult days is a letter from Martin Luther King, Jr., sent to her soon after she enrolled at the University. In it he wrote that he had seen her in church the previous Sunday and that although he made no special mention of her presence, he was very proud of what she was doing.

[14] Charlayne Hunter [now Hunter-Gault] went on to a distinguished career as a journalist in New York and then became national correspondent for the Public Broadcasting Systems' MacNeil/Lehrer Newshour. Hamilton Holmes realized his ambition to become a physician. He became the first black graduate of Emory University's School of Medicine, a highly respected orthpedic surgeon and lecturer at Emory, medical director of Grady Memorial Hospital and board member of the Georgia Foundation. Dr. Holmes died on October 26, 1995. The former Hightower Road in Atlanta was renamed to honor him and his many contributions to Atlanta and to the State of Georgia.

2
FROM BOYHOOD TO MANHOOD

Donald Hollowell's name in 1961 was rapidly becoming synonymous with the legal struggle for Negro rights in Georgia. However, he was not a son of the South. By birth he was a Midwesterner, a section of the country in which Negroes constituted a very small minority.

His arrival on December 19, 1917 in Wichita, Kansas, as the third child and second son of Ocenia Bernice and Harrison Hannibal Hollowell, was noteworthy primarily because of his size. He weighed eleven and one half pounds at birth.

Both of his parents had attended college and were ambitious for a life that would make it possible for their children to achieve more than they. As a young man, Harrison Hollowell had left Mississippi, where his parents, Isaac and Dixie Hollowell, eked out a living from a small farm near Senatobia. He made his way north to Little Rock and enrolled at Arkansas Baptist College. While studying and playing football, he met and married the young Ocenia Davis, who was teaching school in the area. She had studied at Lincoln Institute[1] in Jefferson City, Missouri, and later at Western University in Quindaro, Kansas. Her industrious parents, Jefferson Lee and Cora Scott Davis, supplemented his income as a bank custodian by operating a five-acre truck farm outside of Independence in southeast Kansas.

During the winter of Don's birth, the front page newspaper stories in Kansas focused upon the distant conflict in Europe. The United States had entered the war that was to end all wars on April 6, but the fighting showed no signs of stopping.

For Americans of color, though, there was good reason to be even more concerned about the situation in their own country. Their recently re-elected President, Woodrow Wilson, who told the Congress that the world had to be made safe for democracy, had been busily implementing policies of racial segregation in all federal agencies since his first election in 1913, the fiftieth anniversary of the Emancipation Proclamation. Even more frightening, a national wave of lynchings and other atrocities against Negroes was at full flood. Fearful whites throughout the country were responding with virulent anger to the hard-won economic and social gains of Negro Americans over the past five decades.[2]

By the time baby Donald was a year old, the combatants in the "Great War" had finally signed an armistice agreement. About half of America's 370,000 Negro soldiers and 1,400 commissioned officers had served with distinction on the battlefields of Europe. "Colored" regiments as well as individuals received citations for valor and bravery. Yet their contributions did nothing to stay the wave of lynchings or to stem the killings of other American Negroes in race riots. Before Don's second birthday in 1919, the eruption of racial hysteria across the country generated twenty-six of these riots.[3]

The Hollowells were fully aware of these crises, but their immediate concern was with the survival of their growing family. Despite their education and zeal to achieve, opportunities for Negroes were sorely limited. Donald's father scuffled hard to pick up odd jobs as a custodian and porter to support a family that now included a baby sister, Iris, as well as Don's older siblings, Harry and Corinne. (Another child, Wendell, had died in infancy.) His mother, an excellent cook, began to develop her skills as a pastry chef whose products were in high demand. None of the Hollowells ever went hungry. Although the parents spent most of their waking hours at work, all of the children's memories are of a closely-knit family. They had a mother and father who loved and provided for them and imbued in them the values of truthfulness, trustworthiness and a constant striving for excellence.

Ocenia Hollowell was an enthusiastic reciter of aphorisms. When she had exhausted her supply of such tried-and-true sayings as "Always hitch your wagon to a star," she would invent her own: "If you can't be a tree, be the best bush you can." When something unexpectedly good occurred, she would describe it as "just like a bird's nest on the ground," and she often urged her children to greater achievement with calls of "Let's get high and handsome."

She was especially determined that nothing would stand in the way of her offspring receiving a solid education. On one occasion during their elementary school years, chicken pox spread through the community. Harry became the first of the Hollowell children to contract the contagious disease. Since his mother didn't want her other children to miss school, she carefully instructed them not to tell anyone why Harry was absent. (Corinne, however, simply could not resist sharing with all of her schoolmates as soon as she arrived the interesting news that her brother was infected.)

Wichita in those times was a booming city of eighty-six thousand inhabitants. The discovery of oil in the area had fueled its growth, and local business people also were determined to establish their community as the "Air Capital of America." The city's growth and prosperity also had attracted enough Negroes for the white citizens to have determined that its school system should be racially segregated. Young Don entered first grade at the all-Negro Toussaint L'Ouverture Elementary School, named for the black general who had liberated Haiti from colonial domination a century earlier. Before the end of the school year, though, Harrison Hollowell, in search of better job opportunities, moved his family to Augusta, some twenty-two miles to the east. Since that town's leaders did not find the presence of only a handful of Negro families to be a threat, the schools remained integrated, and Don was sent to Ms. Sawyer's predominantly white first grade.

At that young age, he took no special notice of racial differences and encountered no overt racial prejudice. Curiously, even the Ku Klux Klan, which had an active klavern in Augusta, held no menace. Since the Negroes in town clearly posed no threat, it functioned as an extra-legal correction agency for whites. Its not-so-secret membership, which apparently included many of the town's leaders, assumed responsibility for punishing white philanderers and others whose behavior they considered an affront to community moral standards. When they held their rallies, which included cross burnings in a field only a few hundred yards from the Hollowell home, it was deemed completely appropriate for the Negro families of Augusta to attend them too.

As a young boy, Hollowell was stubborn and truculent. His school grades for deportment tended to range from C downward to D's and F's, and his obstinacy continued at home. One day the six-year old failed to respond after his mother asked him to perform a chore. She dispatched Harry to bring his younger brother to her for a spanking. Don endured the punishment in silence, but as soon as she released him, he ran into the yard yelling, "It didn't hurt, it didn't hurt!" His mother, who weighed more than two hundred pounds, again directed Harry to retrieve his younger brother, whereupon she pinned him to the floor and sat on him until he recanted. On another occasion, after the family had put on their Sunday best and walked to church, Don stood adamantly at the front door and refused to enter the sanctuary.

He himself recalls testing the limits of authority when he was about seven years old by sneaking off to puff on cigarettes and chew tobacco. There was no need for parental discipline on those occasions after both the smoking and the "chaw" made him painfully ill.

Even at that early age, Don displayed a fascination with the intricacies of the English language. He might resist authority, and his academic performance might be erratic, but he almost always scored an A in spelling. In later years he would represent his class and school in various spelling competitions.

As presaged by his birth weight, young Don was bigger and stronger than most children his age. These traits suited Harrison Hollowell's theories of child-rearing well. He firmly believed that children should go to work as soon as they could dress themselves. Even as a first-grader, Don was already helping his father. Early each morning the two boys would go to work with him in Augusta, where he performed janitorial duties for several of the stores in town. While Harry helped with the dusting, sweeping and mopping of the drug store and the bank, Don's first job was to sweep the sidewalk in front of the drug store and to empty the wastebaskets. An occasional bonus for this assistance might be an Eskimo pie or an ice cream ball—special treats for a boy who had a passion for sweets.

By the time Don was in third grade, the family had returned to Wichita, where his entrepreneurial father now operated a taxi service as well as a small store and restaurant. His mother, who had baked for many of the stores and restaurants in Augusta, worked in the kitchen. That stay in the city also was short-lived. Harrison Hollowell's search for ever-improved employment opportunities next took the family sixty-eight miles east of Wichita to Eureka. After the discovery of oil, that once sleepy community in the middle of cattle country became a boom town, and Don's father was determined to cash in on the spillover of the new wealth. People could now afford to pay for all kinds of help, he reasoned, and by cleaning the white folk's buildings, washing their cars and being alert to any other services they might need, he felt he could generate much of the income needed to support his family of six. His wife quickly found employment as a domestic servant for Ward McGinnis, rumored to be the richest man in town.

Eureka, like Augusta, had only a few Negro families, and the Hollowells' diligence and deportment earned them the respect of the white citizens. They worshipped in a white church, and the children attended white schools. Harrison Hollowell, no doubt influenced by memories of growing up in Mississippi, was careful, nevertheless, to be cautious about any appearance of success. The racial ethos of small-town Kansas life may have been relatively tolerant, but he had a keen appreciation of the need to make sure that no one perceived the family as doing too well economically or appearing to rise above their proper station. Therefore, for example, after he bought a new 1932 Chevrolet, he prudently did not drive it downtown until several months had passed and its fresh appearance had been tempered by use.

To escape the kind of psychological pressure brought on by his constant wariness the senior Hollowells periodically would load the family into the car and travel back to Wichita or El Dorado which had larger Negro communities. There they could regain some sense of racial identity by attending Negro churches and visiting with friends. Other favorite trips, especially for the children, were the visits with their maternal grandparents in Independence. There Grandfather Jeff Davis would take them for rides between his farm and town in a horse-drawn buggy. In later years those excursions became even more exciting after he purchased a Model T Ford.

As the children grew, Harry emerged as the star of the family. During the next six years, while he proceeded through junior high school and high school, his athletic and musical prowess gained increased renown. Don, who idolized him, also began to show signs of athletic ability after outgrowing his younger chubbiness, but he still was an indifferent student. He continued to have a short emotional fuse, and his stubbornness and bad behavior regularly earned him more than his share of whippings both at home and at school.

There were good times too, with many of them centering around music. Their parents made every effort to introduce the children to the world of culture through attendance at band concerts and the occasional staging of operettas and other artistic presentations. Music filled the home as well. Harry, who had demonstrated his abilities at an early age, played trombone. Corinne was fairly adept on the violin, and both the older siblings and Iris learned to play the piano. Don impatiently tried his hand with piano, trombone and cornet for several weeks at a time but then quit. He experienced a sudden change of heart, though, after his sisters and brother returned from a state music competition. Although they excitedly reported on the talents of the contestants as well as several guest artists, what impressed Don most was the report that participants received enormous ice cream cones. Here was some motivation to which he could relate. By the time of the next year's contest, he was playing an E flat tuba in both the school orchestra and band. (He eventually worked his way up to the first chair in the bass section where he played the double B flat Sousaphone.)

He was starting to come into his own and winning approval for some of his accomplishments. Especially enjoyable was the chance to participate in some Methodist Church-related activities of the Epworth League, particularly the evening programs for teenagers. His athletic abilities continued to develop as he played on church and school teams.

Yet, on balance, these formative years were lonely ones for him. There were no other Negro boys his age in the town. He went to church and school and played with white youngsters but those associations did not ripen into true friendships. He also carried the psychological wounds from his first direct and painful encounter with racial prejudice. The school basketball team on which he played as an eighth grader had traveled to Fredonia for a tournament. After the final game in which he had played a starring role, the Eurekans went to a local restaurant, which refused to permit him to eat in the same room with his teammates. Later that evening they all returned to their home town and made their way to the

Greenwood Cafe to celebrate. When Don joined his teammates at their table, the management quietly escorted him from the dining room and made him eat in the kitchen.

Ocenia tried to be supportive of all her children. She attended as many high school track meets as possible, standing right behind the rail that separated her from the runners. There, with her right hand cupped to her mouth for added volume and her left hand waving frantically, she would urge all of the home town athletes, but especially her boys, toward the finish line.

Her husband, on the other hand, was a hard taskmaster. He clearly loved his children but could not bring himself to demonstrate a great deal of warmth toward them. His primary concern seemed to be making sure that everyone pulled a share of the financial load. Since the sixth grade Don had been earning enough money, usually by shining shoes, to buy his own clothing.

Resentful of his father's demands, unable to spend much time with Harry, who was caught up in his own studies and far-ranging extra-curricular activities, and becoming increasingly aware of bigotry, Don brooded a great deal. It did not improve his mood when the family moved again, this time to Emporia where his parents opened a small restaurant. The Hollowells also hoped that Emporia, home to both The College of Emporia and Emporia State Teachers College, might eventually provide an opportunity for their children's undergraduate study.

They left behind Harry to complete his senior year of high school in Eureka. Prompting that decision were the strong urgings of the principal, the coach and the music director, none of whom wanted to lose the talents of the high school's most outstanding athlete and fine arts student. At the time it was virtually assured that upon graduation Harry could matriculate at the University of Wichita.

Don was fourteen years old when the family moved. That summer, for the first time, he officially joined a church, the Baptist congregation whose sanctuary stood next to his family's restaurant on Commercial Street, the town's main thoroughfare. While in Eureka, his various part-time jobs had forced him to miss Sunday School and Sunday morning worship, but his new schedule permitted a fuller exposure to both worship and fellowship opportunities within the Emporia congregation.

Their influence began to have a noticeable effect on the still-growing adolescent. He became more sociable, and his quick temper moderated.

Within four months of their arrival in Emporia, though, it was time for yet another upheaval. Don's father received an appointment to a full-time job as a guard at the state prison in Lansing. Although it would mean leaving the community in which they had hoped that some of their children might attend college, the parents decided to move to Leavenworth, five miles from the prison. They rationalized that they would be relatively close, instead, to the institutions at which Ocenia Hollowell had attended college.

Soon after the relocation to Leavenworth, Don and his younger sister, Iris, became very active at the Independent Baptist Church, whose leaders and members welcomed them warmly. There Don participated fully in the programs of the Sunday School, as both a student and then a teacher, and the Baptist Young People's Union, of which he eventually became President. He also sang in the choir, became a member of the Usher Board and actively involved himself in any other opportunities that presented themselves. The experiences had a profound impact upon his life as, for the first time, he began to have a truly grounded sense of self-appreciation and leadership potential. As he learned to study the Bible, he also began to gain a budding sense of the value that lay in service to others.

During the first summer after the move to Leavenworth, the fifteen-year old Hollowell took another step toward fuller maturity. Harry made the case to his parents that Don should be permitted to spend the school vacation with him in Eureka. He had to make it forcefully. While recognizing the tempering influence that church life had exerted on their younger son, they still questioned his ability to stay out of trouble if he left home. Harry, though, finally convinced them that his brother would do well. Eventually, with great reluctance, they permitted Don to return to Eureka for the summer.

Away from his strict father but under the guidance of a kind but firm older sibling whom he idolized, Don thrived. He succeeded Harry as the operator of a shoeshine stand, so Harry could take a better-paying job to earn money for his freshman year in college. That experience of receiving and justifying his older brother's confidence in him bonded the two with emotional ties that remained tight and strong for the next six decades. Not surprisingly, at the end of that profoundly influential summer, Don begged his parents to let him stay with Harry. They instead summoned him home to Leavenworth.

That town drew its character primarily from the twin monoliths of the military and penal systems, represented by the Army's disciplinary barracks and a federal penitentiary. It also was just across the river from Missouri, where the historic white stance toward Negroes had always been less tolerant than in Kansas. Don began to receive more concentrated exposures to racial bigotry than he had ever experienced.

Leavenworth High School had a strong academic program, and Negro students attended classes with their white counterparts. Yet, when it came to non-academic pursuits, the system shunted the Negroes into the racially segregated Colored Student Activity Club. Despite his size, strength and ability, school officials would not permit Don to suit up for football and forced him to play on an all-Negro basketball team (although, with bewildering inconsistency, the high school fielded an interracial track team). These unfamiliar patterns of systematic discrimination generated a seething rage in the powerful young man, one that sorely challenged the other emerging call he felt to a life of Christian humility and charitable behavior.

Offsetting these racially motivated humiliations were the efforts of Professor Earl Lawson, the principal at one of the local Negro elementary schools. Lawson, a commissioned Army officer during the Great War sixteen years earlier, was now an acknowledged community leader who also coached the Negro high school basketball team on which Don played. He did everything in his power to bolster the self-esteem of the teenagers with whom he worked and to encourage their preparation for college.

Don's adolescent moodiness steadily waned, and as he found the strength to manage his temper, the signs of his leadership abilities became more pronounced. His powerful frame, his natural abilities and an emerging self-confidence in public speaking began to attract adult attention. His mother took note of these attributes as well as his obvious enjoyment of church activities. One day when he was sixteen years old she exclaimed to him, "Boy, if you don't become a preacher, you'll miss your calling."

However, as the Depression continued to deepen and damage the financial stability which the Hollowells had struggled for years to achieve, the notion of a call was far from Don's mind. Increasingly, survival was becoming the name of the game. He soon found himself unable even to secure the kind of part-time employment with which he had customarily met his needs for clothing and entertainment. The final blow came late in the summer of 1935, as he was preparing to begin his senior year of high school. His father determined that he simply couldn't afford to support his younger son any longer. Harrison Hollowell informed Don that he would have to leave school and find a full-time job.

Don was furious. Filled with anger toward both his father and the economic conditions that had forced this disruption in his life, he spent little time in search of work. After all, grown men were unemployed. Instead, he went out to Fort Leavenworth and somewhat spitefully sought to join the 10th Cavalry Regiment of the U.S. Army. Since he wasn't yet eighteen years old, his enlistment required parental signatures. Both Harrison and Ocenia Hollowell were shocked by their son's decision, but they reluctantly gave their consent.

Military historians designate Kansas as the cradle of the U.S. Cavalry, and the state then served as headquarters for two of its regiments—the 9th and 10th. By the time Don enlisted, these two units had amassed a seven-decade tradition of distinguished military service. They came into being in July, 1866, as all-Negro regiments commanded by white officers. During the fierce fighting of the Indian Wars against the Kiowas, Cheyennes and Apaches, the members of these units, as well as of the 24th and 25th Infantry Regiments, acquired a nickname—the Buffalo Soldiers.[4]

By 1935 white Americans had forgotten or chosen to ignore the proud history of the 10th Cavalry. The Army had reduced its functions to those of a service unit within a thoroughly segregated military system. All of its officers were still white. Nonetheless, the soldiers in its ranks had retained a remarkably high *esprit de corps*.

The young Donald Hollowell who impetuously enlisted on September 6, 1935, was a powerful seventeen-year old. He weighed only one hundred and seventy-four pounds, but he was so well developed physically that the Army had to custom-order his uniforms from the quartermaster. The supply officers who were outfitting him discovered that they had to slit the regular issue breeches from the ankles to the knees in order to stretch them over his enormous calf muscles.

When the coaches of the regimental football team spotted the strong young newcomer, they were quick to recruit him. They wasted no time in ordering him another kind of uniform and putting him to work on the base gridiron. That fall, despite the rigors of basic training and playing football, he continued to eat well and to grow. By Christmas the heavily muscled young man weighed in at more than two hundred pounds.

Hollowell blossomed under the disciplined and purposeful regimen of the 10th Cavalry. Although his horsemanship was not distinguished, he became a better-than-average rifleman. From the start he had no difficulty with the transition from civilian life, and his familiarity with military order and procedure, gained from high school ROTC, stood him in good stead. Making life even more enjoyable for him was the arrival of his revered older brother, who left college after one year and enlisted in the same regiment.

Harry quickly achieved the rank of Company Clerk, and Don in time became a Stable Clerk, with responsibility for all of the routine paperwork. Spotting an advertisement in the post's daily report for a used typewriter, he promptly purchased it. Then he prevailed upon Harry, already an accomplished typist, to give him a lesson in the use of the machine. Harry obliged and also presented him with a manual which his younger brother faithfully studied to teach himself the touch-type system. It was a skill that proved highly useful for the next forty years, and one about which Hollowell, normally a self-effacing man, enjoys bragging.

Even more important, he used the time in the 10th Cavalry to enroll in correspondence courses through the Kansas State College Extension Department. By diligently working his way through the lesson plans and submitting the results by mail, he was able to complete all but one-fourth of a point in the credits needed for certification as a high school graduate. By the fall of 1938, Private First Class, Specialist Five, Donald Lee Hollowell represented the transformation of a rough-hewn, tempestuous adolescent into a disciplined, studious and self-controlled young adult.

ENDNOTES

[1] The historically Negro college founded by members of a "colored" regiment after the Civil War.

[2] Vicious race riots had erupted in East St. Louis, Illinois, the previous summer. Although the NAACP organized a silent protest parade down Fifth Avenue in New York City that drew thousands of Negro marchers, the violence did not diminish. Within a month of that dramatic demonstration, a riot broke out in Houston, Texas, between members of the Negro 24th Infantry Regiment and local white citizens. When the fighting ended, two Negroes and eleven whites were dead, and by December, thirteen soldiers had been hanged after being found guilty of participating in the bloodshed.

[3] During the shameful "Red Summer" of 1919 these riots exploded in South Carolina, Nebraska, Texas, Tennessee, Arkansas, Virginia, Washington, D.C. and Chicago. Whites lynched seventy-six Negroes, ten of them U.S. military servicemen. These eruptions of violence continued the next year in Atlanta and other cities.

[4] The origin of the title is a subject of debate. Some believe that it refers to the thick overcoats the soldiers wore during the harsh winters on the plains. Others contend that the Indians recognized a resemblance between the soldiers' hair and the thick pelts of buffaloes. A widely accepted theory is that the Native Americans who revered the buffalo transferred the term to their dark-skinned adversaries as a sign of respect. Whatever the derivation, members of these units have always accepted the name as a badge of honor.

Some historians contend that George A. Custer, who would later command the infamous 7th Cavalry Regiment, declined to command these units after the Civil War because he was unsure whether they would remain intact. Other scholars feel his reluctance stemmed from a more basic disdain toward being associated with Negro outfits. John Pershing had no such reservations. In later years he commanded them during the Spanish-American War (hence his nickname of "Black Jack"). They fought gallantly beside Theodore Roosevelt's Rough Riders in Cuba, and, according to some military chroniclers, were responsible for saving that force from defeat.

The 10th Cavalry had another claim to fame. Henry Ossian Flipper, the son of a distinguished Georgia family, had served with distinction in the unit. He was the first Negro graduate of West Point in 1877, but he was later framed in a racist plot by fellow white officers, court-martialed and dishonorably discharged, a sentence that required decades of appeals after his death and later burial in Georgia for his sentence to be overturned.

It would take more than fifty years and the appointment of a black soldier, General Colin Powell, as Chairman of the Joint Chiefs of Staff, before the Army would formally dedicate a monument to the Buffalo Soldiers.

3
ALMA MATER

Despite all of his new maturity, Donald Hollowell was not giving especially careful thought to the future. Countries were at war in Europe, but that conflict was very far away and didn't involve the United States. There seemed to be no pressing reasons to leave the safe situation in which he had established a secure niche for himself. For the time being he could relax in the familiar, relatively comfortable and well-ordered routine of peacetime Army life. Ahead of him stretched the prospect of a professional military career during which he could continue to rise steadily through the ranks.[1]

Frank Holbert, an older friend from Atchison with whom Hollowell had been involved in church activities and sports, emerged as the instrument for engineering a radical change in Hollowell's plans. Holbert's uncle owned some property in Bowling Green, Kentucky, to which his nephew had been driving him regularly for several years. In the fall of 1937, the pair had made the trip again. One afternoon, as Holbert was walking past the Negro high school's playing field, he noticed a football team running through its drills. He was especially impressed by their shiny blue and red uniforms. Further inquiries produced the information that the team came from a small Negro institution in Jackson, Tennessee, called Lane College.

The local high school coach had arranged the stopover in Bowling Green for Lane's team which was on its way to Xenia, Ohio, for a game with Wilberforce University,[2] another historically Negro college. Holbert, a tall, two-hundred pounder introduced himself to Lane's coach, Edward Clemons. Clemons, impressed by the size of the young man who stood before him, encouraged him to come to Lane for spring practice the following year. If Holbert performed well, said Clemons, he'd give him a scholarship the next September.

The immediacy of the offer flustered Holbert. Perhaps he was a bit nervous at the thought of taking this kind of step by himself. At any rate, he responded by describing his friend, Don Hollowell, to the coach. Hollowell, he told the coach, was just as big and strong and could play football too. Holbert went so far as to assert that he couldn't come to Lane without Hollowell. Clemons replied that both of them would be welcome to try out for the team.

Holbert returned to Kansas with the news and began the task of convincing his friend that it was time to leave military life. After a few months, Hollowell finally decided to take this precipitous step. He was careful, though, to safeguard his security by enlisting in the Regular Army reserve forces. Both of his parents applauded the decision. He withdrew the hundred dollars he had scrupulously saved from monthly pay checks that never had exceeded thirty-five dollars, purchased a steamer trunk and a train ticket and set out for Lane College.

Lane, founded in 1882, was one of several institutions of higher learning established by the Negro denomination originally called the Colored Methodist Episcopal Church.[3] Heightening the college's close ties to the Church was the presence in Jackson then of the C. M. E. publishing house, which produced all of its religious education and other printed materials.

The financial status of Lane was always precarious. Many of the other dozens of private, historically Negro colleges that were founded by northern white denominations could count upon a steady if not especially generous stream of support from them. Lane's constituency was Negro and primarily poor. Yet the institution, while lacking in many material advantages, was rich in spirit. Driving its leadership was the passion to produce leaders for the Church and for Negro society.

The small Negro colleges of that day, especially those in small towns and rural areas, were educational and cultural havens in an otherwise hostile Southern terrain. Virtually everywhere else in the region, Negroes were fair game for harassment and abuse by any member of the white community. Yet, in one of many curious unwritten codes of the time, these campuses stood as protected enclaves. Generally off limits to overt hostility, they were able to establish a liberating atmosphere. There the values of academic achievement, social decorum, respect for African

American history and a sense of self-worth received nurture and honor.

In Jackson, there were also some practical considerations that enhanced the tolerant feelings of the white community toward the institution. The C. M. E. publishing operations, located in downtown Jackson, were a significant economic resource for the town and assured its post office of a strong rating.[4] Hollowell quickly acclimated himself to the spirit and style of the college. It became a true alma mater — a "nourishing mother" — under whose care and interest he would blossom. The first order of business was to make the football team in order to assure himself of scholarship support. Although Hollowell had not been able to come to spring practice, Holbert had shown up and done well — so well that Clemons was anxious to meet the other young man who Holbert claimed was an equally good player.

Football practice started several weeks before the beginning of the academic year. Accustomed to the all-male milieu of military life, Hollowell easily slipped into the routine of training. His athletic ability, as Holbert had promised, impressed the coach and quickly secured him a place on the roster. By the start of the season, he was the second-string fullback. His teammates discovered that Hollowell in uniform was serious and even intense, but that off the field his easy-going manner made him good company.

Even as he was adapting himself to the rigors of undergraduate academic life, the twenty-year old freshman also was becoming a student of the Deep South. It was a new and different country for the young man who had grown up in a state with a very small Negro population. He had, to be sure, attended segregated institutions and had felt the stings of racial prejudice, but, on balance, they had not dominated his experiences.

He soon came to recognize that Lane's campus boundaries were indeed a buffer against daily affronts and that his college life had an artificial quality when compared with the lot of Negroes elsewhere. Nothing had prepared him for the apartheid he encountered as the football team played its away games with other Negro institutions. Traveling through Tennessee to Nashville, Memphis and Knoxville, riding the team bus to Xavier University in New Orleans and Talladega College in Alabama, visiting Atlanta for contests with Morehouse and Morris Brown Colleges, he was stunned by what he observed and experienced. Everywhere they went he encountered a white-dominated society whose primary passion seemed to be the isolation of the races and the demeaning of all Negro citizens in every imaginable way.

Hollowell watched closely and asked questions. Many Southern Negroes gave the appearance of having adjusted to the system. As he delved deeper, though, he discovered the simmering of sorrowful outrage.

There were many who sided with Booker T. Washington and his arguments for gradualism and industrial education. Washington had said, "I would set no limits on the attainment of the Negro in arts, in letters or statesmanship; but I believe the surest way to reach those ends is by laying the foundation in the little things of life that lie immediately at one's door." However, the more "radical" notions of W.E.B. DuBois were rapidly gaining in popularity. DuBois proclaimed, "The Negro race is going to be saved by its exceptional men...."[5]

The lot of Negro Americans came to dominate young Hollowell's thinking. Nevertheless, he really didn't know what he could do to change the situation. Besides, he faced the more immediate challenges of staying in school and playing football. His leadership abilities soon surfaced during that freshman year. His first public speech — a testimony during a campus-wide prayer meeting—captured widespread attention. It was all the more notable because the remarks came from a powerful football player who didn't fit the usual stereotype of the pious Christian.

Finances were still tight for Don, as they were for most of his fellow undergraduates. Harry and Iris now and then would send small gifts of money and clothing, but there was no room in the budget for luxuries of any kind. In one of his lettters to Harry, Don described a dance on the Lane campus. Because he and Frank Holbert[6] had only one suit between them, they divided its use. Midway through the evening event, Holbert left the festivities and returned to the dormitory where Hollowell was waiting. As soon as Holbert slipped off the formal wear, Hollowell immediately climbed into it and made his way back to the hall for the second half of the dance.

Hollowell also played on the basketball team, and his great physical strength won him the position of discus thrower and shot putter on the track and field team. The freshman class elected him president, a position he continued to hold through his sophomore and junior years. Everyone on the small campus soon knew "Big Don."

Those leadership abilities were not lost on the football coach. Clemons (better known behind his back as "Ox") gave little evidence of the graces generally associated with members of a college family. He was coarse and unpolished, in many ways the antithesis of the studious, grammatically correct and devout Hollowell, whom he had taken to calling "Fessa" (short for "Professor"). Yet, he was also a good coach who knew what it took to assemble a winning team.

By the time of spring training during Hollowell's freshman year Clemons realized he had a problem. Most of the members of the football team belonged to one of the two fraternities with chapters at Lane — Alpha Phi Alpha and Omega Psi Phi. The intense rivalry between the two was hurting team performance. Loyalty to fraternity had started to transcend team spirit. The first- and second-string quarterbacks, both of whom were Alphas, couldn't always count upon the Omega backs and linemen to respond to their signals.

Clemons, himself an Omega, realized he had to do something drastic. Early during spring practices, he sat down with Hollowell to discuss the situation. He knew that his strong, second-string fullback was planning to pledge Kappa Alpha Psi even though that fraternity didn't have a chapter on the Lane campus at that time. "'Fessa,'" he said, "I want you to try running this team."

Hollowell did just that for the rest of the training season. All of the players respected him, and his neutrality on the Alpha-Omega issue offered no grounds for fraternity-inspired disloyalty. There was now a team spirit that made it possible for what already was an impressive collection of physical talent to coalesce into a very good football team.

By the fall of Hollowell's sophomore year he was the starting quarterback. As he recalls, "I wasn't a hot-shot passer or one of those triple-threats, but I could get those fellows to play together." Jack Gilmore, a back from Beloit, Wisconsin, was the team's most versatile member with the ability to run, kick and throw, and the line was exceptionally big and strong for a small-college squad. Hollowell's elevation to the first string didn't deter his studiousness. As they traveled, while the rest of the team played cards and told jokes, he invariably was absorbed in a textbook.

The football schedule that fall included a home game with Florida A & M in Tallahassee, coached by the already-legendary Alonzo "Jake" Gaither. The Rattlers, as was their custom, dominated the Southeastern Intercollegiate Athletic Conference. Lane College, like many of its peers, had never defeated this powerhouse. Nonetheless, Clemons clearly had a premonition that his team, led by its new quarterback, could match up better than usual with the Florida team. He established contacts with friends and fellow coaches throughout the conference and began collecting scouting reports on the Rattlers. The team dedicated many of its practices to learning a whole new set of defenses against them.

The Floridians arrived in Jackson, well-prepared as always but certainly not worried about the game. From their perspective, it would be a breather between more important matches. Their starting line-up included four members of the All-American team selected annually by the *Pittsburgh Courier*, the nationally read Negro newspaper.

Lane's team had already won several games, but the betting members of the crowd who showed up that Saturday night had their money on the Rattlers. Most of the people in the stands were there to watch the high-stepping Florida A & M band. Its national reputation for inventive music and movement was every bit as great as the football team's image.

By halftime, though, when the members of that famous band strutted onto the field, the spectators in the bleachers had something else about which to be excited. Little Lane College, accustomed to being annihilated by the Rattlers, had scored against the powerful Florida team and held it to one touchdown. The score was tied 6-6.

The next thirty minutes of football were the stuff of legend. Coach Clemons' scouting had paid off, and his specially-designed defenses kept the visiting team from scoring again. With Hollowell calling all of the plays, one touchdown came on a powerful end around sweep. Then he faked a quick kick and lateraled to the team's scatback, who threw a fifty-yard touchdown pass. The Lane offense produced a total of nineteen points, and when the game ended, the vaunted Florida team was on the short end of a 25-6 score. The fans' reaction swung between hysterical excitement and stunned disbelief. The supporters back on the Tallahassee campus were sure there had been a mistake. When the telegraph transmitted the score, they immediately wired back for confirmation, certain that the numbers had been transposed.

No one was more shocked and disturbed than Coach Gaither. It was customary for traveling Negro college teams in the segregated South to spend the night on the host campus after an evening game. They would have breakfast there the next morning before departing. This time, though, Gaither had no intention of playing the part of gracious loser. Although it was late, as soon as his players had taken their showers, he loaded them on the team bus. They drove through the night to Chattanooga, where he finally permitted them to have breakfast.

"Big Don" and his teammates were campus heroes that Sunday morning, and his place in Lane College history would have been assured had he never done anything else of significance. Yet, it was typical of his seriousness that he soon set aside that achievement and continue his other pursuits. The football team was to have another good season his junior year. (It narrowly missed a second upset over Florida A & M when a late field goal attempt by Lane saw the ball hit the crossbar between the goalposts and bounce back, leaving a final score of 7-6.) But Clemons' quarterback, "Fessa" Hollowell, was growing and stretching on other fields of endeavor.

His leadership was influential in establishing a Kappa chapter at Lane toward the end of his sophomore year. A few of the undergraduates were members of that fraternity, but they had been "made" at the Alpha Theta chapter on the campus of Tennessee State A & I College, the public Negro institution in Nashville. He started the process by organizing a pledge club — the Would-Be Scrollers — and serving as its president. The WBS Club prided itself on the high academic standards of its members and the organization's commitment to service. By the spring, a new Beta Lambda chapter was an official part of the college's Pan-Hellenic life, and Hollowell was its first Polemarch.[7] He had a strong, clear voice and loved to sing. One of his particularly fond memories is of the evenings when the Kappas, carrying their lighted shield, would march across the campus to serenade the coeds beneath the windows of the girls' dormitory.

Although a loyal fraternity brother, even then Hollowell made it clear that he was also an independent thinker who was ahead of his time. Initiation ceremonies and hazing in those days still could be fairly brutal affairs. The students themselves referred to this rite of passage as "crossing the burning sands." Hollowell disapproved of these practices. He himself was willing to withstand a severe paddling, but thereafter always wielded a light hand when new inductees joined the chapter. As he puts it, "I always thought there were better ways" to conduct an initiation.

During his freshman and sophomore years, Hollowell, who had been an average but generally indifferent student during high school, steadily came to the realization that he had a true aptitude for scholarship. His excitement about learning and increasingly disciplined study habits soon made him a consistent "A" student.

By his junior year he was managing an incredibly busy regimen of both academic and extra-curricular activities. He was class president; editor of the *Dragonette*, the college newspaper; active in inter-collegiate athletic competition and a fraternity leader. To help pay for his tuition, he also worked as a secretary for the college registrar, Joseph H. Stevens, a position in which the typing skills acquired at Fort Leavenworth stood him in good stead.

While still a freshman, Hollowell had formally joined the C. M. E. Church and thereafter remained active in the religious life on campus. He came to the attention of Dr. B. Julian Smith, who would later become a leading bishop of the denomination. Smith was the C. M. E.'s General Secretary of Christian Education and he put Hollowell to work on various projects whenever the young man had a few spare hours. That association in time led to Hollowell's participation in a wide range of church youth activities and conferences around the country, including the Methodist Youth Conference in Estes Park, Colorado, during the summer of 1941. Indeed, as a varsity athlete, class officer and leader in both fraternity and religious organizations, he may well have been one of the most widely-traveled undergraduates of his time.

Members of Lane's administration (like Dean P. Randolph Shy, who also would later become a renowned C. M. E. bishop) and faculty began to harbor hopes that the impressive young transplant from Kansas would feel a call to the ministry. His deep Christian commitment, his keen mind and his speaking abilities all suggested that he had the potential to be a mighty church leader. However, before there would be an opportunity for him to ponder that option, Hollowell received a summons from another authority—the United States government, which recalled him to active military service.

ENDNOTES

[1] Harry Hollowell made the decision to take that route. Determined to gain a commission, he entered the regiment's first officer candidate school to which Negroes were admitted but, as he recalls, did not do particularly well in weapons handling or horsemanship. However, in 1942, he went to the Army's bandleader school in Washington, D.C. As a band officer, he joined the 45th Engineer Regiment in India and began a career that was to take him around the world for the next 22 years.

[2] Another historically Negro institution, which bore the name of the English statesman who fought for the abolishment of slavery in the British Empire.

[3] Created as a separate and racially segregated "jurisdiction" of white American Methodism, the C. M .E. Church in later years became independent and autonomous. It adopted a new name, the Christian Methodist Episcopal Church, and received the authority to establish its own organization and episcopacy. Lane College's name derived from one of the early bishops of the denomination.

[4] Jackson in those days had a relatively strong economy. It functioned as a railroad center (both the Illinois Central and Gulf, Mobile & Ohio lines had roundhouses there), employing significant numbers of Negroes as firemen and brakemen. In addition, Jackson also was home to the West Tennessee Medical Center. All of this activity in turn helped to stimulate the growth of a solid Negro business community on the south side of the town.

[5] Both quotations are taken from *The Education of the Negro in the American Social Order* by Horace Mann Bond, himself an exceptional man. The book was published by Prentice-Hall, Inc. in 1934, a few years before Hollowell enrolled at Lane.

[6] Frank Holbert disappears from the narrative at this point. However, a few more words are in order about the man who played a key role in propelling Hollowell in the direction of higher education. Holbert went on to the pharmaceutical school of Drake University in Des Moines. He subsequently operated a small pharmacy until his partner died, while his wife, Alice, was a librarian at the university. Holbert had always been exceptionally gifted with his hands (and, indeed, helped to support himself at Lane College by keeping the buildings and equipment in repair). He then became a machinist and later organized a small landscape business. Throughout his adult life he was also active in Des Moines civic affairs. He and Hollowell remained close friends until Holbert's death.

[7] The Kappa tie was to become a highly significant and lifelong bond for Hollowell. In 1968, at its national convention, the fraternity recognized his commitment and leadership when it awarded him that organization's supreme honor—the Laurel Wreath.

4
FIGHTING FOR FREEDOM

Seventy-eight years earlier, Frederick Douglass, the fiery Negro abolitionist had sat at his desk in Rochester, New York, scribbling furiously. He was composing an impassioned plea for men of color to enlist in the Union Army — to add their strength to a force that was fighting, no matter what some might contend, to abolish slavery. It was a cause that Douglass had championed since the day the South seceded from the Union. The government, however, had been reluctant to welcome Negro soldiers into its ranks. Massachusetts, at last, had relented, and Douglass wrote:

> By every consideration which binds you to your enslaved fellow-countrymen and to the peace and welfare of your country; by every aspiration which you cherish for the freedom and equality of yourselves and your children...I urge you to fly to arms, and smite with death the power that would bury the Government and your liberty in the same hopeless grave.[1]

Now the United States of America was preparing for another war with an enemy whose avowed goals included the establishment of racial purity. Much more wholeheartedly than in 1863 or even in 1917, the government this time was ready to extend Negro men the call to military duty. Hollowell responded willingly. He hoped, as had all American soldiers of color before him, that his contribution might help to speed the full acceptance of American Negroes by their own country.

Fifty years after that experience, Hollowell can still reflect with dispassionate but deep appreciation upon the benefits he was able to distill from his military experience. Yet during five years of duty during World War II, he also had to weather a steady barrage of bitter racial affronts. They began the day he crossed the State of Tennessee and reported for duty to the Induction Center at Fort Oglethorpe in North Georgia.

Oglethorpe had no record of the young Army veteran's recall and assignment to that post, and the Sergeant of the Guard was clearly taken aback by the appearance of the young Negro who stood before him. In a fashion familiar to all soldiers, there had been a snafu in the military paperwork and communications network. For whatever reasons, Hollowell's orders from the segregated Army also had failed to take note of his race. When no one else seemed to know what to do, the noncom assigned him to an eight-bed tent by himself and said he would report the young man's presence to the Officer of the Day the next morning. Hollowell made his way to the tent–canvas stretched over a wooden frame that rested upon a concrete slab. It was quickly becoming apparent to him that he was the only Negro soldier in the entire Center.

The next morning he appeared for breakfast in the mess hall. There he was told that because he was a Negro, he would have to eat in the kitchen. It was, with cruel irony, July 4, 1941 — Independence Day.

Hollowell refused the instruction and instead reported the incident to the Sergeant of the Guard, who in turn relayed the information to the Officer of the Day. That officer claimed there was nothing he could do. It was a matter that required the attention of the commanding officer, who was absent for the holiday. Hollowell staved off hunger for the next twenty-four hours by dipping into his slim cash reserves and purchasing his meals at the post canteen.

The next morning he reported to the commanding officer. "Sir," he declared. "The people at the mess tent don't seem to understand that I'm a soldier. I'm not just a recruit, but a Private First Class of the Regular Army. As such, I don't eat in the kitchen."

The major didn't apologize for the affront to Hollowell. However, he did say that he would order the mess officer to draw up a meal schedule that would make it possible for Hollowell to eat in the same quarters as everyone else. Later that morning, after returning to his tent from a round of test-taking, Hollowell found a crudely-lettered note on his bunk. It bore the title, "NEGRO EAT," beneath which ungrammatical phrase was a list of times when he was to report for meals. All of them immediately preceded the regular mealtimes of the inductees. That day, and for the rest of his brief stay at Fort Oglethorpe, Hollowell would appear in the mess hall and find his table at the rear, on which would be arrayed a full pitcher of that meal's beverage, an entire plateful of bread and a pound slab of butter. He would carry his tray past the steam table, receive the rest of his food, take it back to his table and eat alone.

Having completed all of his tests for that first day and drawn the initial issue of clothes and equipment, Hollowell found himself with time on his hands. He wandered over to the day room where table tennis was a principal form of recreation. The Ping-Pong protocol, called "rise and fly," dictated that the winner continue to play until a challenger could beat him. Hollowell was a very good player and held the table for long periods of time. It clearly angered those white soldiers who didn't want to compete with a Negro. They carried their gripe to the First Sergeant. In short order Hollowell found himself barred from the day room too.

On his third full day at Fort Oglethorpe, Hollowell completed a new battery of tests in the morning, drew another issue of gear and then was detailed by himself to mow the grass around the orderly room tent. While he disposed of this assignment, the white recruits, who had drilled all morning, were raking and policing the parade grounds.

He finished cutting the grass and presented his work for inspection to the sergeant, who dismissed him to take a shower. Hollowell returned to his tent and stripped off his sweaty fatigues. Wrapping his robe about him and gathering his toilet articles, he proceeded to the latrine that he had initially been told to use, despite the fact that a small sign outside the entrance designated it as a "white" area. (The Army had demonstrated its versatility and a kind of economy by making all of these signs on the base reversible, with one side labeled "white" and the other "colored;" Since Hollowell was the only Negro soldier in the Center, all of the signs still displayed their "white" sides.)

As he began to shave, he heard someone behind him yell roughly, "Hey!" Hollowell continued what he was doing. The voice was louder the second time. "Hey there, boy!" He looked around slowly to discover a knot of some fifteen or twenty white recruits clustered in the doorway. Several of these angry-looking young men in blue denim fatigues and caps were still carrying the sickles and rakes they had been using to clean up the parade ground.

Another one of them barked, "You can't use this latrine!"

Hollowell replied quietly, "This is the one they assigned me."

"Who told you that?" a belligerent voice demanded.

"The first sergeant," said Hollowell, all the while trying to calculate an escape route and wondering whether he could make it to the other door before he was caught.

"Well, there's somebody around here that's more important than him, and we're saying you can't use it." The angry-looking recruits seemed ready to rush Hollowell when the burly first sergeant anxiously pushed his way through their ranks from the rear and stopped in front of Hollowell.

"Say, boy, what the hell are you trying to do? Commit suicide?"

Hollowell feigned ignorance. "No, sir. What do you mean?"

"Well, that's what you're about to do. Now collect your stuff and get back up to your tent."

It was an order that Hollowell was only too happy to obey. A short while later, the sergeant appeared again with the news that his one Negro soldier was to move to a tent beside the orderly tent that he himself occupied. Hollowell spent the rest of the day and that night in the new location. The next morning he was told to move yet again, this time to one end of the frame building that had been converted from a mess hall to a guardhouse for the prison compound. It was positioned as part of the security perimeter with a barbed wire fence attached to each side of it. The guards occupied the portion of the building that had been the kitchen. From this station they controlled access to a gate through the wire enclosure to the prison compound.

Hollowell was given a folding cot in the section that had been the dining room. Since the connecting door between the two areas was nailed shut, whenever he needed to use the lavatory, he would have to leave his side and walk outside to the other end of the structure. There a guard would open the gate to the compound so Hollowell could then proceed to the prisoners' toilet facilities.

Many years later, Hollowell reflected aloud upon his brief re-introduction to Army life that summer:

> You have no idea what impact that situation made upon me during those nine days at Fort Oglethorpe. Here I was, a black man in the United States, who had been in the Army

for three years, had been in college for three years and was now being called back to serve my country — yes, even to give my life if necessary. Yet I was treated with less dignity, less acceptance and less common courtesy that even prisoners.

Virtually every soldier of color who served during that period can offer a personal litany of indignities to which he was exposed. One of the saddest set of stories revolved around incidents in which German prisoners of war were being transported through the South by trains under the guard of Negro soldiers. When the trains would stop, these same prisoners— many of whom may have been responsible for killing white and Negro Americans—were welcome to eat in the local restaurants while their Negro guards were denied admission.

Small wonder that tensions regularly reached flash point. One month after Hollowell rejoined the Army, a Negro private and a white military policeman were shot to death during a racial fight between soldiers on a bus in North Carolina. Situations like these continued throughout the war.

Five days later, the Army transferred Hollowell to Fort Benning, outside Columbus, Georgia. He quickly discovered that his experiences at Fort Oglethorpe were no exception to Army life elsewhere. There were even separate buses for Negroes from Columbus to the Fort. Once on the base, he was assigned to the Reception Center of Headquarters Company, processing inductees before they were sent on to posts around the country. All of the company's senior officers and the first three grades of non-commissioned officers (Master, Staff and Technical Sergeants) were white and virtually all were Regular Army. Hollowell estimates that as many as ninety per cent of the Negro soldiers in Benning's Headquarters Company — none of whom held a rank above sergeant — had earned bachelors' degrees, although he doubts that any of their superior non-commissioned officers had ever seen the inside of a college classroom. This educational disparity served only to exacerbate the racial antagonism. Many of the Negro soldiers were subject to a great deal of hostility.

By September he was a corporal. His responsibilities that month included assisting with arrangements to bring a group of young women from Atlanta to a mixer at the base. Most of them were students at the

Apex Beauty College. One of their chaperones was an attractive young woman by the name of Louise Thornton, who immediately caught Hollowell's eye. He had occasion to speak with her briefly when she arrived with her charges from Atlanta, but his duties as one of the organizers of the event prevented continued contact that afternoon.

The events on that September 28 included dinner in a wooded area not far from the barracks, after which there was dancing in the Day Room. Just before it was time for the young women to return to Atlanta, Hollowell extinguished the pipe on which he had been puffing and invited Miss Thornton to dance with him. It soon became clear that she had been very aware of Hollowell too. She rather directly let him know that if he were to come to Atlanta, he should look her up.

Louise Thornton was a spirited and vivacious young woman with a great drive to achieve. Born in what then was Decatur County in southwest Georgia to Benjamin and Lillie Scott Thornton, she grew up in Iron City on a small plantation in the Cypress Pond community. The property, only a few miles from the Florida state line, belonged to her paternal grandmother, Diller Thornton, who gave Louise's father a portion of it. He in turn built a house on his seven acres, on which he farmed and sold the produce from it. That income supplemented the wages he received from Mr. Hagan, a wealthy white man in town, for whom he worked five days a week. By the time "Lou" completed elementary school, her parents, who were later divorced, had separated.

There was no other schooling available for Negroes in the immediate area. To assure the young girl a continued education, Lou's mother and maternal grandmother, Mary Ross, moved to Bainbridge some fifteen miles to the southeast. There they enrolled her in Hutto Junior High School. Louise subsequently completed her studies at the Commercial High School department of Edward Waters College, a small African Methodist Episcopal institution in Jacksonville, Florida. While taking the prescribed commercial courses, she also enrolled in much of the college preparatory curriculum.

After working in Florida for a year, Louise made her way to Danbury, Connecticut. From there, where she lived with a friend from Florida for a few months, she proceeded to New York City, and her mother joined her. In Harlem she studied cosmetology at the Apex Beauty

College, one of a small chain of schools owned and operated by Madame Sarah Spencer Washington, a successful Negro businesswoman of Atlantic City, New Jersey. That training led to employment with the Modelle Beauty Salon — an upscale establishment on Seventh Avenue, near 136th Street, that had a wealthy and influential clientele.

The energetic young woman with small town roots adapted well to big city life. Within two years she had established herself as a beautician whose services were in high demand. It could have been tempting to make New York her permanent home, but Mrs. Washington's enterprises had need of her elsewhere. The Apex News and Hair Company's operation in Atlanta was in serious jeopardy, threatened by the loss of its license. Despite Lou's youth, Mrs. Dorothy Chapman, the manager of the New York operations, recognized her abilities and offered her the position as manager and head teacher. In short order, she was boarding a Pullman car at Pennsylvania Station and returning to the South. Upon arrival in Atlanta, she quickly began reorganizing the affairs of the small beauty college at 229 Auburn Avenue. One of her other first steps was to take the State Cosmetology Board's examinations, on which, she was told by the examiner, she recorded the highest scores he had ever seen. Miss Millie Mae Shanks, who operated the professional department of the beauty school, helped Louise find lodging with Mrs. Mattie Billings in the neighborhood. A year later, Louise opened her own Modelle Beauty Salon, a modern and handsomely appointed shop at 237 Auburn Avenue that she staffed with operators from the beauty college. Mrs. Gertis Saunders, assisted by Louise's mother, managed the thriving new venture for about three years.

Although both the salon and the Atlanta Apex operations were now running smoothly, Louise had even greater ambitions. She enrolled in evening courses at Morris Brown College,[2] determined to earn an advanced degree.

Several weeks after the first encounter between Hollowell and Louise, Lane College was scheduled to play a football game at Ponce de Leon Park in Atlanta. Hollowell decided that he would like to see his former teammates and arranged to make the trip from Fort Benning. He didn't call Miss Thornton, but, as luck would have it, she was also in the stands. One of his friends was planning dinner at his house with a date, and he invited both Hollowell and Miss Thornton to join them. They accepted, although she had to leave early for a date with another soldier — a sergeant in Hollowell's outfit.

Yet another football game — the annual match-up between Morehouse and Tuskegee in nearby Columbus — became the occasion for the further advancement of their relationship. Hollowell wrote Miss Thornton a letter, making it clear that if she planned to attend the game, he would be pleased to serve as her escort. She replied by mail that she would indeed be at the game and that she had fully expected Hollowell to be her date.

When the couple visited the local USO canteen after the game, a potentially embarrassing situation arose. One of the first people they spotted was the sergeant whom Miss Thornton had previously dated. Unfortunately, that young man had also invited her to attend the game with him. She had declined, informing him that she planned to stay in Atlanta, and now had to excuse herself to straighten out the situation. It was clear that the courtship between the former Buffalo Soldier and the woman he thereafter referred to as his "Georgia Peach" was underway in earnest. At every opportunity she traveled to Columbus to see him or he made his way to Atlanta.

Hollowell was determined not to remain a corporal. The War Department in October, 1940, had called for the "opportunity for Negroes to qualify for reserve commissions" in racially integrated schools and classes. He applied to Officer Candidate School at Fort Benning. Despite additional orders from the Secretary of War, though, the first ten of the OCS classes at Benning had included only a smattering of Negro candidates. The Army was still reluctant to integrate its officer corps and employed a variety of delaying tactics. Fewer than thirty Negroes were admitted during the first six months.

Hollowell's first physical examination rated him as "obese" because he weighed two pounds more than the highest weight permitted. The medical chart also noted that his blood pressure was elevated. He persisted in his demand for another examination, and the second one produced a description of his build as "heavy musculature." The physician now found his blood pressure to be normal. He offered the opinion that the previous examination's finding probably was due to the fact that

Hollowell had been checked just before the lovely Louise was scheduled to arrive for a visit.

Hollowell was clearly smitten, and the emotion stimulated his already great fondness for language. Returning from a trip to see her in Atlanta, he wrote, with an ornate script that matched his flowery rhetoric:

> *Yes, darling, I'm here again — S-l-e-e-p-y. However, I have withstood the day program quite well. We arrived here, that is, in Columbus, at three o'clock [a.m.] But, we could not get transportation to Benning until after five. As a result we got here just in time to change clothes and fall out for reveille. You can bet that I will retire early tonight.*
>
> *I could draw upon my literary, linguistic, scriptorial resources and still not pool my phrases in a manner to sufficiently express the pleasure derived from being with you again over the weekend. May I cut short and let those three little but greatly significant —yes, immortal — words supplement? <u>I love you</u>!*

The visits and the letter exchanges between him and his new love intensified. In another, undated note to Louise, he declared:

> *...Your letter was such a sweet and enjoyable one. Don't you know that embers will burst into flame when fanned in the open air? Your pocketbook must be fat, young lady. Have you ever thought that you might be compelled to pay a doctor to treat a scorched heart? (smiles) ... You make it very enticing for me to return to Atlanta. You know I like and want to come to see you, don't you? ...Don't let your sugar crystallize, sweet thing....*

At long last, Hollowell became a member of the OCS-11 class with sixteen other Negro candidates, the largest number in the school's history. Their first quarters were in a separate barracks about two hundreds yards down a trail and over a hill from the rest of the compound. The Army's decision to isolate them backfired, however. No one remembered to send anyone to wake them up, and they all missed reveille the first morning. After that incident the Sergeant of the Guard was required to come to the Negro barracks and blow his whistle as he did for the other trainees. All of the men ate together without incident the first day. That practice stopped for a while after the order came down to enforce racially segregated meals, but the Negro candidates all complained strongly enough to reinstate a desegregated mess hall. The dispute illustrated the overlay of racial harrassment that never completely disappeared. However, any personal affronts to Hollowell did not last long. One day as the candidates were going through a bayonet drill, it was his turn to attack the dummy. He parried and thrust in prescribed fashion and then delivered a vertical butt stroke to the dummy so hard that it crushed the stock of his rifle. Word of his strength spread rapidly around the camp, and no one ever hassled him again. Hollowell wrote to Louise:

> *Well, we have moved since I received your...letter. When I saw you, all the colored were in one barracks. Now, we stay on the floor of the [same] barracks in which our platoon is located. However, we are in small rooms which are located at the end of the respective floors. [Drawing inserted to illustrate the arrangement.] We preferred the original set up, but this will be good discipline for both the colored and white candidates. I think I told you that most of the fellows here are from Mass. (I took a shower with a fellow from Miss. last night, however, to my surprise, he was interesting and nice.) So there, my dear, you never know....*

The training was tough, often keeping the officer candidates going from pre-dawn until well after dark. He described the routine in several letters

> *8:10 P.M.*
> *For the first time since 6:30 a.m. I have more than five available moments for my own personal use... I hope the ride home didn't prove too uncomfortable over the rear-wheel... You know, darling, the more I see you and am with you the more I believe (wrong word: KNOW) I love you.*

> [undated]
> *I had good intentions of going to chapel this morning but after breakfast we started a little separate class on the machine gun which lasted until dinner hour. We even cut off the radio and let "Wings Over Jordan" slip by. You see, we are to have our G.T. (Graded Test) tomorrow afternoon. We have covered an immense amount of material on the m. gun in the past two weeks which has been a bit complex and difficult—thus the extra study. I feel somewhat confident that I can make out o.k., that is, with my knowledge of the gun and its supplements plus "your support." I do not believe I shall be found wanting. (smile)...*
> *...my love for you seems to grow with each meeting and each letter... nothing will come to sever or even dampen that exquisite...attitude that seems to exist between us — nothing.*

> [undated]
> *...since writing you I have taken my Machine Gun test. My persistent and conscientious study paid dividends. Although we haven't received our papers back, we have received the test solutions. I have no fear of my grade; just hope I do as well on those that will follow... I have missed you during our three weeks separation... Be sweet, as you ever appear to me....*

After yet another weekend visit to Atlanta, he wrote:

> *I arrived at the station in time to catch one of the three buses which were leaving. We pulled out about 12:30 a.m. and arrived in Columbus at 3:45 a.m. However, I did not get to bed until 5:45 a.m. (Got up at 6:15 a.m.) I made it through the day ok by forcing myself. The G.T. didn't appear particularly hard. I feel quite confident that my mark will be very satisfactory. Just hope I can do as well on subsequent ones...*

The long night-time bus rides between Atlanta and Columbus provided Hollowell with ample opportunity to engage in one of his favorite acts of resistance against the South's racial taboos. Whenever possible he would surreptitiously remove the "COLORED" sign on the back of the bus seat behind which Negro passengers were forced to sit. Then, after slipping it beneath his jacket or down the sleeve of his overcoat, the innocent-looking young soldier would calmly disembark with the hidden trophy of his sabotage. Louise, raised to fear the retaliation that could fall upon Negroes who challenged the system, never failed to be both frightened and thrilled by Hollowell's refusal to be intimidated.

On January 18, 1942, he shared these thoughts with her:

> *It's such a beautiful afternoon here; have you had your daily walk? You must get enough exercise for both of us for a while; for it's work-to-meals-to-work-to-home in the barracks at an hour after seven o'clock in the evening. After thirteen or more hours, I don't want much exercise... [continuing the next morning] you should see the crescent, star-surrounded moon these mornings about six o'clock. Its presence, when I am out for reveille, causes me to make pleasant associations which to me are quite nice to... have as a preface for a long nap... It so happened that I too noticed the moon on that particular night and thought of you... The analogies made in your letter were also beautiful. Although I like 'Romeo and Juliet,' I have always thought of the Brownings as having had an almost perfect affair. Haven't you heard that history repeats itself?...*

The flow of correspondence continued:

> *January 28, 1942*
> *How are you, darling? Between work at the College and your regular duties you must be very busy. Do be careful and don't overdo yourself. We ambitious people are prone to do such. Mom has constantly cautioned that brother of mine and me about the same...*

> *Saturday, March 28*
> *Hello, my Love,*
> *As I start this anniversary letter "I Don't Want To Walk Without You" is being swung out as the No. 2 song of the week. The title of the song is at least very appropriate in my estimation...*

> *This week has been a rather strenuous one, but we have had an occasional break. Two night exercises, two G.T.s, plus other activities just about wore us down. We cherished the coming of the weekend. This afternoon was also a very busy one ... We ordered our uniforms... I must admit that officer's clothing knocks one out financially, but the initial allowance the government gives us will serve to counteract the exorbitant prices. Wednesday we begin our eighth week...*
>
> *Much love, darling and "Here Is A Kiss" (X) (sung by Jessica Dragonette tonight)...*

On May 12, 1942, Hollowell became another one of the U.S. Army's ninety-day wonders. He remembers vividly the poignancy of his mixed feelings the day his class graduated and lined up for a group photograph. Only a few weeks before, Hollowell had seen the truck transporting those candidates who had washed out of the course disappearing over a hill in the distance. He still ached for the men who had gone through the hell of training only to fail to qualify, but he was "mighty glad" to be in the picture.

The new Second Lieutenant's first assignment was to report to the 795th Tank Destroyer Battalion at Fort Custer, Michigan, on May 22.[3] He, though, didn't want to take the chance of leaving Louise Thornton behind and unattached. Realizing that his 10-day 'delay in route' didn't leave him much time, he quickly purchased both an engagement ring and a wedding ring. Then, on May 14, as they made their way to a dance in Atlanta, he turned to her and asked, "Say, when are we going to get married?" Louise, taken aback by the suddenness of the question, replied, "Maybe in the fall." Satisfied by the fact that she hadn't declined his "offer," Hollowell then pulled the engagement ring from his pocket and persistently suggested that there was no point in waiting any longer. She agreed, and only later discovered that her confident suitor already had also selected a wedding ring for her.

The couple decided that he too should wear a ring, so the next day Hollowell made his way to Kay's Jewelry Store in Five Points. Attired in his flattering tropical worsted uniform and overseas cap, the handsome young officer became aware that two of the white clerks were watching him closely. The reason for their close scrutiny was unclear until, as he left the shop, he overheard one say to the other, "The army sure has glamorized some of them." From the shop he proceeded to meet Louise and to obtain a marriage license. They thought they were keeping their plans private (and, indeed, did not formally announce that they had wed until the fall). However, a friend who worked in the area spotted them that day as they prepared to enter the courthouse and, as she later told them, thought to herself, "That couple's fixin' to get married."

The hastily organized wedding took place on the evening of May 18 in the home of Dr. Joseph W. Nicholson, a faculty member on the campus of Gammon Theological Seminary in South Atlanta. There was only a slight delay when the wedding party had a flat tire on the way to the ceremony. The minister was the Rev. R. Edward Reid, a Lane College graduate who was now a divinity student at Gammon. Hollowell paid Reid for his services by presenting him with the nearly new suit in which he had just been married. After a modest reception, the bride and groom returned to her shop on Auburn Avenue, where she cooked breakfast for them. They checked into the honeymoon suite of the Savoy Hotel about three o'clock in the morning. Only a few hours later, his new wife awakened Hollowell by gently laying a cold cloth over his eyes. She informed him that three of his buddies had arrived to pick him up for the long automobile ride to Michigan. The honeymoon was over.

Three months later the 795th, an enlarged cadre of the 184th Field Artillery, was continuing its training in Northern Michigan. One day, as Hollowell was conducting a machine gun firing exercise, Major General Benjamin Lear from the Second Army arrived to inspect the battalion's readiness. He paid special attention to the authoritative way in which Hollowell was commanding the exercise. Finally the general walked over to speak with him. He began by congratulating him on his performance and then asked him about his military experience and career. As Hollowell learned later, Lear, before leaving the base, had recommended to Lt. Col. Theophilus Mann, battalion commander, that Hollowell be promoted to the rank of First Lieutenant. Another period of happiness that summer was made possible by a three-week visit from Louise, who also returned to Battle Creek, Michigan, for a brief stay at Christmas time.

Hollowell's next set of orders arrived in January, 1943. They called for him to report to Camp Hood[4] for additional training in tank destroyer warfare. He was able to interrupt the long train trip to Texas with a welcome stopover in Leavenworth to visit his sister-in-law, Harry's wife, and her baby Louise. It was an opportunity to attend a basketball game and then to sit up half the night sharing stories.

He was in good spirits as he continued on his way to Texas. The train stopped at the station in Wichita, his birthplace, and there he scribbled one of the many letters he would write during those years of Army duty.

So far this trip has been most enjoyable, although this train is over two hours late. We left K.C. about 9 a.m., one hour late, and have continued to lose time. I'm due to arrive at Killeen, which is just out of Camp Hood, early in the morning. It would be lovely having you along. You would enjoy the trip, I believe. Chicago, Kansas City, Wichita, Oklahoma City, Forth Worth. Maybe we can take such a trip for our honeymoon, huh?

The days that followed called for him to revise his thinking on the subject. Racism, he quickly discovered, was also alive and well at Camp Hood. Initially he kept his temper in check and resolved to get through the experience as painlessly as possible.

Then one evening Hollowell decided to catch a movie on the post. He bought his ticket from the cashier and entered the theater. Since the film hadn't started, the house lights were still up, and he found the officers' section without difficulty. As he settled into his seat and waited for the beginning of the show, a young, white corporal appeared beside him. The noncom nervously invited him to take a seat in the last row of the theater. Hollowell was angry, but he calmly replied that he was already quite comfortable. The corporal disappeared — but not for long. He soon returned, this time with the message that Lieutenant Hollowell would have to move. Hollowell was already seething at the first affront, but he kept his voice low and asked for the source of that order. When the corporal said it came from the Theater Officer, Hollowell suggested that the corporal send him out to deliver that order personally. The agitated young man disappeared again.

Instead of the lieutenant in charge of theater seating, a short and pompous little major, attached to headquarters, blustered up. Hollowell remembers him as bearing an uncannily striking resemblance to Adolf Hitler.

"You want to take a seat in the back row?" he snorted, quietly but aggressively.

"No, sir," replied Hollowell.

"Well, either do it or leave," the major shot back in a harsh whisper.

"I'll leave, sir."

The major seemed both ruffled and relieved by Hollowell's cool politeness. "I'm sure they'll refund your money," he offered.

Hollowell told him he wasn't interested in a refund and left the theater—his posture erect, his face betraying nothing, and his emotions raging. The incident had been all the spark needed to ignite a gaseous build-up of frustration. Returning to his quarters, he sat down and in cold fury typed a hard letter addressed to post headquarters. With measured, steely phrases he documented in detail the exclusion of Negroes from the camp's officer facilities as well as a list of other indignities. It concluded with a recitation of that evening's episode. When he had finished the first draft, he showed it to Captain Stewart, another officer from his outfit who also had trained at Fort Custer. Together, the two of them made further revisions, and Hollowell then typed a letter-perfect final copy.

This manifesto of the young lieutenant proved powerful enough to attract quick attention. It generated a meeting between the regimental commander whose desk it had reached and some eight or nine other Negro officers who were in training and housed in Hollowell's barracks. This colonel seemed sympathetic, but his message offered no relief. He noted that their stay at Camp Hood would be relatively brief and that the "situation" was bound to change in time. The colonel counseled patience and suggested that they drop the matter.

It was tempting for Hollowell to follow this advice until the colonel asked him to withdraw the letter. He replied that he would do so if the commanding officer would endorse it back to him, thereby taking official action. He doubted that would happen, and he was not to be surprised. The colonel declined, and Hollowell told him to let the letter continue its way up the chain of command in the direction of headquarters.

Several days later the captain charged with administration of the officers who were at the camp for advanced study pulled Hollowell from the line of march as they were returning from a training exercise. He relayed the message that the lieutenant was to report to the base command by one o'clock that afternoon. Hollowell hurriedly showered and put on a clean uniform. By twelve-thirty he was being driven by jeep to headquarters. There the secretary informed him that Colonel Miller, Chief of Staff for the post, was at lunch but would return very soon.

Hollowell didn't have to wait long for the colonel, a very tall and powerful man in his late forties. The young officer came to attention, clicked his heels and reported.

"So you're Lieutenant Hollowell," said the Colonel, staring at him with great curiosity. "Well, the General will be here in just a minute."

Hollowell suddenly realized that his letter had made it all the way to the top of the command chain more quickly than he expected. He was nervously swearing to himself, but there wasn't much time to compose his thoughts. Almost immediately he heard the sound of boots in the corridor and saw a Major General rush by him into a private office. The colonel followed him in and then returned to summon Hollowell.

Hollowell presented himself in his best officerial manner, breaking a salute with a snap that must have sent shock waves across the room before he took the seat offered him. In front of him, on the general's desk, he could see his letter, with the label, "CONFIDENTIAL," stamped across the first page. "Who wrote this letter for you?" demanded the general.

Hollowell began to speculate that he might be under suspicion for association with Communists or the kinds of so-called "fellow travelers" who had been pressing for integration of the armed forces. He temporized by responding, "I'm not sure I understand the general."

"Did someone help you to write it?"

Hollowell assured him that the work was his own.

Seemingly satisfied, the general lowered his voice to a calmer level and began to speak in a more conversational and easy-going fashion, "Lieutenant Hollowell, I had an old colored mammy, and if there was ever anyone that we loved in our family, it was that old colored mammy...." As he continued in that shallow vein, seeking to establish his credentials as an unprejudiced human being, Hollowell, not a profane man as a rule, could only think, "Oh, shit!"

Having certified, at least to his satisfaction, a close identification with Negroes, the general began to warm to his subject. After making it clear that he had been up North "to Cincinnati and St. Louis" where he had observed customs to be somewhat different from Texas, he then tried to elicit Hollowell's sympathy. "When I first came to Camp Hood, they wouldn't even let Negro soldiers off the train in Killeen. I had to go around in the community, speaking to groups in churches and the like, to get people to be tolerant, lieutenant. Tolerant! " He made it abundantly clear that those efforts had stretched his capabilities for social engineering as far as he intended them to go. Then he concluded quickly by reminding Hollowell that the lieutenant was at Camp Hood for a course which would not last long and that he should get his work done and drop the matter. "Is that understood?"

Before Hollowell could even say "Yes, sir," the general concluded his rambling discourse by barking, "That's all, lieutenant!" Hollowell was military enough to understand that he dared not even open his mouth. He made his exit, the only consolation being that he had at least made his point. Recalling that course of events, Hollowell notes, "I don't know what happened to that letter. It may be in my military record. I hope it is."

Another visit from Louise took some of the sting from that miserable winter in Texas (she stayed with a minister and his wife in Temple, and Hollowell would slip off base whenever possible to be with her). Then, abruptly, his unit was sent to the Army camp at Lake Ponchatrain outside New Orleans for firefighting training. The reason for the shift from tank destroyer duties wasn't immediately clear, but after Louise met him in New Orleans for a brief visit, he was able to notify her that they would next be transferred to Camp Patrick Henry in Virginia. From there he sent her word that he would soon be shipping out from Newport News.

Anxious to see him one last time before his departure, she caught the train for Virginia. Yet when she arrived at the USO early on the day that they had arranged to meet, he was nowhere to be found. Deeply upset, not sure whether he had already left for overseas, she paced and fretted through the afternoon. That evening Hollowell sauntered into the

USO hall where his happy but nearly hysterical wife threw herself into his arms. In response to her questions, he explained that he had decided to pay a visit to the campus of Hampton Institute, the famous Negro college, several miles away.

Some friends gave them a bedroom for what they thought would be their last night together for a long time. Hollowell and his men had received the boat order number; their bags were packed and stacked on the stanchions, waiting to be loaded aboard the troop ship. Yet when Hollowell reported the next morning, prepared to leave for Europe, he learned that a radical change in plans was underway. Despite the intensive training it had received, the Negro 795th Tank Destroyer Battalion was being dismantled and would see no action. The African campaign against Rommel's forces had demonstrated that the U.S. Army's equipment was inadequate against the superior German panzers. Headquarters company of the battalion, under the command of the same Lt. Col. Mann under whom Hollowell had trained in Michigan, was converted into a port company and left immediately for the European theater. The line companies, including a detachment commanded by Hollowell, reported to Camp Pickett near Petersburg for additional training in firefighting. Several of the firefighting units left for Europe later that summer, but by the time Hollowell's company had settled in at Pickett, he was eligible for a long leave.

Louise traveled back up from Atlanta to be with him, and the two finally could enjoy their long-deferred honeymoon. They spent a portion of that summer in nearby Blackstone and capped the time together with a trip to New York. Before leaving that city they obtained tickets for Carmen Jones, saw Cab Calloway performing in Harlem and visited some friends from Louise's days in New York when she had lived in the Dunbar Apartments.

They returned by train to Virginia by way of Washington, where they had to transfer to a Jim Crow car at Union Station. It was hot and the "colored car" had no cooling system. Opening the windows permitted some fresh air to enter, but since there were no screens, the breeze also carried in the filthy smoke and cinders from the locomotive. With perspiration dripping from their dirty faces, they clambered off the segregated rail car in Blackstone. They were in love and still in a honeymoon frame of mind, but Hollowell nonetheless recalls the bitter stabs of irony he felt when he remembered that he was preparing to go oversees to protect this "way of life."

In the fall Hollowell's detachment moved on to Camp Miles Standish near Taunton, Massachusetts, and then, after more than three years since his recall to active duty, Hollowell's outfit finally received orders to proceed to Europe. On November 4, 1944, after Louise had come north one more time to say good-bye, Lieutenant Donald L. Hollowell and his men shipped out from Boston.

They disembarked in France and spent a month assembling their equipment before making their way east across the French countryside to Dijon. From there, after a brief stay, they proceeded northeast to Epinal on the Moselle River. Trained as soldiers, they were now only fire fighters, so they swallowed their frustration and settled in for the better part of a relatively quiet year, away from the fighting. It was an opportunity for Hollowell to make friends with the local fire chief and other civilians and to acquire fluency in the French language.

One of the few surviving letters of the many that he sent home during that period was this one:

> *Baby:*
>
> *Today was Valentine Day, and some controlling Being must have known it. For we had the most beautiful day we have had in months and now the starry sky above is picturesque. One of those kinds of nights, you know.*
>
> *I recall Valentine's Day of three years ago. You came to Columbus to the party. As I recall, we did enjoy ourselves immensely even though the other wolves tried to stick in a howl. However, there was a bit of difficulty getting together at first, wasn't there?*
>
> *The following year I believe I sent you candy from Custer — a heart-shaped box. Was it not the same last year? Oh yes, I remember. We were in New Orleans, having just arrived. My first trip into the city was for the purpose of obtaining the candy for "My Valentine."*

> *This year, darling, I have only my love to send. But it is sincere, devoted love that seems to increase with the passing of the years. The kind that is to take me back to the States and you without having been too much affected by the length of my absence.*
> *I love you "My Valentine."*
> *Don*

The major assignment of Hollowell's detachment was to assist with the protection of several Army field hospitals and other installations in the region. The detachment it relieved moved on toward Germany but had to return within three weeks. The German army, although badly weakened and with its ranks spread thinly across several fronts, was still a formidable force. In mid-December of the brutal winter of 1944, it launched a counteroffensive. The fighting in the Ardennes Forest took place along an eighty-mile line being held by an inadequate number of U.S. troops. The infamous Battle of the Bulge, which would rage from December 16 to 26 and lead to seventy-seven thousand American casualties, was underway.

Soon the call went out for junior grade infantry officers. Hollowell was giving serious consideration to volunteering and transferring back to the infantry. Surely the Army could put to good use his extensive training in officer candidate school and in tank destroyer warfare. Then he learned that the Army had also made it pointedly clear that it was not looking for officers of color. He vowed that day never again to volunteer for duty in a combat unit. That winter, he and many of the other Negro troops—still fiercely patriotic—had to content themselves with listening to the sounds of bombardment some sixty miles away and cheering from below as the flying armadas of American bombers roared above them in the direction of German targets. Many of them yearned to be engaged in the kind of action in which some Negro soldiers and airmen, like the heroic 332nd fighter squadron in Italy, found themselves.

On March 8, 1945, as the combat units of the American Army moved eastward, Hollowell's letter to his wife included these lines:

> *Hey, Baby:*
> *Yes, "Baby" is what I like to call you best next to "Sweetie" and "Lou." Don't know why. You will*

recall that I told you once that before meeting you and marrying you, I did not like "babe" or "baby." But I guess it's all in the way you say it and the feeling behind it, huh? Just like saying "Donnie." There are people I wouldn't let call me that. But, when you say it, I don't mind at all. As a matter of fact I don't know but what I like it sometimes. Again, it's all in the way it's said and of course by whom.

I am quite tired tonight having traveled about 800 miles in the past three or four days. [The sector in which he served was a large one.] Included in my travels was Paris. It is certainly quite a city. Enjoyed the short time I was there and was a very good boy. (Smile) Saw Col. Mann while there. Also saw Lts. Wilson, Hopkins and Hancock at another place that I can't mention [because of military security]. All of them were well and sent regards. Returned here today to find seven letters. Was I tickled? Yes Indeed!...Across the hall I can hear "Sweet Slumber" which is quite in order, for I'm going to bed tout [de] suite and hope I dream sweet dreams of you...."

The war in Europe officially ended two months later. On May 7, the eve of V-E Day, Louise wrote to her husband:

My dear Don:
  ...Have been thinking of you so much, your coming home again, and what our future plans are to be.... Well time will tell what we shall do. Anyway, if you are fortunate enough to come home for good I shall thank God and be happy for the privilege of having you with me.... However, when you get home I promise to have decent closing hours that I can be with you in the evenings. We are so lucky to have each other that I think we should try at all times to be together. Unless it is a very short absence for business reasons on your part...

  Well Sweetie, Commencement is just around the corner. Lacks one day of being one month. Much can happen between now and then but pray that I keep my courage and perseverance to the end. The grades were sent ... and I am among the highest in the class. In fact

> *there is a tie between three of us and it was left for the Registrar's office to choose the Valedictorian [Geneva Barker, Mae Harrison and me]. I had the next highest number of votes. Perhaps I shall be Magna Cum Laude. If not, Cum Laude is certain. Anyway, I am glad to finish even without honors.*
>
> [continuing the next morning, V-E Day]
> *...just got out of bed fifteen minutes ago and decided to tune in [the radio] for absolute certainty [about V-E Day]. Celebrations may be in order, but I think I prefer to pray instead.*

For the next eleven months, the Hollowells corresponded frequently, each of them writing at least four or five letters a week. Most of his letters are now lost, but her epistles to him provide a poignant picture of wartime life for a young, vivacious Negro woman, separated from her soldier husband:

> *June, 1945*
> *...Your cablegram was received on the morning of June 15th. Thanks a lot Sweetie for your best congratulations... No husband in the world could be more thoughtful than you. Yes, with letters, remembrances and gifts, too... Went shopping last Friday and bought myself a black, sheer summer dress. Had planned to pick it up on Saturday, but got too busy & failed to do so. You will like it when you see it. I am buying it from your savings account & considering it as a graduation gift from you... The price was rather steep for a summer dress but I wanted it. May use it for any dress-up occasion–like a tea, bridge party, or any sort of formal daytime or early evening affair. Price $45.00 & $2.00 to shorten the skirt. Hope I do not get a spanking, dear. (smile)*
>
> *[undated]*
> *...[graduation picture enclosed] How do you like me in my mortar board and gown. Not so bad, huh? Looks right co-ed-ish, if I do say so myself...*

June 18, 1945
...I was very glad to hear that mom & dad [his parents] have bought a home in California... It will be swell to take a trip with you all the way across the continent. Did you say by plane? Well, I will think about it dear. The Pullman accommodations may be equally desirable. Do you know that will be a long, long trip? Probably read a couple of books while crossing the continent in addition to entertaining my husband. It will be lots of fun I am sure!

Still have my fingers crossed for you and I am hoping that the revision of the point system—to be announced next month—will help you somewhat in being released...

A week later, Louise wrote:

Hello Don:
On last evening at eight thirty I listened to the "Amer. Album of Familiar Music" and made believe, as usual, that you were sitting beside me also listening to same. As expressed by the author of "The Things He Wrote to Her" I could feel your presence...

Sorry Baby but I was lazy again on yesterday. Did not get to church. Mother went all alone & I stayed and did a bit of cleaning and reading. When she returned I had only put the beans on to cook, with all the rest of the dinner to be cooked by her. I must have been a "wee bit" lonesome for my Donnie, for I smoked two cigarettes & drank one highball which caused me to fall asleep only to find mother calling me to get ready for dinner. She said she understood what the trouble was. (smile) I laughed because I knew she was right...

You know I have been thinking of a little dream house darling for you & me. Perhaps, this is a little too much anticipatory planning, huh? We must first decide where we want to live and then begin working toward our goals. Well time will tell! Anyway I have a yen for some dirt under my feet–you know at least a little in the back yard. Not too far out in the country though. Far enough away from the city to get some fresh air.

> Saturday, July 4
> ...The C. M .E. Church is observing its 75th Anniversary in Memphis, Tenn. from Aug. 22-25. I thought I would send ...five dollars as a donation for you, since they are having a drive to raise several thousand dollars. Would that please you? Only thing that you will question is that I should have sent more. (smile). Just paid five on my pledge of $20.00 to Big Bethel A. M. E. Hope to pay the remainder of it by September...

> July 4, 1945
> ...I am spending a quiet July 4th at home. So far I have done very little in the way of work. Had a nice dinner which was very easy to prepare—cold sliced lamb for a change... warm potato salad, steamed cabbage and fresh cornbread—also another scanty item on our menu.
>
> ...Do they play baseball in France the same as here? If so, you may attend a few games for a diversion. The Black Crackers have been doing rather well for themselves so I see by the papers. Not having an automobile I find it most inconvenient to get to and fro from Ponce de Leon Park. Tonight Louis Armstrong and his band will be here. However, it is not being promoted by Neal [Montgomery–local entertainment promoter]. Seems to me some white man is "muscling in" on him. That always seems to happen sooner or later, especially when one appears to be doing very well...

Another letter from her in early July that year made it clear that she was cherishing the thoughts of domesticity:

> My dear husband,
> ....Went to see "Wuthering Heights" on Monday evening—Addie and I—and I must say it was even more enjoyable than before.
>
> On last evening Neal Montgomery... & Callie took us out Simpson Street to see their new home. Oh, but it is a beauty! Lovely both inside and outside with a sunken garden in the rear and hedges all around. The lawn is so green and pretty and extends the whole length

> *of the lot on one side. It will be swell for al fresco parties, sunbathing and the like. There is a fish pond with a large spray of water falling over it–a bird fountain, a double garage beyond the rear lawn. Cost them about ten thousand for the place to say nothing of the expensive, modern furnishings. I am happy for them for they deserve it after nineteen years of hard struggling together...*
>
> *August 2, 1945*
> *...The war situation in Japan seems to be "red hot." Let us hope it remains so for a while that each will realize the hopelessness of all this hostility, atrocities and crime and decide to try and be brothers, respecting human rights regardless of color or creed.*
>
> *I see a tough fight ahead for my race but, as futile as it appears right now, I think a change for the better is inevitable whether some people like it or not...*

Soon thereafter Hollowell and his men finally moved into Germany for an uneventful stay in the Franconian city of Bamberg. As he cooled his heels in Europe, Louise sweated her way through a hot Atlanta summer. Her letters to him, though, made it clear that life in the States was slowly returning to normal and that she missed him very much.

> *Saturday evening*
> *[August 11]*
> *...Just listening to the "Hit Parade" for a change. Can you imagine me having finished my work early enough to indulge in such pleasure? Well, here I am! All dressed and ready to walk out except that one of the operators has a customer, so I must wait for her to finish before leaving... Wish for you now that we could take a nice walk together as we once did. That is, if there are not too many "drunks" on the street. It is probably a little early yet for them.*
>
> *...Oh, baby, everybody is expecting V-J Day on this side... Darling, the synopsis of "Valley of Decision" was certainly a comprehensive one and was most intelligible. I think I could relate the story most accurately by following it. The picture has been here already and, unfortunately, was booked by one of the*

theatres where colored people cannot visit... Say, the weather has actually broken and we have had two nights which were perfect for sleeping. Almost needed a blanket, but used a crinkled bed spread instead. Had you been home, I suspect a sheet would have been sufficient... Shall be expecting you to come home after V-J Day. Perhaps that will greatly alter the situation in Europe as well...

*Wednesday
August 15, 1945*
...This morning everybody is rejoicing over the "unconditional surrender" of Japan and the end of the war... Of course you can imagine how I feel over it all. Having a dear husband, uncle, cousin, and brother-in-law in the Army affects me four-fold, but thank God they will be coming home in the not too distant future, and life for me will take on new zest and enthusiasm for years to come. I realize, too, that there will be problems and difficulties facing us, yet we shall ultimately triumph over them. With courage and patience we are bound to win...

There was a note of sadness which seemed to hover over things last evening despite the fact that there was much hilarity and excitement created among the general public. I could not let it completely overshadow my sober, serious thinking of those persons on both sides who have lost so much in death and wounded—those who are so grief-stricken as a result of same. Before turning in for the night I prayed for the recovery of those who are mentally and physically handicapped and for the safe return of all, & a permanent lasting peace... Here's hoping the end of the war will bring about a speedy revision of the point system.

*Monday morning
August 20, 1945*
...Now that Lois is here again to assist with the work at the shop I thought I should take a few days of well-deserved rest. On tomorrow I expect to leave for New York... There is a young lady at the "Y" who is head of the business dept. at Morris Brown College. She and I shall probably get together and see a few

shows and plays. I tried to postpone this trip but thought I should get away for the change. Besides, I am fed up with "Jim Crow" theaters and the like and once a year is not too often to get away from it all...

*2588 7th Avenue, Apt. 3-L
New York, N.Y.
Aug. 24, 1945*

*My darling husband:
Here I am in big, old New York without my Honey. And although I am alone, with the exception of a few friends, you are more than missed. My mind reverts to last summer when we were here together for only a few days which proved to be most enjoyable to say the least...*

Arrived Wednesday night between nine and ten. The train was about three hours late. Grabbed a cab and taxied up town alone which I never expect to do again. The driver talked to me a little too much. At least I felt that he did. Perhaps he thought it was my first trip to New York–I don't know–but I soon got him straightened out. (smile) Next time I shall ride the subway and pick up the bag the following day...

*New York, N.Y.
August 30, 1945
...Yesterday marked the end of my first week here. So far I have had a swell time. Got in two movies— "The Corn is Green" and "Rhapsody in Blue"—and enjoyed them both.*

Harry [Hollowell's brother] came over Monday night and we played "Chinese Checkers" and then went to the "Lenox Lounge" for supper.

On Tuesday night I met Harry at South Ferry and he took me over to Staten Island to hear his orchestra perform at the Recreation Center. Afterwards he brought me home. My, but I enjoyed the evening! Some of the fellows asked me for a dance and after I had the first one with Harry I consented to take a few with some of them...

Plan to see a play on Friday or Saturday, "Anna Lucasta." [Philip Yordan's play featured an all-Negro cast.] ...Saturday morning I hope to see a musical comedy entitled "Song of Norway" ...then embark for Atlanta at 6:55 p.m. Have Pullman reservations so I should be allright as far as comfort is concerned.

Monday night
November 20, 1945
...Thursday is Thanksgiving, so I shall have to get these customers ready for the [football] game. By the way, I think I can make this one—the first for me this year. Should enjoy it after so long a time... As usual, we wished for you to enjoy the [Sunday] dinner with us. Had the same type...we had during the ...rationing program. However, we have enjoyed some beef and lamb since the program relaxed... Oh, baby, they reduced the points for officers from 75 to 73. That should help a little, huh... Thanks a million, dear, for the extra $20. Shall use ten of it to get my coat out of storage. On second thought, I think I will take the money you send next month and buy a gift for myself. Do not know yet what I want. If I see that I can do without the extra check I will let you know early next year. Then you can buy the bonds.

November 24, 1945
Dearest Don:
Had a rather delightful time on Thanksgiving Day. I attended the game which was M.B.C.'s homecoming and the annual Turkey Day Classic for the city of Atlanta. My, but there were people there! Seemed almost like old times, except that I missed you terribly... We have an invitation to the annual Joymen's dance. You know the one we attended when our marriage was announced. I only wish you were here to go with me next Friday night...

Wednesday night
December 3, 1945
...Received no letters from you on last week, so I began wondering if you were on the way home. Evidently you are still there, for two letters came Monday attesting to the fact that you had not left on

November 28th... Surely you will get here by Feb. if not before. Let us continue to hope for the best. Keep sweet and remember in the language of the song "I am saving myself for you.

December 4, 1945

My darling husband:
... I went... to church... Chaplain Chas. H. Hunter, recently returned from the Italian theatre of war, preached for us, and then was our guest for dinner. He is a former pastor of Atlanta and Macon, and a friend of long-standing, who knew me when I was attending high school in Florida. He certainly enjoyed his visit, and he expressed a desire to meet you. Said he could see from your photo and from what I said that he will like you. Just the fact that you are my husband was enough. (Smile.)

Chaplain Hunter, his wife and little girl [Charlayne, whom Hollowell would represent sixteen years later] reside in Covington, Georgia. They have bought a home there; in fact, he said Mrs. Hunter bought it from his salary that he sent her during the 31 months in Europe. Not a bad investment, huh?...

I have just two weeks more to go to classes. Then return on January 3rd, I believe, to complete the other three weeks before the semester ends. That will be six hours on my master's (at Atlanta University). At least I have had the opportunity to see what is expected of a graduate student...

December 6, 1945

...Went down to the basement early to get some washing done. Finished by nine fifteen and was back in time to enjoy a good breakfast...Bacon and eggs— now that is something! All rationing has been lifted with the exception of sugar...

December 23, 1945

...On your birthday the points were again reduced to... 70 for officers, You can imagine how happy I was to hear of same. Also 48 months service for officers. So you can see that you are eligible for two reasons. By

the way, honey, you are going to get your promotion from what I understand, provided you have an efficiency rating of 40... You will be home before you realize it...

Christmas, 1945

Hello darling:
Today has been one of rest for me with the exception of a few hours to prepare dinner. After it was cooked I decided to take advantage of the peaceful quietness of the day by taking a long nap. Of course I awoke at intervals and listened to the beautiful Christmas carols. Thought of you and wished for a magic carpet to take me to you, at least for the day."

December 28, 1945

My dear Don:
You should have seen me hanging around the house this morning waiting for the letter carrier to come... So you are smoking cigars now. Well perhaps it is all right but they smell a bit strong to me. I suppose though that I can get used to them. Probably no worse than a very old pipe that has been neglected...

There are a good many conclaves being held now in various cities. Do not know where the Kappas are holding theirs. The Sigmas are in St. Louis; Omegas in Wash.

Oh, Lane College is to play football in the "Flower Bowl" in New Orleans on January 1st. Tenn. State and Texas College in the "Vulcan Bowl" at B'hm, Ala; "All Stars" to play at Harper's Field here on the first of Jan.

January 8, 1946

...It will certainly please me when you get your orders to come home. What's the idea of not training more firefighters for replacements. They didn't expect you to stay there forever, did they? You need not make it quite this severe when you talk to the Colonel. (smile)

Relative to your staying in the army, I had also thought of it from the same angle you mentioned but I wondered if you would be able to keep the present rank *and salary. Or if you would have to revert to the previous enlisted status of corporal or private first class. Well, if you knew where you were to be stationed, it might not be so bad. However, I do not fancy living in the piney woods of Miss., the wilds of Texas or the isolated regions of the far west. (smile)...*

It was announced by radio over the week-end that troops overseas would probably remain another ninety days in order to get sufficient replacements. What a break! I only hope the order for you has already gone through...

Early in 1946, Hollowell took advantage of a special tourist deal for soldiers and traveled through southern Germany and Switzerland to Italy. Upon arriving in Rome, he placed a telephone call to Louise. By February he had finally accumulated enough service points to qualify for a return to the States. He assumed command of a bi-racial quartermaster "filler" company (so named because it was composed of men from a variety of units who also qualified to go home). The company proceeded to Antwerp, Belgium, and in March it boarded ship for New York.

The crossing was a long one with a goodly share of stormy days, The night before they docked, Hollowell went up to the deck of the crowded troop carrier. Off the starboard side the welcome sight of the amber lights along the Long Island coastline came into view. The next morning the ship reached its berth in New York City, and his feet touched native ground again after an absence of more than eighteen months. Hollowell would later receive a promotion to the rank of Captain while in the Reserves, but he was more than ready to write an end to this military chapter of his life.

Thousands of Negro servicemen were killed and wounded during the war, but many more did return. Army statistics record a total of 1,154,729 inductees or draftees and 7,768 commissioned Negro officers in the service by the time of V-J Day in September, 1945. Like Hollowell, most of them could describe a wide assortment of indignities and abuses they had to endure while performing military service for their country.[5] The experiences scarred some of them so profoundly and lastingly that it became virtually impossible for them to lead full lives.

What made it possible for Hollowell to resume civilian life with the essentially positive attitude that would continue to stand him in good stead for the next forty-five years? In his words:

> *I grew considerably in the military. Certainly the experiences of leadership were important. I learned how to work with men and to guide them; to administer an office; to be disciplined in conduct and habits. At the same time there were many bitter experiences that were sufficient to cause a man to hate. And I am confident that but for the fact that I found Jesus along the way back when I was about fifteen and had practiced a relationship with Him, I would have entered civilian society with a heart full of hate. But that was not the situation. I did not like many of the experiences I had...but I also knew that hate consumes one and that one has to use that energy constructively in an effort to change those diabolical aspects of life which impinge upon him and others of his race. That's what I chose to do.*

ENDNOTES

[1] Douglass, Frederick, "Men of Color, to Arms!" from <u>Life and Times of Frederick Douglass</u>, as reprinted in <u>Black Protest</u> (Editor, Joanne Grant), Fawcett Publications, New York, 1968.

[2] Morris Brown, an African Methodist Episcopal college, was a member of the federation of contiguous, historically Negro institutions known as the Atlanta University Center.

[3] Although commissioned as an infantry officer, to his joy he was never to serve a day in the infantry.

[4] Lt. Col. Theophilus Mann, Hollowell's battalion commander, would later be elected Grand Polemarch of Kappa Alpha Psi, Hollowell's fraternity.

[5] On July 26, 1948, President Harry S. Truman, who had managed to rise above his personal racist attitudes to make civil rights a federal priority for the first time since Reconstruction, issued Executive Order 9981 directing "equality of treatment and opportunity" in the U.S. armed forces.

Donald L. Hollowell as 2nd Lieutenant in the U.S. Army

Louise Thornton prior to her marriage to Donald L. Hollowell

Chattahoochee County Courthouse, Cusseta, GA, built with slave labor in 1854. Site of a 1958 murder trial defended successfully by Attorneys Donald L. Hollowell and Albert Thompson

Georgia Governor and Mrs Zell Miller
at the Intergenerational Tribute to Donald Hollowell

Attorney Hollowell, accompanied by his legal team, being interviewed by press after court case involving desegregation of public transportation in Atlanta. Includes, l - r: Attorneys Donald Hollowell, S.S. Robinson, A.T. Walden, Romae Turner Powell and R.E. Thomas

Attorney Hollowell arriving with papers for release of
Dr. Martin Luther King, Jr. from the Reidsville State Prison

Attorney Hollowell escorts Dr. Martin Luther King, Jr.
and Rev. Ralph D. Abernathy from the Reidsville State Prison in 1960

Hollowell, Dr. Martin Luther King, Jr. and
Rev. Ralph D. Abernathy leaving the Reidsville State Prison

King being interveiwed after release to Hollowell,
as Abernathy looks on

The Fulton County Daily Report shows Hamilton Holmes leaving the University of Georgia after registering in 1961

Donald Hollowell, Constance Baker Motley and Horace T. Ward, principal attorneys in the University of Georgia case

E.H. Gadsden (Superior Court Judge, Ret.) of Savannah, GA and Thomas Jackson (Former City Judge) of Macon, GA, co-counsels with Donald Hollowell in other Georgia cases
(Photo of partner, Bobby Mayfield, deceased, unavailable)

Mary Frances Early, the first Negro graduate student, and Charlayne Hunter and Hamilton Holmes, the first Negro undergraduates, to graduate from the University of Georgia

Supreme Court Justice Hugo Black and Hollowell

Members of the defense counsel, with Donald Hollowell, in the 1962 Augusta, GA "Delta Manor Trial" of nine Negroes accused of murder. Attorneys Frank D. Reeves (Wash. DC.), Robert L. Carter (NY), John Ruffin (Augusta, GA) and John D. Watkins (Augusta, GA). (Hollowell not shown)

Receiving an honor at Berean Seventh Day Adventist Church with godson "Chip"

Brochure from Hollowell's 1964 Candidacy for Superior Court Judge

Donald L. Hollowell with Duke Ellington at a New York City fundraiser for Hollowell's 1964 Superior Court Judge campaign

Cleopatra Johnson (wife of Senator Leroy Johnson), (Mrs.) Jimmy Bentley (wife of the State Insurance Commissioner), Azira Hill (wife of Atlanta Life Insurance Company President Jesse Hill) and Louise Hollowell at the first integrated Commerce Club Luncheon

Donald and Louise Hollowell leaving the Atlanta Biltmore Hotel following the first integrated Bar Association Dinner in 1965, where Dean Rusk was the speaker

Donald Hollowell, with Franklin Roosevelt, Jr.,
at the opening of the EEOC office in Atlanta

"Daddy" King, Franklin Roosevelt, Jr. and Donald Hollowell
at the opening of Hollowell's EEOC office in Atlanta

Attorneys Donald L. Hollowell and Horace T. Ward, with successful murder trial defendant Preston Cobb and family members

Attorneys Donald Hollowell and Howard Moore, Jr., with defendant Preston Cobb

Group photograph at Donald and Louise Hollowell's 25th Wedding Anniversary

Senior members of the 1960-1966 law firm Hollowell, Ward, Moore and Alexander, left to right: William H. Alexander, now Superior Court Judge; Horace T. Ward, now Federal District Judge; Donald L. Hollowell, retired civil rights lawyer and Regional Attorney, EEOC; and Howard Moore, Jr., internationally famous trial lawyer (circa 1968)

Donald L. Hollowell receiving the "Laurel Wreath," Kappa Alpha Psi Fraternity's highest award from Grand Polemarch Ernest Davenport, in 1968. Seated are Rev. Leon Sullivan, a Laurel Wreath Designee and C. Roger Wilson, a 1968 Laurel Wreath Laureate.

Donald L. Hollowell and C. Rodger Wilson, Kappa Alpha Psi Fraternity Laurel Wreath Laureates, on the cover of the 1968 *Kappa Journal*

Kappa Boule' of Sigma Pi Phi Fraternity
at Christmas Dinner Dance (circa, 1970)

Deputy George "Duke" Beasley and Atlanta Mayor Maynard Jackson,
(standing) at Hollowell's 1976 Ten-year EEOC recognition

Donald L. Hollowell visiting with Presidential Candidate Jimmy Carter at a 1976 Voter Education Project Dinner

The Donald Hollowells and Senator Ted Kennedy, in 1978

Donald L. Hollowell being sworn in as an honorary member of Phi Alpha Delta Law Fraternity on 1978, with Attorneys Wiley Branton (former Dean, Howard University School of Law); and Vernon E. Jordan (former Director, National Urban League). At far right is former U.S. Supreme Court Justice William O. Douglas. Inset: Walter J. Leonard, Oxford University Fellow/Lecturer and former President, Fisk University

Donald L. Hollowell and Georgia State Senator Leroy R. Johnson, with World Boxing Champion Muhammad Ali (then Cassius Clay) in Atlanta

Donald L. Hollowell with frequent co-counsel,
the late Attorney Chevene B. King, Sr. and his wife Carol King

James M. Hinton, Roy Wilkins and the Hollowells
at the 1978 NAACP Freedom Fund Dinner

The September, 1981 Gate City Bar Association and Georgia Conference of Black Lawyers' Tribute to Donald Hollowell for Law, Human Relations, Human Rights and Civil Rights

Louise Hollowell as Professor of English, Emeritus, at Morris Brown College, and with Charlayne Hunter-Gault at the Gate City Bar Association Tribute to Donald L. Hollowell

Donald Hollowell, Charlayne Hunter-Gault and Dr. Benjamin E. Mays, at the Gate City Bar Association Tribute to Hollowell

Donald Hollowell, Charlayne Hunter and Julian Bond at the 1981 Gate City Bar Association Tribute

Donald Hollowell is congratulated by Judge Elbert P. Tuttle, of the U.S. 11th Judicial Circuit, at Hollowell's 1985 Retirement Dinner.

Donald Hollowell, Hamilton Holmes and Judge William A. Bootle (U.S. District Judge for the Middle District Georgia), trial judge in the Holmes, et al., v. Danner (UGA) case, with 1988 UGA commencement speaker Charlayne Hunter-Gault

Photographs   P - 27

Atlanta Council President Marvin Arrington congratulates Donald L. Hollowell at Gate City Bar Association Retirement Dinner.

Edwards Abrams, Donald L. Hollowell and Vince Dooley, 1989 National Council of Christians and Jews "Brotherhood" Awardees

Hamilton Holmes, Charlayne Hunter, first University of Georgia Black undergraduates, with their Attorney, Donald L. Hollowell, at the UGA Bicentennial Celebration

Mary Jordan (Vernon's mother), Althea Hunter (Charlayne's mother), Isabel Holmes (Hamilton's mother), Attorney Hollowell, Louise Hollowell, Vernon Jordan, Marilyn Holmes (wife of Hamilton), Hamilton Holmes, and Charlayne Hunter, on the UGA campus

Mrs. Coretta Scott King making remarks at the 1989 Ebenezer Baptist Church's Intergenerational Tribute to Donald Hollowell

Harry H. Hollowell, Donald Hollowell's brother, at the piano, during the 1989 Intergenerational Tribute to Hollowell

Donald and Louise Hollowell in his office in the Citizens Trust Bank while hosting guest at the 1990 Annual meeting of the National Bar Association

Donald and Louise Hollowell, at the 1989 "Tradition of Excellence" Award Reception at the Savannah (GA) First City Club

Louise and Donald Hollowell with Atlanta Council President, Marvin Arrington, at the 1990 dedication of the Conference Room at Arrington's Mitchell Street Law Office

Donald and Louise Hollowell,
guests of
Judge and Mrs. Albert Thompson,
at the 1991
Sigma Pi Phi Fraternity Dance,
in Columbus, GA

Judge amd Mrs. Albert Thompson,
of Columbs, GA
at the 1991
Sigma Pi Phi Fraternity Dance

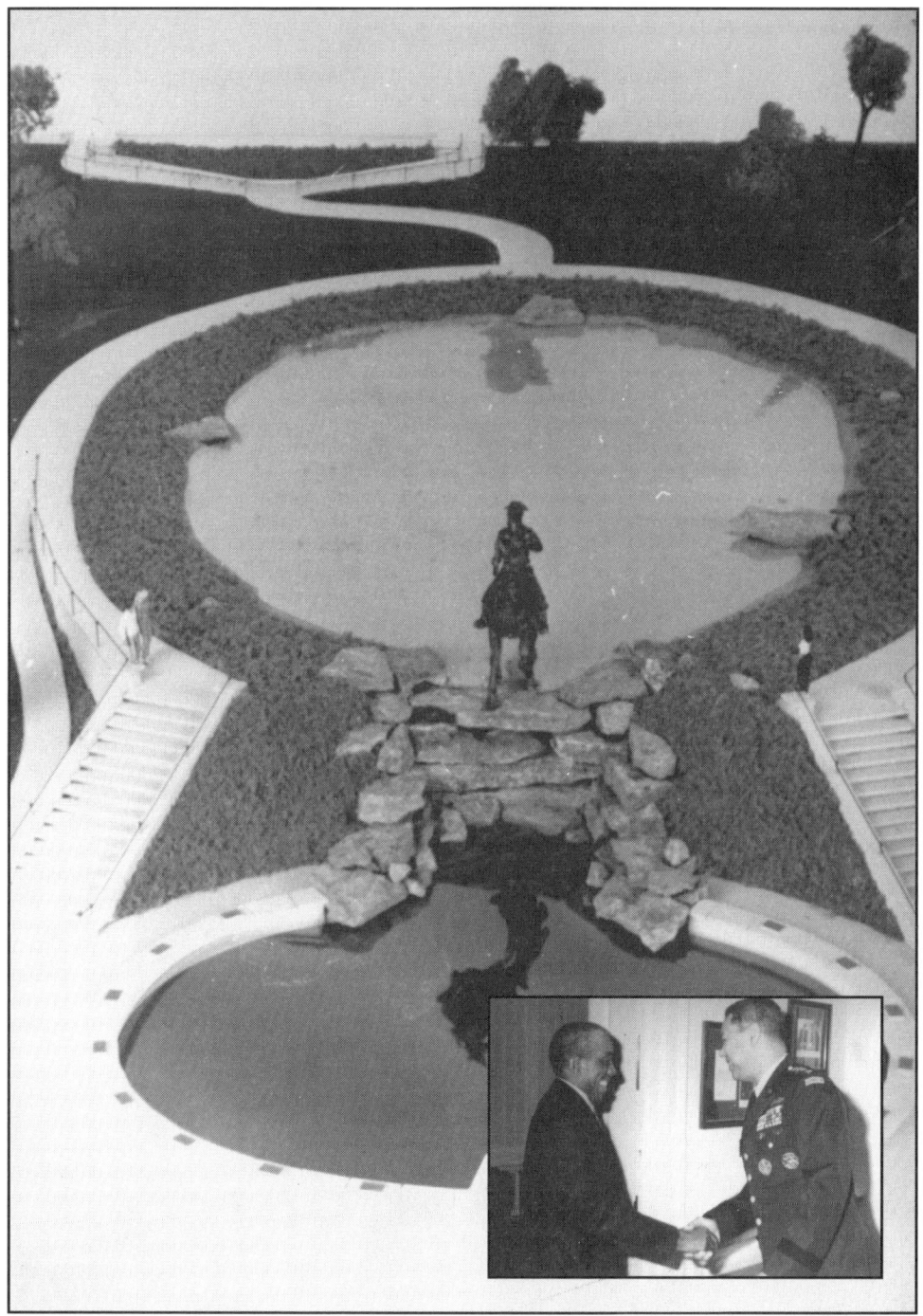

The Buffalo Soldier Monument, at Ft. Leavenworth, Kansas, dedicated in 1992. (Inset: former Buffalo Soldier, CWO4 Harry H. Hollowell and former Chairman of the Joint Chiefs of Staff General Colin Powell, at the dedication.)

Judge Thelma Wyatt-Cummings, Donald L. Hollowell, and Emory University President James T. Laney with Marvin Arrington, Senior Partner of the firm of Arrington and Hollowell, at the announcement of the Donald Hollowell Civil Rights Professorship at Emory Law School

Hamilton Holmes, Ozell Sutton, Jean Young, Jesse Hill, Donald and Louise Hollowell, and Mayor Andrew Young, at the presentation of a portrait of Hollowell, by the Voter Education Project (VEP)

Donald L. Hollowell recipient of the Honorary Degree, Doctor of Laws from Clark Atlanta University, with Clark Atlanta University President Thomas Cole and Spelman College President Johnnetta Cole

The Hollowells with President Clinton
in the East Room of the White House, in 1994

Donald L. Hollowell on the Fall 1993 cover of
A MIND IS, A Publication of the United Negro College Fund,
where he served two terms on its National Alumni Council (NAC)

Atlanta Alumni Chapter, Kappa Alpha Psi Fraternity 50 year members at the 1992 Founder's Day Observance

Kappa Alpha Psi "Laurel Wreath" Laureate, Hollowell, with Grand Polemarch Robert L. Harris, at the head table during the Atlanta Alumni Chapter's 1994 Founders Day Observance

President William H. Minnix of the Wesley Woods Geriatric Center reads the citation preparatory to having Vernon Jordan, Jr. place the "Heroes, Saints and Legends" medallion around the neck of Donald L. Hollowell. (Ritz Carlton Hotel - Buckhead)

Vernon Jordan, Jr., Honorary Chair, making remarks at the "Heroes, Saints and Legends" tribute to Donald Hollowell

Ben Johnson, First Dean of the Georgia State University College of Law, with Donald Hollowell, the recipient of the 1995 "Ben Johnson Award" and Marvin Arrington.

Judge John H. Ruffin, Jr., Judge Horace T. Ward, Attorney Hollowell, and the late Attorney R. E. Thomas discuss their legal careers, in 1996

The Donald and Louise Hollowell *Family & Friends*

Harrison and Ocenia Hollowell, Donald Hollowell's mother and father, at their 50th Anniversary Wedding Ceremony

Mr. & Mrs. Harrison Hollowell, Donald Hollowell's mother and father, at their 50th Anniversary Celebration

Lillie Scott Thornton, Louise Hollowell's mother

Donald, Iris, Corrine and Harry, siblings in the
Harrison Hollowell Family

Sister, Iris; wife, Louise; Donald L. Hollowell,
Hollowell's mother; and niece, Nora at his Atlanta installation
as Regional Director of EEOC

Eddye Wiley Peacock,
Hollowell "Goddaughter,"
an Academic Specialist
in Writing and Reading
at Morris Brown College

Jean C. Dodd,
Hollowell "Goddaughter,"
Chair, Strategic Planning
Committee of the
Atlanta Board of Education

Hollowell "Godson" Dr. Albert J. H. Sloan, President of Miles College, Emma Sloan, his wife and Nicki, their first daughter

Frances Pauley, long-time collegue in the struggle for civil rights, and Donald L. Hollowell at The Open Door Community (1977)

The Hollowell Family Reunion in Atlanta, Georgia (circa, 1981)

Thelma Hollowell, wife of Harry Hollowell; Eddye Peacock, Hollowell Goddaughter; Harry; and Iris and Corrine, sisters of Donald Hollowell, at the 1989 Intergenerational Tribute to Hollowell

Toby, the Hollowell's German Shepherd

Butler Street, CME Church
Donald L. Hollowell's Church

Bishop Othal H. Lakey
Sixth Episcopal District (GA)

Rev. Anthony M. Alford
Pastor, Butler Street, CME

Allen Temple, AME Church
Louise Hollowell's Church

Bishop Donald G. K. Ming
Sixth Episcopal District (GA)

Rev. Dr. Charles E. Wells
Pastor, Allen Temple AME

5

THE WAY BECOMES CLEAR

It was great to be home again after an absence of nearly four years. Hollowell and his wife were ready to begin building the foundation of a marriage that had been forced to rest upon a honeymoon of only a few hours, a handful of intermittent visits and a lengthy exchange of correspondence.

The city to which he returned was still a bastion of segregation and horrible living conditions for most Negroes, but change was in the air. Heavy Negro turnout in a special election for the Fifth Congressional District seat early in 1946 had sent the white Helen Douglas Mankin, an unapologetic liberal, to the U.S. House of Representatives to fill the unexpired term of Robert Ramspeck.[1] In March, just before Hollowell's return, a group of Negro veterans marched on City Hall to demand the hiring of Negro policemen. Then, in April, the U. S. Supreme Court ruled against the whites - only Democratic primary system of Georgia.

Against this backdrop of modest social change, Hollowell considered his career options. Although pleased by these harbingers of improvement for the condition of Negroes, he also was emotionally drained. The continual barrage of racial harassment he had encountered for the past five years had badly demoralized his spirit and left him less than optimistic about the future for his race.[2] The longer he thought about it and discussed the subject with Louise, the more attractive seemed the dreams of a calm and financially stable future. Hollowell concluded that he would prepare himself to be a dentist who could operate comfortably within a segregated system. Having reached that decision, he decided to change his major from sociology to biology. They postponed the trip they had hoped to take to California, and he instead returned to Tennessee for the summer session of Lane College to take the science courses he would need to be accepted to dental school. She in turn, having graduated *magna cum laude* from Morris Brown College,[3] returned to her studies in English literature at Atlanta University.[4] Although she was ill that summer, necessitating his return for several days, his enterprising wife was determined to earn a master's degree.

The Lane College family joyfully welcomed back its star student and athlete. Coach Clemons lost no time in issuing him a football uniform, and the undergraduates elected him President of the Student Council. In that position, Hollowell received an invitation early in the fall to serve as Lane's delegate to a special student conference. The Southern Negro Youth Congress was planning a convocation in October. It would be held on the campus of Allen University, a small African Methodist Episcopal school in Columbia, South Carolina.

Although Hollowell had never heard of the organization, it had been in existence since 1937. That year five hundred and thirty-four young Negroes assembled in Richmond, Virginia. They declared their determination to work for the full citizenship of all people. Like the National Negro Congress, created a year earlier and composed of some five hundred organizations, it sought to protest racial segregation and discrimination across a broad front. Its printed materials balanced powerful rhetoric with practical suggestions. In one of its newsletters, for example, the student organization called for the support of anti-poll tax legislation but simultaneously urged its members to pay the tax in order to become eligible to vote. (During the coming years of the McCarthy era, "Red-hunters" would identify the organization as one of those infiltrated by Communists.)

Hollowell still was essentially apolitical. Indeed, he had never even had the opportunity to vote in a public election. Nonetheless, the more he learned, the more intrigued he became about the opportunity to be part of the session in Columbia.

The invitational brochure for the organization's seventh conference read more like a call to battle. Dominating its cover was an artist's illustration of angry young Negroes, clutching ballots in their clenched right hands and breaking through a stone wall that bore inscriptions like "No Vote," "Jim Crow," "White Only," "Bigotry," and "Discrimination." The printed message read:

> **THE SOUTHERN NEGRO YOUTH CONGRESS**
> Summons you to —
> **THE SOUTHERN YOUTH LEGISLATURE**

The language on the inside of the program struck a responsive chord within Hollowell. The authors addressed their message to young workers, farmers, students and "yesterday's warriors," members of a "generation of victory, who fought a war and dreamed a dream of free citizenship in a free South and a free world."

> This vision, it continued, gave meaning to the million youth of our generation who — though Jim-Crowed and humiliated up to the very point of death on the battlefields — extended themselves heroically in the defense of our country and the people of the world from the bloody tyranny of the fascist Axis.

In its concluding call for attendance, it trumpeted:

> We must win the battle for the unrestricted right to vote.... The mark of a free citizen is his right of suffrage. We refuse to accept the verdict of Klansmen and their collaborators that we shall be a voteless and a voiceless people.

A special bulletin issued by the Youth Congress bore endorsements from Negro leaders like President Benjamin E. Mays of Morehouse College and Dr. D. V. Jemison, President of the National Baptist Convention. Hollowell quickly made arrangements to travel to South Carolina.

A few months later an NAACP report would declare 1946 to be "one of the grimmest years in the history of the organization." It cited "reports of blowtorch killing and eye-gouging of Negro veterans freshly returned from a war to end torture and racial extermination" and went on to say, "Negroes in America have been disillusioned over the wave of lynchings, brutality and official recession from all of the flamboyant promises of post-war democracy and decency." The many young American Negroes who had worn military uniforms felt an especially intensified conviction that change was long overdue and that the responsibility for this change was in their hands.

On October 18, Hollowell joined the ranks of the delegates and visitors to the Youth Congress' legislative session. There, with hundreds of other young Americans, as well as delegates from India, China and the Soviet Union, he heard Congressman Adam Clayton Powell of New York deliver a stirring keynote address. He attended powerful discussions with labor leaders, educators and journalists, whose ranks included Dr. Herbert Aptheker, the controversial historian and author. There were opportunities for deep conversations with other students, many of whom were military veterans like himself. Grace Towns Hamilton from the Atlanta Urban League, who would later become one of Georgia's leading Negro state legislators, and C. A. Scott, Editor of the *Atlanta Daily World*, were also present.

On Saturday evening, at the International Youth Festival, he listened to performances by Paul Robeson and Josh White. Howard Fast, the author of *Freedom Road* and *Citizen Tom Paine*, brought greetings. The next afternoon Hollowell witnessed the presentation of a special award to the renowned educator and writer, Dr. W. E. B. DuBois.

Of all the impressions that he soaked up that weekend, though, Robeson's words and songs had the most powerful and inspirational impact upon Hollowell. As a boy, he had heard recordings of Robeson performing "Climbin' Up," but the experience of personally witnessing and hearing Robeson sing that powerful song stayed with him for the rest of his life. Like most American Negroes, he knew of Robeson's astoundingly illustrious football and academic career at Rutgers University in New Jersey. He had seen the internationally acclaimed actor and singer in *The Emperor Jones*, *Show Boat*, and *King Solomon's Mines*. He was aware that Robeson had gone to Spain to perform concerts in 1938 as a gesture of solidarity with the Negro brigade that fought with the Loyalists. But to be able to meet and to shake the hand of this passionate, charismatic, angry, impatient advocate for Negro rights stirred him in profound new ways.

That 1946 convention was to be one of the watershed experiences of Hollowell's life. When he returned to college he was a transformed and recharged man. For the past eleven years most of his decisions — made within the strictures of organized institutions — had revolved around the fairly immediate needs of his personal life. Now his initial post-war decision to become a dentist suddenly seemed to be a narrow and self-serving career choice. For the first time he began to see the possibilities of setting a course that could be guided by greater motives. There might indeed be ways to use his talents to bring about political and social change.

In 1919 the same Paul Robeson who had stimulated Hollowell's imagination had delivered the valedictory address to his own graduating class at Rutgers. In that speech Robeson declared:

> We of the younger generation especially must feel a sacred call to that which lies before us. I go out to do my little part in helping my untutored brother. We of this less-favored race realize that our future lies chiefly in our own hands. On ourselves alone will depend the preservation of our liberties and the transmission of them in their integrity to those who will come after us.

Hollowell had heard the sacred call. He re-declared his sociology major and began filing applications for admission to law school and graduate school.

That weekend of epiphany in Columbia, South Carolina, also led to another break with the past. Hollowell had planned his weekend trip to Allen University knowing that the football team did not have a game scheduled. Soon after he made his travel arrangements, though, Coach Clemons called for a Saturday practice. When Hollowell asked to be excused, Clemons refused to honor the request. Hollowell's reasoned arguments failed to move him. The coach, accustomed to ordering around young undergraduates, seemed to have forgotten that he was now dealing with a twenty-eight year old veteran of military service who had been married for four years. Instead of seeking accommodation with Hollowell, he simply dropped his quarterback from the team. Other college faculty members would have supported his case for reinstatement, but Hollowell chose not to push the matter. The importance of inter-collegiate competition had shifted to the periphery of his new vision and sense of direction.

Later that school year, the University of Illinois accepted him into its master's degree program in social work, and the law schools of New York University and Loyola University in Chicago also admitted him. A professor and good friend at Lane had attended Loyola and assured Hollowell that he would be treated fairly there. After further consideration, he decided to respond to the offer from the Chicago school and to prepare for a career in law.[5]

After attending summer school to complete the requirements necessitated by his change of major, Hollowell graduated *magna cum laude* from Lane. Because he needed funds for law school tuition, he began applying for various federal jobs. The process required completion of the infamous Form 173, on the back of which was a lengthy list of organizations alleged to be "un-American." All would-be employees of the U.S. government had to indicate whether they had belonged or had other ties to these suspect groups. Hollowell, who considered himself a thorough patriot, barely glanced at it. Anticipating nothing that he felt could be detrimental to his candidacy, he left the page blank and sent back the form.

In short order, he received a letter that challenged his association with the Southern Negro Youth Congress, which he had failed to notice on the list of suspicious organizations and therefore had not checked. The letter's author, who clearly was aware of Hollowell's attendance at the Southern Youth Legislature the previous fall, asked whether he would like a hearing.

Hollowell responded with a lengthy letter. In it he documented his personal history, his war service and that of his brother and brothers-in-law, his exemplary college record, and his church relationships. He concluded by questioning how the government could dare to question his loyalty. Soon thereafter, he accepted the invitation to appear before an interviewer, who quickly approved his application for employment. However, despite the subsequent offer of a position as a federal investigator for the postal service, the challenge to his loyalty offended him deeply. He chose instead to spend the remaining summer period of 1947 as an

Assistant Registrar for Lane.

That summer was dominated by contradictory racial messages in the United States. Jackie Robinson became the first Negro professional baseball player of modern times when he joined the Brooklyn Dodgers, followed soon thereafter by Larry Doby who was signed by the Cleveland Indians. At the same time, Freedom Riders from the Congress of Racial Equality and the Fellowship of Reconciliation were risking their lives as they rode buses through the South to test compliance with court-ordered desegregation of interstate transportation. In St. Louis, thousands of Roman Catholics protested the integration of their parochial schools until Archbishop Joseph E. Ritter threatened them with excommunication.

When Hollowell arrived at Loyola University's Law School in September, 1947, one of his first challenges was to find a job. Louise Hollowell, worn from the strains in her own life, had become ill, and he had used most of his summer earnings and cashed in his savings bonds to pay for her medical expenses.

He managed to find part-time employment at the Canal Street branch of the post office and set about trying to juggle work and study. The academic regimen of law school, he soon discovered, was much tougher than his undergraduate studies. The rigor of his classes, the constant shortage of cash, concern about his wife's health and the bitter cold of the winter collaborated to make it a grueling first year for the would-be attorney. Even the opportunities afforded by holidays for trips home could be a mixed blessing. Travel between Chicago and Atlanta in a Jim Crow passenger car was long and wearying. Small wonder that his weight dropped by almost twenty-five pounds.

Some of the pressure eased for a while during the summer of 1950 when Louise arrived to do special research for her master's thesis on William Vaughan Moody, the American poet and playwright, at the University of Chicago. Nonetheless, Hollowell's second year of law school was even more difficult than the first, so much so that it took its physical and academic toll upon him. Thus, he did not attend law school the following year, but worked as a billing and assistant rate clerk with Bridgeway Trucking and then went to work "pulling tonnage" on the dock of the Lipshultz Company. It was backbreaking labor that involved a crew of four men loading and unloading freight with a 4 x 8 flat hand truck, and being paid on the basis of the total weight moved by the team. Still and all, it paid fairly well.

He was able to return to class in September 1950. With much of the financial pressure removed, he quit all outside jobs in November and, by dint of scrimping, did nothing but study. As a result, he sailed through the final year of legal training with relative ease. In the meantime, Louise Hollowell had completed her master's degree and joined the faculty at Morris Brown College.

There was a predictable period of apprehension as Hollowell, who had returned to Atlanta, waited for the telegram that would confirm his successful completion of law school. The good news finally arrived, prompting his mother-in-law who received the wire to shout aloud and break into a dance. It was a day that he describes as one of "pure joy and great thanksgiving."

The law school held its 1951 graduation ceremonies in a movie theater just off the North Shore campus in Evanston, Illinois. At the time few people paid special attention to the marquee which announced the current feature starring Alan Ladd. Hollowell, though, clearly remembers looking up and taking note of the film's portentous title, *Appointment with Danger*.

ENDNOTES

[1] A political fluke made possible when Democratic party leaders carelessly neglected to hold the usual whites-only primary.

[2] His pessimism was well founded. In May, 1946, the Ku Klux Klan held a widely-publicized cross burning on Stone Mountain. That summer Eugene Talmade was conducting an especially nasty, race-baiting campaign for election to the gubernatorial seat he had once held for three terms, and in July the gruesome lynch murders of two Negro couples in Walton County made national headlines.

[3] See her letters to Hollowell in Chapter 4.

[4] The graduate school from which the Atlanta University Center, the renowned federation of historically black educational institutions, derived its name.

[5] In retrospect, it seems significant that the many accomplishments of Paul Robeson, Hollowell's new hero, included graduation from Columbia University Law School.

6

A NEW BATTLEFIELD

Many of Hollowell's new friends from the Chicago area urged him to remain there. Opportunities for Negro attorneys seemed to be good. Two classmates, Lawrence Carroll and Mark Jones, would pursue careers in that city and in later years rise to positions of judicial leadership.

Oakland, California, where his parents now lived, also beckoned. Both of them had spent the war years managing canteens for the Army. Harrison Hollowell was in charge of one of the largest operations at Fort Leonard Wood before he and Ocenia moved for a time to Arizona. At Fort Huachuca he took over a similar enterprise while she ran the canteen for the base hospital.

After returning home, though, they realized that they had no compelling reason to stay in the Midwest. All of their children were grown and married. The region's extreme summer and winter temperatures were increasingly burdensome for them. Furthermore, as the country disassembled the enormous infrastructure that had sustained the war effort, civilian jobs with the military were becoming less secure. When they heard reports that Negroes fared better in California than elsewhere in the country, the senior Hollowells joined the westward migration.

A brief stay in Los Angeles, though, was enough to convince them that Southern California was too warm for their liking. They moved farther north to the Bay Area, but San Francisco's damp and foggy weather also bothered Harrison Hollowell. Across the bay in Oakland, however, he found just what he wanted: a moderate climate that didn't, as he put it, "punish" him.

Not long after finding a job with the post office, his entrepreneurial instincts reasserted themselves. Everywhere he looked he saw a post-war boom economy driven by civilian housing needs. With a partner he began to build what would become a successful real estate practice. From that financial base he offered to assist his younger son in establishing a law practice in Oakland.

It was a tempting option for Hollowell. His sisters and their husbands had also relocated to Oakland, and Jeff Davis, his favorite grandfather, had moved in with Ocenia and Harrison Hollowell.

Nonetheless, Louise already was living and teaching in Atlanta, and that community, even then, had the reputation of being somewhat more progressive than other parts of the South. It was certainly no more dangerous than many northern cities. During the summer of 1952 a mob of whites several thousand strong rioted in Cicero to protest a Negro family's attempt to move into that all-white city. Governor Adlai Stevenson of Illinois had been forced to call out the National Guard.

On one of Hollowell's trips back to visit his wife in Atlanta, he had an encouraging conversation with Austin T. Walden. The esteemed dean of the city's small coterie of Negro lawyers and arguably the most significant Negro in the community told him that an attorney of color with good judgment and the ability to "blow it out like a lawyer" could do very well in Atlanta.

Harry Hollowell believes that less pragmatic factors were the driving forces behind his brother's decision to go South. He insists that "Don wanted a place where he could fight."

During the summer after graduation from law school, Hollowell worked as a clerk for the Illinois Military District. Then, after weighing all of the factors, he returned to what would become his adopted city.

Negroes in Atlanta during the early 1950s had severely restricted housing options. Poorer families tended to live in the southeastern section of the city called Summerhill or that pocket called Pittsburgh/Mechanicsville. By the time the Hollowells began to look for a home, middle- and upper-class Negro families were continuing to move steadily into the west section of Atlanta along the Hunter Street/Mozley Drive corridor. Indeed, to be able to establish residence on that side of town was becoming a major indicator of both economic achievement and elevated social status. However, as young professionals just getting their start, they chose instead to settle in the older, more established Fourth Ward, just east of the downtown area.

The neighborhood in which they put down their roots was electric with round-the-clock energy. Auburn Avenue was the main street of the Fourth Ward. By day it hummed with the enterprises of business and trade; by night it jumped as people socialized in restaurants and clubs that presented the world-famous acts of Negro entertainers. On Sundays, members of the city's major Negro churches thronged to them for worship and fellowship. Auburn Avenue never seemed to sleep.

Within a stretch of two blocks were the headquarters of the Atlanta Life Insurance Company, Citizens Trust Bank and the Mutual Federal Savings and Loan Company. Together they constituted the largest concentration of Negro financial institutions in the United States. As William Calloway, a long-time Atlanta realtor and black civic leader tells the story, John Wesley Dobbs[1] christened the street "Sweet Auburn" after hearing the saying, "There's nothing sweeter than money."

Here, too, were the offices of the *Atlanta Daily World*, the nation's first Negro daily newspaper, and of J. B. Blayton, Atlanta's first Negro certified public accountant[2] and founder of Mutual Federal. WERD, America's first Negro-owned radio station, had its studios on Auburn Avenue, and on nearby Butler Street, whose principal edifice was the Butler Street YMCA, Attorney Walden occupied the small office building he had constructed.

The Sweet Auburn neighborhood also included the first Yates & Milton drug store, Alexander & Company, a pioneering property and casualty insurance firm established by T. M. Alexander, Sr., and the King Real Estate Company. Interspersed among these businesses were other symbols of Negro economic achievement—restaurants, mortuaries, doctors' offices, night clubs, retail and service shops (like Louise Hollowell's salon), proprietary training institutions like the Apex Beauty College and the Paro Beauty School and a few small hotels. Grace T. Hamilton, the head of the Atlanta Urban League, directed her organization's operations from space in the Herndon Building, and the office of the relatively new NAACP chapter office was on the fourth floor of the Odd Fellows Building.

The Hollowells set up housekeeping in the Wigwam Apartments[3] at Auburn Avenue and Randolph Street. It was the same building in which Louise, with her mother and cousin, had first established residence in

1942 while she waited for her husband's return from military service and law school. The first order of business for Hollowell was to study for the state bar examinations. While doing so, he also directed the local membership campaign for the NAACP which in those days did not have a professional staff. Despite the fact that he, as a Negro, was banned from taking the bar review course available to all white attorneys, Hollowell passed the examination without difficulty in September, 1952.

For one year he shared office space with Cassandra Maxwell Birnie[4] at 864 Hunter Street on the west side of the city. The association provided Hollowell with a good base for beginning his practice. A staunch Republican, knowledgeable political observer, and respected attorney, she graciously provided him with additional door-opening introductions to the community. Within a year, though, his new colleague needed the space that Hollowell was using. In 1953, he borrowed three hundred dollars from a dear friend, Dr. Carol Cotton Bowie, and opened his own office across the street in the newly built Cannolene Building.

Louise Hollowell would not have been unhappy had her husband found other, more secure employment and practiced law on a part-time basis. After all, she had borne her share of a marriage which for eleven years had been marked by tight financial constraints. As the country entered post-war prosperity, she might have welcomed some of the material benefits that were becoming regular features in the lives of other Americans. Hollowell could only reply to his wife that he was thirty-five years old and needed to get started on his chosen career. In effect, he couldn't afford to enjoy the "luxury" of assured income from a steady job. From his small office at 859 1/2 Hunter Street he set about the task of slowly but steadily expanding his practice and reputation.

Much of the work initially was routine and far from dramatic. General practice lawyers drew up wills and handled real estate transactions. Hollowell's clients during those early years included James and Robert Paschal. The two brothers had opened a modest sandwich shop in 1947. Building upon that foundation, they purchased additional property across West Hunter Street to construct what would become a world-famous restaurant and motel. During the next four decades Paschal's was a principal gathering place for Atlanta's and indeed the nation's black leadership.[5]

Hollowell's professional demeanor and performance as well as his civic involvement and church activities were demonstrating his leadership, and his circle of friends in the Negro and liberal white community steadily widened. He was a man upon whom people came to depend for help. Home on vacation from law school in North Carolina, Leroy R. Johnson[6] discovered that side of Hollowell. Johnson had acquired a traffic ticket during his stay in Atlanta. After returning to his studies, he scraped together the requisite twenty-five dollar fine — a large sum of money for a student holding part-time jobs in a grocery store and the school library — and sent it to Hollowell with the request that he pay the penalty for him. A week later he received a letter from Hollowell, who informed Johnson that he would indeed take care of the matter. Enclosed with the letter was the money. It was a kindness that Johnson never forgot. In the years to come the two men and their wives became even closer friends. They worked closely with each other on many projects, and both became members of the prestigious Kappa Boule of Sigma Pi Phi, a Negro fraternal order of business and professional men.

Even as Hollowell was establishing himself in the community, the Inc. Fund, which had been successfully challenging segregated education in a series of cases elsewhere around the country, targeted Georgia for an assault on its university system. The carefully chosen plaintiff was Horace T. Ward. Ward had graduated from Morehouse College a year after Martin Luther King, Jr. and was a classmate of Lerone Bennett, Jr.[7] and Leroy Johnson.

At Morehouse, under the tutelage of Dr. Robert Brisbane,[8] Ward developed an interest in constitutional law. Several of his fellow graduates immediately enrolled in law school. Some of them even withstood the demeaning and demoralizing "opportunity" to attend institutions that were nominally desegregated.[9] Ward, although interested in a legal education, chose first to complete a master's degree in political science at Atlanta University. His faculty advisor was Dr. William Madison Boyd, who also was President of the State Council of NAACP branches.

Then on September 29, 1950, Ward applied for admission to the University of Georgia's law school. The institution had never admitted a Negro student, but the court-ordered token desegregation of other

Southern universities offered some reason to believe it could happen in Georgia, too.

Walter Danner, the University Registrar, having quickly determined that the applicant was a Negro, passed on Ward's papers to the secretary of the Board of Regents. That official then routinely sent Ward the standard information about the availability of financial aid to assist him with his professional training out-of-state.[10] Ward persisted, however. He declined the offer and filed an official complaint with the Regents.

Months of subsequent correspondence produced only a formal rejection of his application in June, 1951. It offered no reason for the decision. Then followed a tedious series of appeals that consumed the rest of the year. The first was to President O. C. Aderhold of the University. On the basis of recommendations from a committee to which he had referred the matter, Aderhold announced that he found Ward to be "equivocal." The next fruitless appeal went to the chancellor of the state higher education system. Finally, Ward filed an appeal with the Board of Regents itself. The board's response was to appoint a committee which in February, 1952, recommended the tightening of entrance requirements to the law school and the addition of a rigid entrance examination for all applicants.

The Legal Defense Fund team now was convinced that Ward had exhausted all administrative remedies. In May, 1952, its chief staff attorney and A. T. Walden, providing local counsel, filed suit against the university in federal court.

The state's official response was to seek dismissal of the suit. Behind the scenes, as reported by Bill Shipp, an *Atlanta Constitution* columnist, the reaction had been a bit more colloquial. Governor Herman Talmadge named his personal attorney, B. D. (Buck) Murphy, as a special deputy attorney general and issued a pointed order: "Keep that damned nigger out of the University of Georgia while I'm governor."

The Board of Regents informed Ward that he would have to take the new entrance examination in July. The legal jabbing and counterpunching continued well into 1953. During this protracted process Ward served on the faculties of Arkansas A M & N and Alabama State Colleges.[11]

At long last the court scheduled a hearing for October of that year. Even as Ward's attorneys were readying their arguments, however, another unforeseen development blindsided them. Ward unexpectedly received orders from the Selective Service System to report for military duty. (It remains questionable whether his draft was purely coincidental.)

The dauntless Dr. William Boyd, described the surprise with withering understatement when he called it an "unexpected windfall" for the state. It was a devastating blow to him. He had conducted a virtual one-man crusade around Georgia to raise funds for the conduct of the case as it unfolded and to mobilize the Negro community's resolve for challenging the state's segregated education system. Now, just as he and the attorneys were anticipating their long-sought day in court, their key plaintiff was being taken away by the very government whose help they were petitioning.

The Inc. Fund feared that the state might use Ward's absence as a reason to declare the case moot and request its dismissal, thereby erasing three years of painstaking work. Thurgood Marshall, the Fund's director, quickly scheduled a trip to Atlanta. He, Walden and Hollowell, who had joined the defense team, were successful in convincing Judge Frank A. Hooper to remove Ward's case from the court calendar. The motion, accepted by the state's attorneys, called for it to be reassigned for trial on request of the plaintiff. Dr. Boyd announced to the press that the NAACP was still determined to desegregate Georgia education.

The Army inducted Ward on September 9, 1953 and sent him to Fort Jackson, South Carolina, and then to Korea.

§§§

Most of Hollowell's cases were more routine, but even in simple civil cases, he was demonstrating an impatience with the status quo. In the first divorce proceeding that he handled, he used his client's full name when filing her suit. The case went to trial, and Hollowell placed her on the witness stand. When the judge gave his instructions to her, he began by saying, "Now, Mary..."

Hollowell immediately jumped to his feet. "If it please the court, I believe the record shows that the plaintiff's name is Mrs. Mary _____."

The judge was taken aback, but he turned to the opposing attorney and asked, "Do you have any comment about the objection?" "Whatever your honor says," that lawyer replied. The trial proceeded with Hollowell's client being addressed by her full name.

§§§

Hollowell's ascent toward prominence began to accelerate when a criminal defense case came his way. As reported by the newspapers, late on the night of November 4, 1953, Marvin Luther Lindsey, a divorced, twenty-four year old employee at a shoe repair shop, purchased a bottle of whiskey. He then picked up his twenty-two year old girlfriend, Betty Jo Bishop, a widowed mother. The white couple drove to a secluded spot on a dirt lane off Jonesboro Road near the ruins of an old brick factory. About eleven o'clock that night, a Negro man wearing a hat with a "funny crown" allegedly approached the car. He was reported to have hit Mrs. Bishop in the face, and then to have brutally beaten her companion to death before raping her.

The Fulton County Grand Jury had indicted Willie Nash, an uneducated, thirty-nine year old Negro mill hand, for these crimes. The police helped to make the decision an easy one when they testified that they had a partial statement from Nash in which he allegedly admitted the attack. They also produced a fifteen-inch threaded bar with several lug nuts on it that they asserted was the murder weapon. The findings of Dr. Herman Jones, the State Crime Laboratory specialist, included his discovery of human blood on the suspect's overalls. Mrs. Bishop had identified Nash in a police lineup. So had a young couple who claimed to have been approached by a Negro man armed with an iron bar in the same area a week before the murder.

Nash's family initially found a white attorney who was willing to defend him. That young man, however, dropped the case when it became clear that there wasn't enough money to pay his fee. The family had scraped together what it could, and the attorney had even distributed cannisters in the community to collect voluntary contributions, but these efforts had fallen far short of their goal.

In desperation, Nash's relatives turned to the Inc. Fund. That organization still had neither the expanded corps of experienced attorneys nor the funds that it would begin to assemble a year later after the Supreme Court's ruling against segregated public education. Limited in its options, it turned to Hollowell.

The Inc. Fund found a few dollars in its coffers, the family assembled several more, and Hollowell agreed to take the case for the grand sum of fifteen hundred dollars. By the time he met his client for the first time, Nash had been locked in an Atlanta jail cell for seven weeks. He was scheduled to go on trial for his life in just a few days.

Hollowell had never defended anyone charged with a capital offense. The trial was delayed for two weeks while Hollowell did his best to convince a frightened Nash to accept his family's choice of counsel. Nash may have lacked a formal education, but he was no fool. He had a clear sense of the unlikelihood that a Negro lawyer would be able to secure justice for him. Small wonder that he broke down and bawled like a baby in his cell after he had resigned himself to the inevitability of Hollowell's representation. Hollowell himself recounts, "I suspect I would have cried, too, if I had been Willie Nash under those circumstances."

The case, to which the press assigned the titillating title of the "Lover's Lane Slaying," went to trial before Superior Court Judge Virlyn B. Moore in January, 1954. The prosecution had marshaled an impressive array of evidence and testimony to support its case against Nash. It included his alleged confession, obtained by the police in the woods at the scene of the crime, to which they had taken him when he was apprehended only hours after the murder. The county's solicitors general also produced a Negro witness who was prepared to testify that he had seen Nash in the area just before the murder. On the bench sat a white judge. All of the jury members were white. The state's prosecuting attorneys were the most senior men on the solicitor's staff.

Hollowell had his own wits and the assistance of another Negro lawyer. Arthur Combs, a graduate of Howard University's Law School, was working for J. C. Daugherty, an attorney across the hall from Hollowell's office. He had been in practice only a year longer than Hollowell, but he agreed to join the defense. Together these two men

A New Battlefield

nervously prepared to do battle in an arena against odds on which no one could have wangled a bet.

Courtroom observers on the first day of the trial were caught off guard by the novelty of Negro attorneys sitting beside a defendant. The manner of Hollowell and Combs was also cause for astonishment. They dressed impeccably. They spoke forcefully and grammatically. They seemed familiar with both the law and legal procedure. Hollowell, his large frame all the more impressive because of his military-like posture, moved about as if he were in charge of the proceedings. Some long-held stereotypes suffered severe challenges that day and in the days to come.

Hollowell and Combs had no evidence except Nash's alibi with which to counter the prosecution's offerings. Instead, they used all of the technicalities at their command. They introduced repeated but unsuccessful objections to the admission of some of the prosecutors' evidence. They lengthily questioned the potential jurors (none of whom had ever been addressed in such a demanding, albeit courteous, way by a Negro) and challenged, again unsuccessfully, the legality of the jury panel because it included no women.

An unexpected development interrupted the second day of the trial. The prosecution was concluding its presentation and close to resting its case. Assistant Solicitor Frank French was offering in evidence the "funny hat" with its pyramid shape. Hollowell objected to the lack of a proper foundation for the introduction of this evidence. French countered, "Yes there is, your honor." He began to remind the court that his witness, a rather large Negro man, had identified the hat. "It has been described," said French, "by uh, uh ... the man, uh, uh ..." He continued to stammer as he attempted without success to recall his own witness' name and then, pointing to him, he blurted out "... uh, uh, by that fat nigger."

Hollowell was on his feet immediately, objecting strenuously. Citing the legal precedent of a recent federal ruling, he and Combs insisted that the use of that term was grounds for mistrial. French apologized to the court, claiming that his language was inadvertent. Nonetheless, Judge Moore ruled in favor of the defense, "The law is zealous of not injecting the race question, especially when a man is on trial for his life." He then dismissed the jury. The courtroom was stunned. So far as anyone can recall, it was the first time in Georgia's legal history that the court had sustained an objection on the grounds of the use of a racially biased epithet.

Solicitor Paul Webb, Sr. was not willing to lose his case on a technicality. Determined to retry it and secure a guilty verdict for the murder, he and his staff went to work preparing a new case. Meanwhile, Nash remained in jail, although a newly found faith in his lawyers significantly lowered his anxiety level.

By March, Hollowell and Combs were back in court with their client. The second trial lasted a week. Hollowell had secured a transcript of the first trial, which included a description of all the evidence that the state had initially introduced. The two attorneys carefully indexed it in preparation for the cross-examination that Hollowell would conduct. Moving methodically, he seriously impeached the testimony of the murdered man's girlfriend, who became so emotional she could hardly testify. The original statement from one of the arresting officers included his recollection that Mrs. Bishop had defensively told the murdered man's parents, "I know you think I did it, but it was a nigger who did it."

Hollowell had also used a portion of his fee to hire an elderly white investigator. That man's probing uncovered the fact that Mrs. Bishop had another boyfriend who owned a small bar and restaurant in the Little Five Points area. The day after the murder, the establishment was closed and the owner nowhere to be found.

Hollowell further made it a point to highlight the results of Mrs. Bishop's medical examination when she was taken to Grady Hospital after the killing. Going into graphic detail he strongly challenged the contention that a rape had even occurred. Both whites and Negroes in the room stared in utter amazement at the sight of a Negro man challenging a white female in this fashion and actually discussing the intimate features of her anatomy.

Then, under heavy and intensive questioning, Hollowell caught the crime laboratory's physician in a series of statements that contradicted his testimony from the first trial. Dr. Jones had initially analyzed in minute detail how the damage to the victim's head matched the shape of the purported murder weapon. Now his description was completely different.

The state's chief identification witness initially claimed to have seen Nash clearly at the scene. According to him, the defendant had approached his car on the night of the murder. He even went so far as to explain that his clear description of Nash's peaked, pyramid-shaped hat was made possible by the moonlight. Hollowell, though, referring to an almanac, demonstrated that the moon was not visible on that particular evening.

Combs and Hollowell also produced an array of good character witnesses. Nash himself, as permitted by the criminal code of the time, made a strong and passionate unsworn statement on his own behalf.

In his closing argument, Assistant Solicitor Copeland had chosen to use a dramatically wavering voice to describe Mrs. Bishop repeatedly as a "poor little girl." When it was Hollowell's turn for final remarks, he sarcastically wondered aloud how it was possible for the young woman who had been so clear-eyed and stoic during the first trial suddenly to become visibly heartbroken by her lover's death. He also questioned whether a "poor little girl" would have been with an older man on a lover's lane in the middle of the night.

By the time Hollowell and Combs rested, they had presented a powerful collection of arguments in support of Willie Nash's innocence. The white jury clearly agreed, as its members soon brought in a "not guilty" verdict on the charge of murder. The prosecutors were visibly disappointed. They found it difficult to believe not only that they had lost but also that their defeat was at the hands of an inexperienced pair of young, Negro lawyers. The state was forced to release Nash on five thousand dollars bond, pending the disposition of the rape and robbery charges, both of which were subsequently dead-docketed.

Hollowell and Combs were ecstatic. So far as anyone knew, they had recorded a "first" in the South. Negro attorneys had successfully secured the acquittal of a client of color tried for the capital offenses of murder and rape of white victims before a white judge and jury. In characteristically gracious style, one of the first things Hollowell did after leaving the courtroom was to call Judge Walden. After sharing with him the news of the verdict, he thanked the older attorney for all of the foundations laid by his integrity and decorum. His track record, he told the older man, had helped to smooth the way for him and Combs[12] to try a case in "open court" and to be treated with a new level of respect.

Despite press coverage during the trial, the significance of its outcome went largely unremarked in the white community.[13] As word reached the Negro citizens of Atlanta, though, they understood that this remarkable achievement was another sign of change in the wind. The mantle of A. T. Walden, nearly seventy years old, was about to pass to a new legal champion.

ENDNOTES

[1] Grandfather of Atlanta's first black mayor, Maynard H. Jackson

[2] Blayton also established the first Negro-owned soft drink company, bottling a product called "Brown Boy."

[3] The King family, who operated the real estate company on Auburn Avenue and also owned the apartment complex, proudly claimed Native American ancestry.

[4] Cassandra Maxwell Birnie would be a worthy subject of her own biography. She came from a family of "free" Negroes in South Carolina who had never been slaves. Her parents operated a grocery store in her hometown of Orangeburg. She herself attended the high school department of Claflin College, an historically Negro institution established in that town by the Methodist Church, graduated from Spelman College and Howard Law School and became the first Negro woman to have a legal practice in South Carolina. She met her husband-to-be, Dr. James H. Birnie, while he was a member of the faculty at South Carolina State College, the public institution for Negroes, and she was teaching at that institution's small law school while also operating the family store and practicing law. When Morehouse College offered him a position on its science faculty, the couple moved to Atlanta. In 1962 the pharmaceutical firm of Smith, Kline & French lured him away from Morehouse to work at its corporate headquarters, and the Birnies relocated to Philadelphia. There Cassandra Maxwell-Birnie established another law practice and was prominently active in professional, political and civic affairs until her death of acute leukemia in August, 1974, at the age of sixty-four.

[5] Paschal's also would later function as a kind of unofficial headquarters for the Civil Rights Movement in Atlanta (students released from jail after their arrests during demonstrations often received free platters of Robert Paschal's famous fried chicken). In 1960, the brothers added the popular La Carrousel Lounge, one of the very few nightclubs in the South where blacks and whites could mingle and listen to the music of nationally known entertainers like Ramsey Lewis. To this day, although the property now belongs to Clark Atlanta University, businesspeople and politicians use Paschal's as a base for caucuses and press conferences, and black institutions regularly schedule board meetings, news conferences and public forums at this historic location. Robert Paschal died in March, 1997.

[6] Later to become Georgia's first black State Senator since Reconstruction.

[7] Bennett would go on to a distinguished career as an author, historian and editor.

[8] Brisbane arrived in 1948 to establish the college's first political science department.

[9] At the University of Arkansas Law School one of them had to sit in the basement and listen to lectures over a loudspeaker. The University of Oklahoma permitted another in the classroom, but separated him from other students with a specially installed rail.

[10] Setting up an entire system of racially segregated professional and graduate schools would have been prohibitively expensive, so it became the standard practice in many Southern states to "discourage" the attendance of Negroes at their own public professional and graduate institutions and simply to provide them with stipends to further their education elsewhere, usually in the North.

[11] Historically Negro public institutions in, respectively, Pine Bluff and Montgomery.

[12] Arthur Combs moved to California a few years later.

[13] *Southern Detective Magazine* later published an account of the trial under the title, "The Man in the Pyramid Hat."

7

ON THE CUSP OF CHANGE

On a Sunday evening in the late fall of 1954 Donald and Louise Hollowell were driving through southwestern Georgia. It was the homeward leg of a trip to Tallahassee for the Morris Brown-Florida A & M football game. After a sumptuous meal that Louise's mother prepared for them in Iron City, they continued northward toward Atlanta. With them were Oretha Brown Waller, her young nephew, Johnnie, and a Baptist minister friend.

Needing to make a rest stop and to gas up the car, Hollowell began to look for a service station. Like all Negroes who had to traverse the segregated rural South, he knew only too well the daunting challenge of finding clean and decent facilities. However, that concern did not stop him from steering his Dodge into a Standard Oil station in the tiny town of Butler.

His wife urged him to look for another stop. Butler, located on U.S. Route 19 midway between Atlanta and Albany, had an ugly reputation for white brutality toward Negroes. Hollowell, though, refused to be cowed and pulled up beside the pumps. While the owner's young son began servicing the car, the two men and the boy left the women in the automobile and entered the station. As the minister and Johnnie looked for soft drinks, Hollowell started toward the "white only" rest room. The old white man who owned the station ordered him to stop and refused to let him use the facilities. Hollowell curtly replied that he didn't spend his money where he couldn't use the bathroom.

The trembling septuagenarian, clearly frightened by his customer's assertiveness, pulled a .38 pistol from beneath the counter behind which he was standing. With his other hand he seized a shovel handle. Hollowell told his companions to put the sodas they planned to purchase back on the counter and return to the car. When Johnnie ran outside, the women asked him whether he had found a soft drink. The boy replied, "No, that man inside's got a gun at Don." As Louise and Mrs. Waller began to fret, Hollowell stormed outside and snatched the nozzle from the gas tank before the attendant could finish filling it. Then he strode back into the building, walked up to the counter and asked how much he owed. The owner, still wielding the pistol, named a figure. Hollowell, never taking his eyes from him, then asked whether the price included the soft drinks. When the old man said it did, Hollowell told him to subtract the charge for them; he didn't want anything in the store. His much younger wife, who had watched the confrontation unfold, asked her husband whether she should call the sheriff. He replied that he thought the situation was under control, and Hollowell left the building. He climbed behind the wheel of the car and quickly drove away.

Only moments later, as they circled the town square, they heard the sloshing sound of escaping fuel. In Hollowell's rush to leave the station, he had neglected to replace the cap on the gas tank. Over Louise's strenuous objections and warnings he announced that he was going back for it. When he pulled up to the pump again, two wide-eyed Negro boys were sitting on a bench in front of the station. At Hollowell's request, they found the missing cap and screwed it on as the owner and his wife watched nervously from the station. With a carful of frightened passengers and carefully checking his rear view mirror for the next several miles, Hollowell then resumed the trip home.[1]

The incident, relatively mild in contrast to the experiences that other Negroes on the road faced regularly, served as a reminder that Georgia was still a bastion of white supremacy. Especially in the more rural portions of the state, to be a Negro was to live under an almost ceaseless barrage of white harassment and intimidation.

Jim Crow was emphatically a way of life in Atlanta during the early 1950s too, but white attitudes and behavior generally were less raw-boned than in places like Butler. Political and economic realities played major roles in tempering the city's race relations. Negroes in the city were becoming a political force with which city government and civic leadership had to contend. A massive campaign by the bi-partisan Atlanta Negro Voters League after the elimination of the whites-only primary put nearly thirty thousand new names on the rolls, and the mayor, William B. Hartsfield, a moderate by the standards of the day, held office because of that support. A largely symbolic but significant harbinger of changing relationships between the races brought about through Negro political power had been the appointment of the city's first eight Negro police officers in 1948. These men operated from a segregated precinct in the Fourth Ward, changing clothes in the basement of the all-Negro Butler Street YMCA, and they could only patrol the Negro district around Auburn Avenue, but their presence signaled the possibility of other changes.

It is arguable, however, that the single most important factor contributing to the improvement of race relations in the city was the presence of the Atlanta University Center. The four undergraduate colleges — Clark, Morehouse, Morris Brown and Spelman —[2] and the graduate school from which the Center took its name constituted a remarkable repository of tradition, culture and scholarship. Since the end of the Civil War and supported almost exclusively by Northern philanthropy, they had played the major role in the building of an exceptionally strong and stable middle-class Negro community. More often than not, the graduates of these and other historically Negro institutions were bankers, businesspeople, physicians, clergymen, university professors, school teachers and other professionals. Many of them had earned advanced degrees at Northern graduate and professional schools.

Their presence in turn helped to create a dynamic in the dialogue between the races that existed in no other Southern city. Social scientists have spent a great deal of time analyzing what Floyd Hunter would be the first to describe as Atlanta's "power structure" — that small core of influential white men who essentially set the course for the city. The role of the less visible but extraordinary Negro leaders did not receive as much public attention, but when the time came for biracial discussions, Atlanta's most powerful whites often discovered themselves to be across the table from their intellectual and educational equals, or even superiors.

The very gradual lowering of racial barricades encouraged and emboldened other efforts at discourse. Public interracial gatherings still were taboo, but Negroes and moderate whites found ways around that stricture by meeting in private homes. The Hollowells were early members of a local chapter of The Great Books Program which came into being under the leadership of Harry Boardman. Hollowell led a discussion series on "World Politics" with attorney Irving Kaler and later one on "The Supreme Court and Social Legislation" with Dr. Abner Golden, an Atlanta pathologist.

In addition to the Atlanta University Center schools, other institutions began to play a growing role in promoting the improvement of race relations. The Southern Education Foundation, sensing the subtle moderation of community attitudes, moved its headquarters from Washington to Atlanta in 1950. This unique philanthropic institution, one of the nation's first professionally staffed foundations, was a federation of several earlier charitable funds, all of which sought to improve educational opportunities for Negroes. Its bi-racial board included several Atlantans among its membership. Because of the difficulty in finding public meeting places, J. Curtis Dixon, its Executive Director, had raised the funds to build the foundation its own facility where Negroes and whites could gather safely.[3]

Another critical organization was the Southern Regional Council. It was born in a series of meetings of black Southerners, first in Durham and then in Atlanta and Richmond during World War II. Its members were appealing for a vision of a new South and a new nation. Over the next several years the organization evolved into a biracial group of men and women, headquartered in Atlanta, which sought to build a democratic South that could respect itself.[4]

Atlanta's growth and corresponding increase in economic strength also were helping to set the stage for change. The capital of the largest state east of the Mississippi now had a population of nearly four hundred thousand inhabitants. To be sure, some of that growth was artificial; one-fourth of those people were citizens only because Atlanta had annexed thirty-seven square miles of surrounding territory during the early 1950s.[5] Nonetheless, Mayor Hartsfield was ambitious for his city. He and his powerful corporate patron, Robert W. Woodruff, the head of The Coca-Cola Company, had no interest in seeing its prosperity and steadily improving national image sullied by bad race relations.

Atlanta, in short, was emerging as a different kind of urban emblem for the slowly changing South. It was steadily beginning to eclipse other communities like Birmingham, Charlotte, Nashville and New Orleans that had dreamed of becoming the region's hub; and if it was a step ahead of its Southern sister cities, it was several laps in front of much of the rest of the region when it came to race relations. However, that observation does not mean that it was ready to desegregate itself. It may have been, as Hartsfield proclaimed to a National Toastmasters assembly, a city too busy to hate, and its paternalistic white leaders did indeed tend to discourage viciousness and brutality toward its Negro citizens, but Atlanta was not actively searching for ways to interrupt its well-ordered patterns of racial separation. The notion of sharing power was almost unthinkable.

And yet, although reality had not caught up with the rhetoric that implied a state of equity, the city *was* poised on the cusp of change. It had white leaders who, by the standards of the day, were models of moderation. It was enjoying new found prosperity as a regional leader, stimulated in strong measure by its emergence as a hub for air transportation. It could boast a strong, highly educated Negro middle class. There had been a significant evolution of Negro political strength, and some influential white members of the community were willing at least to grope toward better interracial understanding. All of these elements were essential for the new directions in which Atlanta would move during the second half of the twentieth century.

Still lacking, though, was a nucleus around which all of these other developments could coalesce. The missing ingredient proved to be the ruling by which the nation's highest court invalidated racially segregated education in public schools. It stands, with the Declaration of Independence, the Bill of Rights and the Emancipation Proclamation, as one of the essential documents marking the movement of the United States of America toward a society characterized by justice and equity. That unanimous decision by the U.S. Supreme Court in 1954 is one of the critical watersheds of American history. It triggered legal and social shock waves across the country that continue to reverberate.

The justices' ruling renewed the hope of the men and women who had been quietly campaigning for change. It emboldened their fellow citizens who had been standing on the sidelines. They now had a legal basis to begin casting off a social system that many knew in their hearts to be immoral.

For those whose "way of life" it threatened, though, the decision unleashed fierce resistance. In what had once been the Confederate States of America it resurrected old passions and rekindled old hatreds. One of the milder expressions of this newfound rage was the proliferation of "IMPEACH EARL WARREN"[6] billboards and signs across the region. They blossomed forth in such profusion that they might well have been declared the South's official new flowers.

Ninety years earlier the South had taken up arms and gone to war against the Union. This time the state legislatures and the lower courts became the battlefields where lawmakers and lawyers began devising a host of strategies to subvert the Supreme Court decision. The "generals" of the opposing forces often were the state's administrative leaders. Thus, in his inaugural address of January, 1955, Governor Marvin Griffin of Georgia declared:

> I repeat my pledge to the mothers and fathers of Georgia that as long as Marvin Griffin is your governor there will be no mixing of the races in the classrooms of our schools and colleges in Georgia.

Horace Ward returned to the country from military service that same year and resumed his teaching duties at Alabama State. Nonetheless, his dream of becoming a lawyer had not died. The final chapter of the story, though, was not to be a happy one.

William Boyd, severely disenchanted with the progress of the case and also ill with cancer, and the impatient Inc. Fund decided it was time to bring in a new quarterback. They appointed Hollowell as chief counsel, although he was insistent that Walden remain on the team. The two Atlanta attorneys and the Inc. Fund lawyers sought to resume the battle at the point of its artificial postponement in 1953.

The defendants found a variety of new tactics to delay the trial and Ward's entry into the university law school. These obstructions, the fact that Ward was now twenty-eight years old and Dr. Boyd's steadily worsening health brought Hollowell and the rest of the legal team to a reluctant conclusion. They recommended that Ward enroll in another law school with the view of transferring to the University of Georgia if the trial were to produce a decision in his favor. The courageous Dr. Boyd lost his final battle with cancer in 1956, and that fall, Ward matriculated at the law school of Northwestern University.

The case did finally come to trial in December, 1956, with Hollowell as chief counsel. Sitting with him and Walden at the defense attorneys' table, although they did not participate actively, were Constance Baker Motley and Robert Carter, the NAACP's general counsel. Judge Hooper ruled that Ward's matriculation at Northwestern had rendered moot his application to Georgia and dismissed the case. Ward's legal team believed it could win the case on appeal but decided not to carry it forward and delay their client's legal education any further. Though the reasoning was sound, it still forced the swallowing of a bitter pill after a dogged, six-year pursuit of legal remedies to educational segregation.[7]

§§§

That year the Hollowells found new housing as part of another major change in Atlanta's demographic patterns. Although Negroes represented about one-third of the city's population, they still were squeezed onto one-sixth of the land, primarily in the areas around Auburn Avenue downtown and surrounding the Atlanta University Center to the west. The dilemma was particularly acute for well-to-do Negroes who continued to record economic progress but could find only limited housing or land on which to build.

Six miles west of Five Points lay Collier Heights, a tract of largely undeveloped land, its wooded ravines crossed only by Collier Drive and a few dirt roads. About nine hundred residents, most of them white and living in poor, rural homes, were spread across the two square miles of rough terrain. As part of the city's so-called Plan of Improvement and through a complex series of maneuvers and agreements that involved the Planning Commission, the bi-racial West Side Mutual Development Committee, the Atlanta Urban League, and black and white real estate companies, in-depth plans emerged for a new neighborhood. The suburban-like development was one of the first of its kind in the nation to be built by Negroes for Negroes.[8]

Donald and Louise Hollowell were in the initial wave of families to acquire property and build homes there, and Hollowell himself handled much of the legal work for many of these transactions. In March, 1956, they moved to their first and only Atlanta house on Dale Creek Drive, a ranch-style brick structure that felt like a castle after what for Louise Hollowell had been nearly fifteen years of cramped apartment living.

It was to be a busy year along many fronts. Just as Southern Negroes were becoming more organized and systematic in their protests against discrimination and segregation, state officials in the region were finding new ways to disembowel their efforts. In Alabama they had essentially put the regional NAACP office, the first in the Deep South, out of business, forcing it to relocate to Georgia.[9]

In Atlanta the state tax authorities swooped down upon the offices of the local NAACP chapter on Auburn Avenue and threatened its executive, John Calhoun, with fines and imprisonment for having failed to register the organization with the Secretary of State. Their real goal, however, was to obtain the NAACP membership records, which he refused to surrender. Possession of these rolls, which included the names of many teachers and other public employees, could have become a powerful tool for white intimidation and repression.

The state's efforts backfired. Instead of frightening the Negro community, it generated both resolve and legal cohesiveness. Hollowell and virtually every other Negro lawyer of stature in the city[10] joined Walden, the lead counsel, in volunteering their services when the State of Georgia brought suit against the NAACP.

Superior Court Judge Durwood T. Pye presided over the first trial. The courtroom was jammed with Negro onlookers, including Louise Hollowell. It was Hollowell's first encounter with the man who would be his judicial nemesis for the next decade. He and his colleagues quickly discovered, if they didn't already know, that Pye, relatively new to the Superior Court bench, was a diehard segregationist.

However, the days when Negro lawyers might have swallowed their pride and humbled themselves before an antagonistic bench were rapidly disappearing. Instead, the NAACP chapter's attorneys carefully constructed and filed a motion requesting that Pye recuse himself on the basis of his racial bias. The judge reacted in shock. He made it clear that he considered it a serious affront that anyone would dare to believe that he held a bias against "nigras."

"The court," he said righteously, referring to himself in the third person "could not look at itself in the mirror when it shaves in the morning, if it were to consider itself prejudiced." Of course, he further noted, "the court also does not believe in the mongrelization of the races." His response was insulting, but the confused and contradictory imagery also was so preposterous that every Negro present in the packed courtroom was at pains not to laugh.

Pye was not satisfied with having issued that oral reproof. To make official his anger with this newfound Negro uppityness, he quickly issued a "show cause" order against Walden and Hollowell to demonstrate why they should not be held in contempt for impugning his judicial rectitude.

One of the witnesses for the NAACP was Lorimer D. Milton, President of Citizens Trust Bank and one of the city's most respected Negro citizens. A graduate of Brown University, Milton belonged to that handful of dignified, old-style leaders from the Negro community with whom whites would meet for private discussions about race relations. He was, however, also treasurer of the local NAACP chapter. When the state's attorneys sought to discredit the work of the organization, he boldly proclaimed that every Negro in Georgia ought to be a member.

Pye and the other white officials were beginning to realize that they lost the power to intimidate, but he seemed unable to regain control. The trial began to degenerate into a judicial circus. One of the witnesses for the NAACP was the sassy, bright-eyed Eunice Cooper, the organization's office secretary. Her wily answers under cross-examination became increasingly frustrating for the defense. She initially feigned an inability to understand a question about the process by which the order had come to turn over the NAACP records. Hollowell didn't really want her to answer, because he knew that she had a tendency to be loquacious and might volunteer more information than necessary. He quickly offered an objection to the question on the basis of the way it had been framed. "There's no way to answer the question, your honor," he said. Pye responded, "She seems to be doing all right to me." He himself then turned to the witness and asked, "Do you understand the question?" "I'm not sure," she replied. The judge persisted. "Were you in the office when something was delivered by the marshal?" She conceded that she had been. "What did the marshal say?" Pye continued. Ms. Cooper replied, "He said, 'I've got a love letter for you.'" "Did the marshal tell you who this 'love letter' was from?" asked Pye. She turned to the judge with a wicked smile and answered, "Why, yes, your honor, I believe it was from you." The Negro spectators burst into laughter, and even Pye, despite his exasperation, had to smile.

However, he was becoming increasingly frustrated with the proceedings. When Calhoun took it upon himself to open a window to let some air into the overcrowded and hot room, Pye, a stickler for proper behavior by everyone else in his court, threatened him with a contempt citation. Hollowell tried to intercede politely. "I'm sure that he meant no harm, your honor." Pye's response was to place Calhoun in Hollowell's custody to "assure his conformance with court decorum."

When the trial ended, Pye found against the Atlanta NAACP and imposed a fine of twenty-five thousand dollars. Even as the Legal Defense Fund gave leadership to the successful appeal process which eventually went to the Georgia Supreme Court, the state authorities sent its representatives to New York to determine whether the national organization had any assets that they might attach.

The ruling of the state's highest bench in support of the NAACP was, of course, a significant step for Negro rights. The NAACP never paid a fine, nor did it surrender its membership lists. There was, though, another equally important outcome of the legal battle—a growing body of Negro lawyers and other leaders who were ready, willing and able to go to court to secure their rights.[11]

Governor Griffin had opened the year with another State of the State address in which he re-intoned his support of racial segregation:

> There will be no mixing of the races in the public schools and college classrooms of Georgia....I campaigned...with segregation as the No. 1 plank in my platform. We must not desert future generations of Georgians. We must never surrender.
>
> All attempts to mix the races, whether they be in the classrooms, on the playgrounds, in public conveyances, or in any other close personal contact on terms of equality, peril the mores of the South.

After the state legislature passed a series of repressive and discriminatory measures to block race-mixing, the *Atlanta Journal* reported on January 29, 1956:

> No Southern state is willing to go as far as Georgia to maintain segregation in schools....no other state goes to the extreme of proposing to totally scrap the public school system if segregation fails.

In that spirit, the General Assembly, casting about for a symbol of its defiance of federal law, seized upon the device of changing the state flag to incorporate the battle banner of the Confederate Army.[12] The change became law on February 10, 1956. That year the State of Georgia's motto — "Wisdom, Justice and Moderation" — had an especially hollow ring.

One month later, in March, 1956, six Negro applicants became the first of their race to seek admission to the segregated Georgia State College of Business Administration in Atlanta. They received the predictable run-around from the institution and the Board of Regents which denied them admission. The State of Georgia had seen the handwriting on the wall and during the early 1950s began setting up roadblocks for the challenges to segregated education that it saw coming. One of the state's requirements was that applicants furnish letters of endorsement from alumni of the institution — all of whom, of course, were white.[13]

The Negro candidates for admission filed a suit. Their team of local attorneys included E. E. Moore, Jr., Hollowell and Walden, assisted by Robert L. Carter, Thurgood Marshall and Constance Baker Motley from the Inc. Fund.[14] As the case moved through the appeal process, Governor Ernest Vandiver, Griffin's successor, responded by requesting the Board of Regents to cut off all enrollment within the entire university system. He then led an effort to pass "age limit" bills and additional complicated admissions regulations to forestall further attempts at integration.

While the Georgia State case dragged on, Hollowell became involved in the early battle to desegregate public facilities. On June 8, 1953, the U.S. Supreme Court had banned segregation in the restaurants of Washington, D. C. The Inc. Fund seized upon this precedent and began taking other similar cases. In 1957 it joined forces with Atlanta attorneys in *Coke v. City of Atlanta et al*. Coke, a Negro insurance man from Birmingham and a frequent traveler through the Atlanta airport, had brought suit after being denied admission to the terminal restaurant.

This Dobbs House facility was not only racially restricted; it further chose to promote itself through a less-than-subtle identification with a stereotyped Old South. The restaurant's management had placed a large bale of cotton near the entrance. However, not content with that passive symbol, it also employed an elderly Negro man with bushy white hair and an Uncle Remus-like costume, complete with overalls and a red bandana, to cavort outside for the amusement of the patrons and passers-by.

The Inc. Fund dispatched Jack Greenberg as its attorney and retained the services of Hollowell to serve as local counsel for Mr. Coke. The two handily won the case in the U.S. District Court for the Northern District of Georgia.

On the same evening that the court announced its ruling in favor of the plaintiff, Martin Luther King, Sr. and some of his fellow Baptist ministers from Atlanta arrived at the Atlanta airport. They were returning from a conference in Hot Springs, Arkansas, where they had met, dined and revived themselves in the famous baths of that town's segregated facilities. When they deplaned in Atlanta, they decided to test this latest legal ruling by stopping at the Dobbs House for dinner.

Somewhat to their surprise, and to the absolute astonishment of the Negro employees who huddled at the entrance to the kitchen to see what would happen, they encountered no difficulty. The white hostess, long accustomed to denying service to Negroes, seated them graciously. After they had finished their well-prepared and politely-served meal and were readying themselves to leave, she cordially inquired whether they had enjoyed the dinner.

"Daddy" King rumbled in reply, "We enjoyed it very much, and we expect to come back." After the group left the terminal, the venerable pastor of Ebenezer Baptist Church is reported to have announced, "The more I thought about what had just happened and how good the food and service were and about how long I had been denied, the madder I got."

Later that spring, Hollowell's close friend, C. B. King,[15] asked him to come to southwest Georgia to help him with a particularly nasty civil rights case. King had been retained by Mrs. Hattie Brazier, whose husband had recently been killed. As Hollowell soon learned, police officers had arbitrarily stopped James Brazier, a long-time and gainfully employed resident of Dawson, as he was driving through the small town on a Sunday afternoon in April. He protested their action, and his complaints led to an angry exchange of words. Later in the day the police, infuriated by his "smart talk," came to his home, arrested him and threw him into the county jail.

During the night, several men dragged him from his cell and took him away. After beating Brazier senseless, they hauled him back to the jail and threw him on his mattress. By morning his condition was so critical that the authorities notified his family that their prisoner seemed to be "pretty sick." After the doctor they summoned reported that Brazier was in grave health, Brazier's people took him to the medical center in Columbus where he died on April 25.

King learned that there was a witness to Brazier's incarceration, a woman imprisoned in the same jail the night he was arrested. Worried for her safety and realizing that it would take at least several months before a trial date, they waited to interview her until her own case was settled. She was subsequently sentenced to eighteen months in the prison at Milledgeville, where they went to meet with her. She told them that she had seen the sheriff of Terrell County, the police chief of Dawson and three of his officers spirit Brazier away from the county jail and then later dump his brutally beaten and unconscious body in the cell.

It took two years for the case to come to trial in U. S. District Court. Hollowell, assisted by C. B. King, brought suit against the local and county police, as well as the insurance company that represented their jurisdictions, for conspiracy to deprive Brazier of his civil rights and sought $180,000 in damages to be paid to Brazier's estate. Even before it began, the defendants' attorneys first sought to prove that their clients should be dealt with separately because they represented two different jurisdictions. Hollowell and King successfully established that both forces regularly used the same detention facilities and could therefore be sued together.

Their key witness, whom they interviewed again the day before the trial began, still was willing to testify. However, by the time they placed her on the stand, it was clear, Hollowell remembers, that "someone had gotten to her." She was so frightened that her legs were shaking and her knees knocking together, and she denied any knowledge of the events that led to Brazier's death. Even his attempts to cross-examine her as a hostile witness could not elicit any testimony against the defendants.

As the trial began, Hollowell and King had also learned that Brazier's beating probably had occurred in an old warehouse not far from the downtown jail. They found an elderly Negro woman who had known the old, white night watchman at that facility for many years. Since they frequently saw each other and conversed about all kinds of subjects, she was willing to see whether she could obtain any incriminating information from him. They met her at the courthouse and found a quiet spot to give her a battery-operated, reel-to-reel tape recorder and instructions about how to operate it. She agreed to carry it in her shopping bag when she dropped by the warehouse to engage the watchman in conversation late that afternoon.

Even before their attempts at espionage could begin, though, there was a moment of panic. As the woman left the courthouse, she dropped the bag, and all of its contents, including the tape recorder, began bouncing down the front steps. Hollowell, who happened to be a few feet behind her, immediately saw what was happening and raced past her to scoop up the machine before anyone else noticed it.

No one did, and she proceeded on her mission. However, nothing came of the attempt. Although she probed a bit, the watchman would never admit to seeing anything out of the ordinary and claimed that he also had heard nothing because his radio had been playing. Reluctant to place her in further danger, they told her not to persist in the search for information.

Without witnesses or other evidence, Hollowell and King could not build a strong case against the police officers. The court found them not guilty. They then carried their search for relief to the Fifth Circuit Court of Appeals, which heard the case a year later, in July, 1961. Jack Greenberg of the Inc. Fund argued the case. At issue was whether Brazier's death as a result of the violation of his civil rights would support a federally enforced claim for damages to be paid to his survivors. Among the material that the attorneys introduced was what they believed to be a precedent ruling by the Ninth Circuit Court that was so recent it had not even been published. They obtained photocopies of the ruling and handed it to the three appeal judges.

The appellate justices made clear their concern about the blatant injustice of what had happened to Brazier and their desire that it not go unchecked. They noted that federal civil rights law was intended to protect individuals in situations where state statutes failed to do so. Nonetheless, with one dissent, they ruled that because "deficient" federal statutes did not expressly make reference to death caused by civil rights violations or to the rights of survivors (in other words, legislative action had not kept pace with judicial activity), their only recourse was to remand Brazier's case to the state of Georgia. The state, they said, had the responsibility to provide the remedy that the federal government could not offer.

Hollowell and King had no additional evidence with which to establish the guilt of the defendants and no funds to carry the case forward. The power of police to intimidate, the fear of that power in the Negro communities of rural Georgia, and weak civil rights laws had again carried the day. However, although it would take more legal battles, the battle had been joined by the opposition. There were, for the first time, Negro attorneys and clients who were willing to seek justice in places where the established order barely understood the principle of civil rights for citizens of color.

§§§

Finally, in 1959, U.S. District Court Judge Boyd Sloan of Gainesville issued an injunction against racial bias at Georgia State. Sadly though, Judge Sloan, drawing upon the 1954 Supreme Court decision, only ruled against bias. Since he did not order the plaintiffs' admission, the institution remained essentially segregated. The state subsequently found administrative means with which to subvert the judge's findings. Chief among them was to cite a 1953 resolution of the Board of Regents that required applicants to demonstrate "good moral character." Thus, the education authorities were able to document that two of the women seeking admission, even though they later married the fathers, had given birth to children out of wedlock. The moral issue was to become a favorite ploy of the attorney general's office and other lawyers of the state during the years to come. As a result local Negro attorneys and lawyers from the Inc Fund began to take even greater pains to scrutinize the backgrounds of the plaintiffs they represented.

Elsewhere, other Southern universities were succumbing to legal pressure and opening their doors, but Georgia remained defiant. The state had spent the past six years circling its wagons in preparation for the attack. In 1953, even before the *Brown* ruling, Governor Talmadge had secured legislative approval for the so-called "private school amendment" which authorized the state to pay tuition grants in lieu of providing public education. Georgia voters approved the amendment a few months after the Supreme Court decision.

Beginning in 1955 and continuing through subsequent sessions, the General Assembly adopted a series of laws that called for the mandatory closing of desegregated schools, the leasing of these closed facilities to private corporations, the cutoff of state funds and the withdrawal of taxing power for desegregated educational institutions and the punishment of administrators and teachers who participated in desegregation. The catch-all phrase that summed up these provisions in Georgia and other Southern states was "massive resistance." Despite the fact that the Supreme Court had been systematically striking down such laws in other states, Georgia dug in its heels and prepared to fight.

Negro Atlantans, nonetheless, were determined to force the integration of the city's public schools. There had been sporadic legal attempts by courageous Negro teachers like Rheubin and Vera Taylor to secure pay equal to that of their white counterparts, but filing suit could and often did lead to their firing and years of waiting to be reinstated. As early as 1950, using a strategy that the Inc. Fund was pursuing around the country, some two hundred Negro citizens sued the Atlanta Board of Education in federal court. At the heart of their case were the disparities between the funds available for the education of their children and the money spent on teachers, facilities and programs for white children. That suit, however, filed four years before the *Brown* decision, was derailed by the state. Using money from a sales tax for which Governor Herman Talmadge secured passage, Georgia poured money into both black and white public education — seeking, among other goals, to use "equal" spending to preserve a segregated system.

By 1958, though, bolstered by the 1954 Supreme Court decision, a new group of plaintiffs was back in federal court, with Hollowell as their chief counsel. The case, recorded on the docket as *Calhoun v. Latimer*, would drag on for many years. Initially, though, there was some reasonable hope for resolution. Under court order the city had already desegregated its transportation system, libraries and other public facilities. In mid-1959, U. S. District Judge Frank Hooper, after listening to testimony over a period of many months, finally gave Atlanta's schools one year to submit an integration plan. Thirty-five years after that case began, Hollowell still remembers with enormous distaste the public school system's "Sneaky Pete-isms," as he describes the foot-dragging and delaying tactics employed to avoid significant desegregation. The city officials, he notes, were apprehensive to the point of paranoia that school integration would produce the same violent white reaction it had provoked in other Southern communities. Nonetheless, the putative virtue of caution became a smoke screen for obstructing the intent of the law. Thus, for example, the first plan called for only ten students to "integrate" four high schools [16]

§§§

There were some public white voices of moderation. Several hundred Atlanta women formed an advocacy organization called Help Our Public Education (HOPE) that called for the abandonment of resistance to desegregation. By 1960 the General Assembly Commission on Schools (the so-called "Sibley Commission", named for its chairman, James Sibley) was conducting hearings around the State of Georgia and seeking to promote token and gradual desegregation as an alternative to the closing of all public schools. Ralph McGill, who was sharing his growing sensitivity to the evils of segregation in front page editorials of the *Atlanta Constitution*, continued to prod the conscience of the community as he quietly called for the South to accept the necessity of social change. Restrained and temperate in tone, his words offered hope to those who were trying to institute that change. Behind the scenes he encouraged a group of white Atlanta ministers to respond to the infamous Southern Manifesto of the region's governors that declared their opposition to the 1954 Supreme Court decision. In language that seems tame today but was strong enough then to have some of them driven from their pulpits, these clergymen issued their own manifesto, calling for racial peace and harmony. McGill's probing of what Gunnar Myrdal had described as "the moral conflict in the heart of white Americans" also consistently served to inflame the diehards whose battle cry was "never."

It was clear that a tough battle lay ahead. Thurgood Marshall in New York would often sigh and exclaim, "Lord, I get awfully tired of trying to save the white man's soul." Yet when he addressed a gathering of Prince Hall Masons in Atlanta in 1959, his words took on a more assertive tone:

> *They call us agitators, but you know what an agitator is. It's the thing in the washing machine that gets the dirt out of the linen, and that's what we're doing, getting out the dirt.*

It was in this setting that Donald Hollowell was establishing his base of operations and from which he would become one of those "agitators" for a new way of life.

ENDNOTES

[1] Once back in Atlanta, he filed a letter of protest with the Standard Oil Company and also sent a personal note to the owner. In it he both cited the law and appealed to the man's conscience. The oil company responded that its hands were tied because it did not own the station but that it would investigate the matter. The gas station owner never replied.

[2] The Center came into being when Atlanta University, Morehouse and Spelman signed an agreement of federation in 1929. During the early 1940s, Clark and Morris Brown relocated their campuses to adjacent property and became members of the consortium. Joined in 1958 by the Interdenominational Theological Center (itself a federation of historically Negro seminaries) these six institutions would in due course become the largest center of private, black higher education in the world. During the 1970s, the Morehouse School of Medicine joined the Center, and in the late 1980s, Clark and the graduate school merged to become Clark Atlanta University. Hollowell served on the boards of Spelman College and the Atlanta University Center, Inc., as well as of Phillips School of Theology, the C. M. E. member of the ITC, and he also was to become the first lay chair of the ITC trustees.

[3] Indeed, a great deal of the research and writing that would later undergird the plaintiffs' arguments in *Brown v. Board of Education* took place in that small building on Cypress Street.

[4] This all-too-brief sketch of the Southern Regional Council draws upon remarks by one of its former executives, Leslie Dunbar, as reprinted in SRC's publication, *Southern Changes* (Spring, 1993, Volume 15, Number 1). Donald Hollowell was a key director of SRC, and later board president of the Voter Education Project it created. SRC recognized his many contributions some years ago by designating him a Life Fellow.

[5] Dr. Dana White of Emory University has compiled a splendid array of statistical data for this period and coupled it with a series of fascinating analyses and historical insights. His publications are "must" reading for anyone with an interest in Atlanta's emergence as a modern city.

[6] Warren, of course, was the Chief Justice who wrote the historic decision of the Court.

[7] The sour taste never did begin to dissolve until five years later. In 1961 a new legal team successfully challenged the university's denial of applications

from Hamilton Holmes and Charlayne Hunter (see Chapter 1 for a full account). Perhaps the bad taste vanished fully for Horace Ward on the day in 1979 when he was sworn in as a federal district judge in the same courtroom where his case was dismissed when he sought entrance to the state university's law school. It was an historic occasion. All of the other district judges were there, as well as Elbert P. Tuttle and several other justices of the 11th Circuit Court. Hollowell had the privilege of robing the new black judge. It was also the opportunity for him to offer some remarks that reminded the listeners of the roles played by William Madison Boyd, A. T. Walden and others who had spent their lives laying the foundation for this moment.

[8] The original projections called for Collier Heights to be a community of twenty thousand residents, who would have easy access to shopping centers and other amenities. However, the population eventually leveled off at about seven thousand people. White flight from the Cascade Heights and other areas on the far west side of the city, stimulated by massive block-busting, and the corresponding in-migration of middle-class Negro families reduced the pressure on the new suburb.

[9] The state enjoined the NAACP from further operations in Alabama for failing to follow the laws governing "foreign corporations" and ordered it to pay a hefty fine for every day that it failed to release its membership rolls. By a happy coincidence, given the close association that Hollowell was to have with both the NAACP and the Legal Defense Fund during the coming years, Ruby Hurley, its director, chose to locate the new regional office in the same building on Hunter Street in Atlanta where he was a tenant.

[10] Their ranks included E. E. Moore, S. S. Robinson and R. E. Thomas, all of whom, as well as Walden, now are deceased.

[11] Judge Pye never did seek to enforce his contempt orders by holding a hearing on those motions. However, as noted, his path and that of Hollowell were destined to intersect for many more years.

[12] For perhaps the most comprehensive account of the way in which this decision was reached, see Frederick Allen's *Atlanta Rising (1996)*.

[13] One touch of decency found its way into the intransigence of the authorities. If candidates could not find alumni to endorse their applications, the law permitted the clerk of a court to sign their certificates. J. W. Simmons, the white Clerk of the Fulton County Superior Court, was willing to assist Hollowell's clients in this way.

[14] The scope of the Inc. Fund's operations also was broadening. Its steadily increasing numbers of courtroom successes made it possible to attract more funding

and to expand its staff and the number of cases it could handle. As a result, Hollowell and other lawyers in the field could call upon the Inc. Fund for support on a more frequent basis.

[15] See Chapter 10 for more information about C. B. King and his association with Hollowell.

[16] That legal battle with the Atlanta Board of Education lasted for fifteen years, well beyond Hollowell's involvement with the case. Before it ended, a host of local attorneys like E. E. Moore and Inc. Fund lawyers were involved. In February, 1973, it was at last resolved by a settlement that the historian C. Vann Woodward referred to as the "Second Atlanta Compromise." Blacks agreed to stop bringing suits to achieve school integration through such means as busing, and whites agreed that the school superintendency and at least fifty per cent of all staff positions would be filled by blacks. The national office of the NAACP was so upset by this concession that it forced the removal of Lonnie King, the Executive Director, and all of the local board members. And yet, sadly, when all was said and done, the push for integrated public education in Atlanta had become a virtual non-issue as other forces—primarily the flight of white families to the suburbs and the transfer of white students to private schools—led by the 1980s to a system whose enrollment was ninety per cent black.

8

THE MOVEMENT'S NEW ATTORNEY

The combat for which Hollowell had consciously started to prepare himself after World War II was underway, and the protagonists for a racially integrated society were taking and holding some important ground. Yet the progress of their trench warfare through the courts seemed agonizingly slow. Even the historic *Brown* decision, once thought to be just the armament needed to secure the final breakthrough to victory, had failed to deliver on its promises. Something else was needed to turn the tide of the battle.

The "something else" appeared on February 1, 1960. That day four Negro students at North Carolina A & T College, without a great deal of advanced planning, seated themselves on the lunch counter stools of an F. W. Woolworth store in Greensboro. When the waitresses refused to serve them, they refused to leave. It was not the first sit-in. There had been similar protests in many other cities during previous years, but they attracted little attention. This particular incident, though, fired the imagination of other students. They claimed their share of ownership in the struggle and this catalytic surge quickly transformed a cause into a crusade.

Within days undergraduates were protesting in other North Carolina cities and soon thereafter in South Carolina. The students, far more impatient than many of their elders and less bound by economic and other restraints, had entered the battle for civil rights and created "the Movement." For Martin Luther King, Jr., their arrival seemed heaven-sent. He had been searching more than three years for a way to galvanize public imagination and support. King strongly endorsed what the students were doing and encouraged them to fill up the jails.

The Movement quickly began to acquire some organization. In Nashville, the Rev. James Lawson, who had been offering training in non-violent protest since 1959, organized a new series of crash courses for the hundreds of students who were preparing to march.[1] At the Atlanta University Center, however, rebellion foundered for a time on the twin shoals of tradition and political expediency. The city's Negro and white leaders considered themselves more progressive than their urban counterparts in the South. It was their custom, they reminded the students, to work out solutions to racial problems behind closed doors.

Furthermore, even as the student protests had been gathering force, the authorities arrested King. The young minister, who had become the pastor of Ebenezer Baptist Church only weeks earlier, now faced felony tax evasion charges in Alabama. Dr. Samuel Williams, King's professor of philosophy at Morehouse College and the pastor of Friendship Baptist Church, counseled caution. Both he and Dr. Benjamin Mays, Morehouse's president, were concerned that responsibility for the student actions would be laid at King's feet at a time when he was already in trouble. Mays and the presidents of the other Atlanta University Center institutions met with the students and extracted from them a promise to put their demands in writing. Left unclear was whether this proposed statement would be a substitute for or a prelude to action.

The student leaders, with Julian Bond, Herschelle Sullivan and Roslyn Pope functioning as the principal drafters and M. Carl Holman, the beloved Clark College faculty member, serving as their advisor, went to work on the declaration. It won the approval of the college presidents and on March 9, "An Appeal for Human Rights" appeared in both the Negro and white daily newspapers as a paid advertisement. Its message was forceful, but its tone was moderate — even polite. Nonetheless, it took the entire community by surprise.

In response, both white and Negro community leaders called publicly for ongoing negotiations of the kind that had always characterized progress in Atlanta's race relations. However, it soon became apparent that it was too late to ask the students not to make waves. Six days after the manifesto's publication, the tide began to rush in.

Led by young men and women who would emerge as national figures during the coming decades, several hundred well-dressed, mannerly and well-organized students began their march toward downtown. They came from all six of the contiguous campuses of the Atlanta

University Center and fanned out to sit in at targeted eating establishments throughout the center of the city. Some white students from other local colleges joined them.

Even as the students were devising their strategy, someone observed that when arrested — as they surely would be — they would need legal counsel. They found their way to Donald Hollowell.[2] Like King, he realized that the students' commitment might constitute a turning point in the push for civil rights. Perhaps he recognized in their energy something of the spirit of the Southern Negro Youth Congress that had redirected his own life. At any rate, Hollowell readily agreed to represent them. Other Negro attorneys would become involved in the days and years ahead, but it was Hollowell to whom the students usually turned first for legal counsel and strategic advice.

As the arrests began, the situation was tense and volatile. Still, it was not without its moments of humor. Julian Bond met Hollowell for the first time on the day of the initial march and vividly recalls the experience. Prior negotiation between the attorneys and the city authorities had determined that one representative from each group of student demonstrators would appear in court. The boyish-looking Morehouse student, who had been arrested with the group at City Hall, sat with Hollowell on his right and A. T. Walden on his left. The son of a distinguished university dean and former college president, Bond had never before been in a courtroom.

As Bond tells the story, when the judge stared down at him and asked him how he planned to plead, he didn't know what to say. His mind raced. "Was he guilty? Not guilty? Surely he was guilty of doing what we had done." In panic, he turned to Walden for guidance, only to discover that the aging counselor had fallen asleep. Quizzically, he then turned to Hollowell, who whispered sharply, "'Not guilty,' you damn fool." Happily, Bond had the sense to repeat only the first half of Hollowell's direction. Others who were present also recall with delight the way in which Hollowell early during the long proceedings that day politely but firmly requested the judge to instruct the prosecuting attorney in the proper pronunciation of the word "Negro."

Hollowell and his colleagues secured bail bonds for all of the students, and no one stayed in jail. Atlanta's Negro and white leaders, determined to keep order, had managed to abort this first student demonstration before it could reach full term. Nonetheless, many of the student leaders made their way on April 15 to Shaw University, a small Negro college in Raleigh, North Carolina, to organize themselves further. There, with more than one hundred of their peers, they heard speeches from Lawson and Martin Luther King, Jr. Before the conference ended they had formed the Student Nonviolent Coordinating Committee (SNCC), for which Lawson drafted a statement of purpose.

As Lawson was preparing that document, the Atlanta contingent was seeking another rallying symbol. They hit upon May 17, the sixth anniversary of the Supreme Court's *Brown* decision, proposing to celebrate it with a march to the state capitol. They implored King, in court in Montgomery, to march with them. The college presidents, made all the more jumpy by the governor's threat to call out the state police, did their best to discourage the students.

The young men and women, more than one thousand of them, marched anyway. Downtown Atlanta was agog at this show of strength. The *Atlanta Daily World* later reported the comment of a white woman who watched this parade and then exclaimed, "I didn't know there were that many niggers in college." When confronted at the capitol by the promised state police the marchers veered north to Auburn Avenue. There they swung east and paraded down Sweet Auburn to Wheat Street Baptist Church for a rally that became all the more joyous because of King's unexpected arrival from Alabama. Again, though, there were no arrests. The Atlanta authorities still were opting for restraint.

Summer vacation began soon thereafter, and the city's student protests stopped for a time. Other events regained the headlines. The African freedom movement was peaking. Within two months, Zaire, Somali, Dahomey, Niger, Upper Volta, Ivory Coast, Chad, Congo Brazzaville, Gabon and Senegal became independent countries, followed soon thereafter by Mali and Nigeria. On the home front, the Republicans and Democrats held political conventions and nominated Richard M. Nixon and John F. Kennedy as their presidential candidates.

With the coming of fall, the students returned to the Atlanta University Center. Classes resumed, and there were football games to play and homecoming events to arrange. The student movement leaders, nonetheless, kept looking for and planning new ways to keep alive their protest against racial segregation and discrimination. The previous May, Congress had passed and President Eisenhower had signed into law a Civil Rights Act. However, its very weakness had helped to give the Movement further force and organization.

The students found their opportunity in October when SNCC sponsored a conference at Mt. Moriah Baptist Church across Fair Street from the Morehouse campus. King was the featured speaker. Over the course of the next several days, the students finally managed to convince him to join them in a new wave of marches and sit-ins. Donald Hollowell, now SNCC's attorney of record, prepared himself for a busy time in court.

At eleven o'clock on Wednesday, October 19, King stood with a small group of students as they were denied service in the snack bar of Rich's department store above Forsyth Street. When the police who were standing at the ready did nothing, the protesters moved to the more upscale Magnolia Room on the sixth floor. This time the store called for their arrest. All of them, as well as other protesters who had simultaneously demonstrated against restaurants elsewhere in the city, were taken away.

Offered the chance to post bond, King declined and went to jail for the first time. Thousands more protesters took to the streets as Atlanta's civic leaders and elected officials tried to break the impasse. Heightening the tension were rumors that the Klan might stage counter-demonstrations.[3] Mayor Hartsfield's efforts to negotiate King's and the students' release were hampered by their refusal to leave unless the state and the store management dropped the charges against them. By Saturday night, four days after the arrests, white and Negro leaders had fashioned a deal. It featured the important concession that desegregation talks would begin on Monday.

Hollowell, serving as King's attorney, was among those awaiting his new client's release from the county jail on October 24. He did not know the young minister especially well. Some years earlier while still in Atlanta and before accepting the pastorate of Dexter Avenue Baptist Church in Montgomery, King would occasionally poke his head in the door of Louise Hollowell's shop to flirt with one of the cosmeticians.

Hollowell had also heard him preach at Ebenezer after his return to Atlanta and seen him at the Butler Street YMCA.

Unknown to the waiting attorney, though, even as the behind-the-scene deliberations proceeded in Atlanta, legal developments elsewhere were already changing the rules. The students began to straggle forth from the jail, but the sheriff's deputies refused to release King. They announced that they were holding the young minister on a bench warrant that charged him with a different offense.

It took a while, but Hollowell finally tracked the source of the complaint to adjoining DeKalb County. Earlier that spring a policeman had stopped King who, with his wife, was driving Lillian Smith, the liberal white writer, to Emory University Hospital. King, who had moved to Atlanta three months before, still had not obtained a Georgia driver's license to replace his Alabama certificate.

Appearing before Judge Oscar Mitchell in September and represented by a lawyer of his father's choice, he had received a twelve-month sentence — suspended by the judge — and a fine. The same Mitchell now had signed an order to "show cause" why the suspension should not be revoked. It essentially served to keep King imprisoned pending a hearing that would determine whether his arrest at Rich's constituted a violation of his suspended traffic sentence and his promise not to break any state laws.

Hollowell hastily assembled an array of technical arguments in King's defense, including the point that both Rich's and the state had dropped the trespass charges. They fell on deaf ears. Mitchell insisted upon the hearing, and the next day the DeKalb officers arrived in Atlanta to pick up King. Their orders obviously encouraged them to add humiliation and intimidation to their duties. Before pushing King into their car for the short trip to Decatur, they shackled him with arm and leg irons as well as handcuffs.

In the tense and hostile atmosphere of Mitchell's court, Hollowell and the hundreds of King supporters who squeezed into the room heard the prosecutor's demand for a stiff penalty. Hollowell put character witnesses, including Dr. Mays and Dr. Rufus Clement, the President of Atlanta University, on the stand. He had King himself testify that he had not even been aware that he was under sentence. Then Hollowell called

C. M. Clayton, the elderly Negro attorney who had represented King at the September court appearance, to state that he had not made this fact clear to King. Finally, Hollowell presented another series of legal objections. Mitchell overruled all of them. Ignoring the rest of the testimony, the judge quickly revoked King's probation and ordered him to begin immediate service of a four-month sentence on a chain gang. Although shocked, Hollowell requested that his client be freed on bond, pending further appeal. Mitchell denied that motion too.

King's family and friends — and King himself — were justifiably frightened. The life expectancy of Negroes on Georgia chain gangs was always in question. Both Negro and white supporters raced to telephones, trying to reach someone who could sway the judge's decision. As they began this panicky effort to exert political pressure, Hollowell pursued the straightest legal route available to him. He returned to his office and began to prepare a writ of *habeas corpus*. Georgia law, he asserted in his brief, required the authorization of bail for anyone charged with only a misdemeanor.

The next morning Hollowell was awake early. He called the DeKalb County courthouse and asked to speak with the sheriff to alert the officer that he was on his way with the writ. When one of the deputies laconically replied, "He ain't here," Hollowell asked, "When do you expect him?" The deputy said, "I don't rightly know. He took your boy to Reidsville."

As Hollowell pieced together the story, during the middle of the night the sheriff had loaded King into a car and driven him to the infamous maximum security prison southeast of Atlanta. There he was now reportedly in solitary confinement. That report was cause for further alarm. Was King really in prison? Georgia history included its share of stories about Negro prisoners being taken from jail late at night and then released, only to be shot for allegedly trying to escape. As soon as he could reach Warden Balkcom at Reidsville, Hollowell was able at last to satisfy himself that King was probably safe for the time being.

Coretta King, six months pregnant, was frantic when Hollowell called her with the news. She telephoned Harris Wofford, a member of John F. Kennedy's campaign team. That call set in motion a flurry of confused events that eventually led to a much-publicized, albeit reluctant, telephone call of sympathy to her from the presidential candidate.[4]

Martin Luther King, Sr., the powerful pastor and community leader, was taking his own steps. He had lived in the South his entire life. From his layman's perspective, he reasoned that if his son's Negro attorney had not been able to do the job yet, maybe it was time to retain a white lawyer. He peremptorily called in Morris Abram, a prominent Atlanta attorney with liberal credentials who supported Kennedy.[5]

About three-thirty that afternoon, Hollowell received a call from A. T. Walden. The long-time friend of "Daddy" King was in Abram's office, where Charles Wittenstein, a young attorney working with Abram, had made a useful discovery: the required thirty-day appeal period on the September sentencing of King still had a day to run. In other words, there was still theoretically time to file a bill of exception and have it signed by the judge, which might also mean that King would be eligible to be freed on bond.

Hollowell drove to Abram's office immediately and reviewed the relevant statute. As King's counsel of record and the attorney most knowledgeable about the case, he took charge. Commandeering a typewriter, he sat down and, without benefit of notes, began to pound out the first part of the brief. Abram's secretary completed the task, and by late that afternoon the attorneys had finished the legal paperwork.

It was nearly closing time at the courthouse in Decatur, and there was no way Hollowell could get there in time to file the brief. He called Judge Mitchell to explain his predicament and to request a favor. If Hollowell were to slip the papers beneath his door that evening, would the judge be willing to sign them the next morning and back-date them by one day.

Mitchell grudgingly acceded to the request and also agreed to let Hollowell appear before him in the morning to post a two thousand dollar bond for King (the maximum permissible for a misdemeanor). While other reporters were scurrying about in an attempt to cover the political side of the story, Ed Blair, a newsman with Channel Five, the local CBS affiliate, followed Hollowell to the courtroom the next morning. As soon as the attorney had secured the necessary papers to effect King's release, Blair asked Hollowell how he was going to get to Reidsville.

When Hollowell said he planned to drive, Blair offered him a deal. He would charter a small plane for them, if Hollowell would let him be the first to interview King. Hollowell gratefully accepted. He had not been looking forward to the prospect of driving back to Atlanta through rural Georgia with one of the state's most detested Negro citizens.

By the time Blair and Hollowell reached the county airport, the word of King's probable release was spreading rapidly. Ray Moore, another newsman from Channel Two, the NBC affiliate, also chartered an airplane for himself and a cameraman. So, too, did Ralph David Abernathy and Wyatt Tee Walker from the Southern Christian Leadership Conference. A team from Colortone that had been filming events in Atlanta found yet another plane. The little airborne flotilla soon was flying southeast toward Reidsville, where all four craft landed in a field not far from the state security facility.

At the prison, Hollowell presented himself to Warden Balkcom while the cameramen filmed everything. As Hollowell reached out to shake the warden's hand, the prison official noticed the cameras and pulled back. "Hell, no, don't do that," he exclaimed. "You want me to lose my job?" King appeared in prison greens, looking well, and the warden began to relax a bit. "I'm sure glad to see you fellas," he said. "We've about burned out three telephone transformers with all the calls we've been getting." There was more picture-taking. Then King, now dressed in street clothes, gave Blair the interview promised by Hollowell and also spent a few minutes with Moore. The entire ensemble finally trooped outside for a group photograph. Hollowell slipped into the back row as everyone else crowded as close as possible to the liberated Civil Rights leader. As they all dispersed to return to their aircraft, Hollowell remembers hearing a distant voice cry out from within the stockade, "Long live the king!"

Just before six o'clock that evening, the plane carrying a weary Hollowell and his celebrated client touched down at the Fulton County airport.[6] King's immediate family and other well-wishers ecstatically welcomed him home. "Daddy" King ushered his son into a Cadillac limousine for the ride to Ebenezer Church. There, at an impromptu celebration, King Sr. delivered his first public endorsement of John F. Kennedy, whom he credited with his son's release. Meanwhile Hollowell returned without fanfare to his office on Hunter Street.

The next afternoon, a few minutes after Hollowell had given an interview to NBC News, Thurgood Marshall called from the Inc. Fund in New York. He, like everyone else, had been closely following the fast-paced developments of the past several days. "Well, Don," Marshall rumbled, "I see that everybody except the lawyers is responsible for getting King out of jail."

Within a month, John F. Kennedy won the presidential election. A key to his narrow victory, as later analysis would reveal, was the vote he received from thousands of traditionally Republican Negroes.

In Atlanta, however, Hollowell had little time to ponder the vagaries of national politics. The sit-in demonstrations escalated when the promised negotiations between the students and downtown store owners failed to materialize. Adults, even those who had earlier deplored the tactics of the students, now were joining them on the picket lines that sprang up everywhere. The arrests continued.

The defense was also gearing up. Thurgood Marshall announced that the major objectives of the Legal Defense Fund for the coming year of 1961 would be representing the students arrested during the sit-ins (almost two thousand in 1960) and speeding up challenges to school segregation. "To protest against injustice is the foundation of our American democracy," he proclaimed.[7]

In Atlanta, white patience was wearing thin and, in some instances, turning to ugliness. In December, angry terrorists bombed the English Avenue Elementary School. No one was injured, but the blast was a sober warning that even in Atlanta violence lurked just beneath the seemingly peaceful fabric stretched thinly over the social order.

As the demonstrations and arrests continued during January, 1961, and spread to include more than just students, Mayor William Hartsfield pleaded publicly for calm. George F. Whitman, the presiding judge of the Fulton County Superior Court, though, instructed the grand jury to be zealous in carrying out the law.

More often than not the Negro attorneys and their clients found themselves before the bench of Superior Court Judge Durwood T. Pye. Pye was a studious man who had the ability to offer well-reasoned opinions. He also could be extremely pedantic in his delivery of all judicial pronouncements as well as thoroughly uncompromising and extremely strict in matters affecting court decorum.

Hollowell and his colleagues had first encountered Pye at the trial over which we presided when the state sued to obtain the membership records of the Atlanta NAACP. He said about him years later, "If I had a good, meaty case that didn't involve the civil rights of individuals, I would just as soon have had Pye for a judge as a number of other judges before whom I had appeared."

However, in those days it was Hollowell's misfortune to be handling civil rights cases before this justice. Pye, a swarthy, dark-haired man with darting eyes, for whatever his other strengths, made no secret of his militant dislike for Negroes and his contempt for "nigger-lovin' whites." He especially enjoyed stationing the latter group directly in front of his bench, where he could subject these mostly young people to the full brunt of his badgering and taunting, delivered from the full authority of his judicial position.

Pye also had another habit that achieved some notoriety. Whenever he was preparing to deliver himself of what he considered to be an important pronouncement, he would raise and stretch out his arms to either side. The sleeves of his robes would fall back and he would thus shoot the French cuffs and ornate cuff links on his immaculate white shirt. This mannerism became so well-known in the Negro community that John Gibson, a young friend of the Hollowells and a student at Atlanta University, even invented a dance to mimic the judge's movements and called it the Pye-Pye Twist.

Nonetheless, for all the legal power and authority at his disposal, Pye remained essentially a sideshow attraction. The main event for the Negro audience that began flocking to his courtroom was the performance of Donald Hollowell. The spectators who packed themselves into the wooden benches of the county courtroom were in awe of this powerful man with the strong, deliberate voice who gave no sign of being intimidated by his surroundings. Most of them had grown up going to churches where their pastors could climb to rhetorical heights of homiletical excess. The students had the experience of dynamic professors. None from the South, however, had ever seen a Negro like themselves stand erectly on "the Man's" turf and command respect by his sheer presence.[8]

Nearly thirty years later, many of the individuals who were students during the 1960s could still summon back vivid and precise memories of those moments. At a reunion of the Atlanta "veterans," Charles A. Black, a 1962 Morehouse College graduate, said:

> I'll always remember his presence in the courtroom with his huge hands and huge feet and his deep voice addressing the judge by saying, "I submit to you..." He always had the law on his side, and he knew the law much better than the court.

James Felder, President of the Clark College student body in 1959-60, also remembered that Hollowell was always better prepared than the other side.

> Even though the judges ruled against him at the trial level, he always won on appeal. His articulation is what impressed me. His feathers were never ruffled in the courtroom. His demeanor — the way he handled a situation — was just impeccable.... I came to Clark...on an academic pre-med scholarship, destined to go to medical school. Don Hollowell turned all that around as I watched him operate in the Fulton County courts, and it made me decide to go into law rather than medicine.

Ken Crooks, President of the Atlanta University student body in 1962 who became an attorney in Fort Lauderdale, Florida, recalled that:

> Don was very stately, very calm, careful and well-spoken. As he made his presentations in court...it was obvious that 1) he knew what he was saying, 2) he had set a trace in the people who were listening to him, and 3) he was talking sense.

Julian Bond offered this summary of his impressions:

> I think it is arguable that if it had not been for Don Hollowell, black Georgians wouldn't have advanced as far as we have....Not only did he have courage, but he also

had a brilliant legal mind. He out-stripped, out-argued, out-appeared these famous so-called great constitutional lawyers who had erected this barrier of segregation throughout the South. They had the reputation, but Hollowell had the goods.

Small wonder, then, that the students were soon fond of reciting this credo, "King is our leader, Hollowell is our lawyer, and we shall not be moved."

ENDNOTES

[1] Lawson, a longtime activist and student of independence movements throughout the world, was a graduate student at Vanderbilt University's divinity school. The Vanderbilt trustees expelled him for his civil rights activities without a hearing or the consent of the faculty, although he was reinstated after four hundred professors threatened to resign in protest of that action.

[2] No one seems to have had a clear idea of how to go about obtaining an attorney. Ben Brown's memory is that they went directly to Hollowell. Lonnie King recalls someone remembering that the closest Negro attorney to the campus was J. C. Daugherty, a Clark College graduate whose office was at the corner of Chestnut and Hunter Streets, just blocks away. In his account, a small delegation called upon Daugherty and announced their intention to march. Daugherty said he would be happy to represent them but would need three hundred dollars up front as a retainer. King says they then went to Samuel Williams, who was also the head of the local NAACP, and that Williams immediately directed them to Hollowell. As Julian Bond tells the story, the students' first inquiry was to another well-known attorney who said he would have to charge them five thousand dollars. Since the first protests, despite their careful planning, were not textbook exercises and because the rapid-fire development of events at times made everything confusing, all of these accounts may contain part of the truth.

[3] About a dozen Klan members did later arrive on the scene, dressed in their finest robes of red, green, blue and purple. When they began their counter-picket of Rich's, the students fell in line behind them and, for a time, both groups nervously marched on the same outer portion of the sidewalk. There were no serious confrontations, but the police decided to forestall that possibility and moved the Klan members to the other side of the street.

[4] It did not receive the same amount of publicity, but Robert Kennedy had also been on the telephone, vainly urging Judge Mitchell to do something to correct the situation.

[5] As events unfolded, both Hollowell and Abram took the venerable preacher's panic in stride. Each realized that the factor of the attorney's race – or, for that matter, any private pressure upon the authorities – would have to be coupled with a legal basis to resolve the dilemma.

[6] Even as Blair returned to Atlanta with Hollowell to file what he thought would be his exclusive story, Ray Moore was scooping him by flying to nearby Savannah where he "fed" his story to New York from that local NBC affiliate's studios.

[7] The Inc. Fund had organized a cadre of some seventy-five Negro and white attorneys throughout the country. During 1960 it had convened these lawyers at conferences in New York, Washington and St. Paul. At these gatherings, the expanded corps could engage in broad-ranging discussions on legal strategy as well as pick up drafts of briefs and pleadings to use when they returned home.

Years later, in a tribute to Thurgood Marshall, Hollowell wrote, "I sat at his feet as he taught me and others the art of using the Constitution to do our bidding as we sought to help improve the quality of life for those who could not help themselves." Hollowell, in the same op/ed piece for the *Atlanta Constitution*, also remembered traveling "many miles just to hear [Marshall] argue a motion in an important case."

[8] Leroy Johnson offered these comments about Hollowell's performance in the courtroom: "He had a romance with the King's English that was especially intriguing to lay people and a set of mannerisms that supported his lofty language. What he could not convey orally he said with his hands and body."

9
"MR. CIVIL RIGHTS"

As demands for social and legal change gathered force, Hollowell — who was rapidly achieving heroic stature in Georgia's Negro communities — was in high demand. Wherever civil rights cases surfaced, the call invariably went out to him and his associates. Soon thereafter, the powerfully built and dignified Negro attorney with the erect military posture would, in effect, come riding into town. His very presence, which never gave a hint of fear, would send an electric surge of confidence through his clients and their supporters and put the opposition on notice that the rules of the game had changed.

Sometimes he didn't even need to be on the scene to get results. Lonnie King, who described Hollowell as the "hired legal gun of the Movement" in Georgia, made that discovery for himself late one night. The young Morehouse student leader was returning by bus to Atlanta from a speaking engagement in Augusta. In those days before interstate highways criss-crossed the region, travel by public transportation could be interminable, with many stops along the way. King's bus made such a stop in Athens, a town that still was in the midst of the turmoil surrounding the University's desegregation.

The young activist climbed off the bus and wandered into the station. Feeling compelled to challenge the status quo, he entered the "whites only" section of the depot. The authorities, already jittery from the widespread racial unrest, called the sheriff's office. In short order King found himself in the county stockade. When Sheriff H. T. Huff asked him who his attorney was, he quickly replied, "Donald Hollowell." As King recalls the episode, "everybody froze."

Permitted the use of a telephone, he placed a call to the Hollowell residence at three o'clock in the morning. A sleepy Louise Hollowell answered and put her husband on the line. After a brief conversation with King, Hollowell told the young man that he wanted to speak to the sheriff. Recounts King, "I don't know what Hollowell said to the man, but when he hung up the phone, he told me I could go. I suspect he just didn't want to bring any heat on himself."

Increasingly at gatherings of organizations that sought his gifts as a public speaker, the glowing introduction of Hollowell would conclude with the appellation, "Mr. Civil Rights." He, however, had no time to bask in his growing reputation. A flood of new cases had started to swamp his calendar even as he was representing Hamilton Holmes and Charlayne Hunter. Many of his clients continued to be the students from the Atlanta University Center and other protestors who still were launching waves of demonstrations. Most of them had lost faith in the ability of the established Negro and white leadership to negotiate the desegregation of public facilities promised to them the previous fall.

Ralph McGill understood clearly that Atlanta's historic patterns of civilized accommodation were coming to an end. In his column on January 26, 1961, he wrote:

> One of the most persistent falsehoods and the one most troublesome in our present time is the 'stereotype of the Negro into...' 'Amos and Andy,' 'Uncle Tom,' 'Boy, 'Uncle,' 'Mammy...'etc. Most Southerners do not know, or want to know, the facts of Negro development.
>
> This is one reason why the students in their sit-ins, and the pupils who have appeared at elementary, secondary schools and universities, have produced such a revolutionary effect. They have fitted none of these stereotypes.
>
> The new leadership is not in the old style....[It] wants done what is right, and just, and what is constitutional or delineated by statute....Older white leadership, which has earned a reputation for decency and fairness, often is driven to anger and dangerous loss of perspective when confronted by a new Negro leadership which wishes to negotiate on even, rather than paternalistic, terms....

Others, like Fannie Lou Hamer, put it more simply. That gallant fighter for civil rights in Mississippi was credited with a line that became popular throughout the student movement: "I'm sick and tired of being sick and tired."

The summer of 1961 — the season of the Freedom Rides — provided an opportunity for the United States to present its best and worst sides in startling contrast. As idealistic, non-violent, often praying young women and men tested their legal right to public accommodations throughout the South, they were met by profane and violent crowds that cursed and beat them.

There were also other horrible acts of more random but still racially-motivated violence. On July 4, as reported by an FBI agent, Sheriff L. Warren "Gator" Johnson of Baker County in rural southwest Georgia attacked a Negro field hand, Charlie Ware, and beat him on the head unmercifully. Johnson then handcuffed the man, who was a foot shorter than he and weighed one hundred pounds less, and fired three bullets into his neck. Somehow doctors were able to save Ware's life, thereby making it possible for a grand jury to indict him for felonious assault against the sheriff. Ware, however, for whatever reason, chose to defy the time-honored mores of Baker County and refused to plead guilty. C. B. King, a courageous and quixotic Negro lawyer in Albany, accepted his case. Within months Hollowell was to be embroiled in other crucial events in South Georgia and would join King in Ware's defense.[1]

Then, as an increasingly strenuous load of cases poured into the Hollowell & Ward office late that summer, Horace Ward answered a telephone call one September afternoon from Monticello, a small town east of Atlanta. On the other end of the line was a frantic Leathy Cobb with a shocking story. On August 16, after only forty-five minutes of deliberation, a Jasper County Superior Court jury had found her fifteen-year-old son, Preston, guilty of the murder of an elderly white man on whose land she and her children lived and worked. Despite the boy's youth, the jurors recommended no mercy, thereby making the death sentence mandatory. Moving swiftly, Judge George Carpenter had sentenced Preston Cobb to die in the electric chair at Reidsville State Prison on September 22. J. Ben Warren, the boy's white, court-appointed attorney, had not appealed the verdict. Rather, he requested to be released from the case.

Unknown to Ward, though, Vernon Jordan had already learned of the situation from a cousin who was dating Preston Cobb's sister. The two young men sought to persuade the terrified mother to seek legal help. Her fear of white reprisal should she buck the system was so great, however, that she would only meet with them late at night with no lights on at the home of a Negro doctor. There, during a whispered conversation, she agreed to come to Atlanta. since Jordan still had not seen her face, she was to wear a red suit so he could recognize her when she arrived.

By the time she called Ward, Preston Cobb's execution date was only five days away. Jordan met Mrs. Cobb at the Atlanta bus station and brought her to the office where she agreed to retain the firm's counsel. Soon thereafter the Legal Defense Fund accepted the case and designated Hollowell as its chief attorney. Thus began a courtroom saga that would continue for the next several years and attract international attention.

Preston Cobb's memories of his boyhood in rural Jasper County are not unpleasant ones. Most Negroes did live a subservient existence and had to eke out a living by working as tenant farmers or domestics and picking up other menial jobs. Yet Cobb recalls that "there wasn't any name calling and no 'cheap shots' by the white folk." By the same token, those Negroes also had little time to ponder the dead end quality of their lives, and no one was brave enough or sufficiently stupid to challenge long established patterns of race relations. "The preacher," Cobb remembers, "would tell us about how things were going to get better, but there weren't any signs of change."

His father had died, and his mother raised Preston and eight brothers and sisters on a farm between Monticello and Eatonton. The property, once owned by his grandmother, had come into the possession of Frank Coleman Dumas, one of the area's leading white citizens.

Young Preston picked up a smattering of formal education at the elementary school, to which he walked five miles every day. The high school for Negroes in the area was a dilapidated, two-story wooden structure in Monticello with several classes squeezed into each room. He dropped out of school when he was fifteen and, by his own account, started "hanging around with the wrong crowd," most of whom were older than he.

The details of exactly what happened probably never will surface, but Frank Dumas was found lying in a ditch, shot to death. Sheriff's deputies the same day picked up Preston Cobb and a friend joyriding in Dumas' car.

The first step for Hollowell and Ward was to put the brakes on the state's rush to execute their new client. They immediately filed a motion for another trial, thereby effectively staying the execution and giving them time to prepare their case. Hollowell did not have a lot of ammunition with which to fight, and he had to contend with Preston Cobb's alleged — although unsigned — confession to the murder of the elderly Dumas. Since he had no new evidence at that time with which to counter, he elected instead to go on the offensive. The crux of his attack would be an assault on the validity of the jury and on the forcefulness of the defense presented by Cobb's first attorney.

In support of these contentions, Hollowell, accompanied by Ward and Jordan, drove to the courthouse in Jasper County. Approaching the clerk of the court, he asked to see the jury books and explained that he wanted to determine whether there were any Negroes on the list. The clerk's laconic response was, "Look, Colonel, there ain't no niggers on the books, and most of the white folk aren't qualified."

Hollowell and his associates substantiated that contention in meticulous detail. Drawing upon census figures and tax digests as well as high school graduation and voting data, they documented the availability and qualification of Negroes to serve on juries. They also confirmed that to anyone's recollection, no attorney had ever raised the constitutional question about the systematic exclusion of Negroes from juries, although no Negro had served on one during at least the past thirty years.

Even as the attorneys combed the records of Jasper County, the case was attracting international attention. A lawyer in Malaya cabled President Kennedy with a request that he intervene. Two Dutch court officials arrived in Georgia, claiming to speak for more than two million people in The Netherlands. Dr. B. W. Van Houten, a juvenile judge, and Mrs. S. T. Diemer-Lindeboom, a member of a supervisory board in Rotterdam, announced their attention to attend the hearing on Hollowell's motion for a new trial. Eleanor Roosevelt sent a telegram of appeal to Governor Vandiver on behalf of Preston Cobb.

Hollowell appeared with his client[3] before Judge Carpenter in early October. The first order of business was to clear up a nuisance challenge from Solicitor General George Lawrence that nonetheless had serious implications for Preston Cobb. Lawrence filed a motion for Hollowell's dismissal, claiming that Mrs. Cobb had not officially retained him. The confusion surrounding the matter stemmed from the fact that she had initially signed an agreement with Hollowell's associate, Horace Ward. However, although the judge eventually dismissed the prosecution's motion, it added further tension to the proceedings. Had Hollowell not been recognized as the attorney of record, the appeal deadline would have passed, thereby requiring the resentencing of Preston Cobb to the electric chair.

Hollowell exhibited no visible sign of concern. Instead he launched into his argument before Judge Carpenter that the wholesale exclusion of Negroes from the jury had violated Cobb's constitutional rights. He then also asked the judge to take "judicial cognizance" of his contention that Warren had failed his client by not raising the issue.

While Carpenter considered his decisions on the many motions from both the defense and prosecuting attorneys, Governor Vandiver replied to Mrs. Roosevelt's telegram and the hundreds of other messages that were pouring into his office. He would if necessary, he said, grant a stay of execution until the General Assembly could consider changing the law that governed the minimum age for executions.[4] Vandiver also reminded everyone that his authority did not extend beyond stays of execution. Only the three-member State Board of Pardons and Paroles could commute a death sentence, after the conclusion of all court action. The governor further explained to the Dutch observers who had come to his office that even should the legislature change the law, it would have no effect on Cobb's sentence. However, he noted, the Pardon and Parole board probably would be positively influenced by any such action of the General Assembly.

In Jasper County, meanwhile, the mood in portions of the white community was steadily growing uglier. A white minister who was seen speaking with Hollowell soon thereafter succumbed to community intimidation and left town. Sheriff E. R. Ezelle reportedly had expressed concern about the possibility of physical danger to Preston Cobb if he remained in the county jail. Citing the threat of violence, Governor Vandiver announced his intention to sign an executive order to readmit the boy to Reidsville.

Judge Carpenter soon made it clear that he was not moved by Hollowell's arguments. He denied the motion for a new trial, but by the end of the month, Hollowell had filed a writ of error to the Georgia Supreme Court. Chief Justice W. H. Duckworth and his colleagues heard oral arguments on March 12, 1962, as Hollowell again appealed for a new trial. Joining Hollowell and working closely with him on this case as it progressed was the proud and fiercely militant Howard Moore, Jr.[5]

The appeal process dragged on for another three years as Cobb's legal team of Moore, Hollowell and Robert L. Carter, General Counsel of the NAACP, worked unremittingly to save Preston Cobb. It included attempts to introduce the testimony of a witness who claimed that the murder victim's son had confessed to the killing of his father just before he himself died of injuries in an automobile accident soon after the murder. The teenaged Cobb remained on death row during the entire struggle. The attorneys carried their case all the way to the U. S. Supreme Court, which in 1963 refused to review it.

Yet another motion for a new trial on the basis of new evidence[6] finally reached the U.S. Court of Appeals. In December, 1964, that court overturned the 1961 conviction, ruling that "there was no express waiver by Cobb either of his right to challenge the grand jury indictment or the trial jury." The court noted that Cobb was subject to reindictment and could be retried, but that further efforts by the state to do so would have to occur within a reasonable period of time.

Solicitor General Lawrence was determined not to give up his pursuit of a guilty verdict for Cobb. Despite a variety of pre-trial pleas filed by Hollowell and Moore, all of which were overruled by the court, Lawrence succeeded in having the boy re-indicted. They were able to secure a change of venue to Macon, and a second trial began. Hollowell still remembers with enormous pleasure his cross-examination of Sheriff Ezelle. "I ran him back and forth, catching him in all sorts of lies and contradictions. Every time I did, he would grimace and pound the fist of his right hand into the palm of his left, almost as if to say, 'I wish I had you alone somewhere.'"

After presenting its case, the prosecution rested, but Hollowell and his associates offered no testimony. They were convinced that the court's rulings on its pre-trial motions had been in error, and they also realized that because they had presented no testimony, they would have the opportunity to open and close when the time for arguments came.

An article in the *Macon Telegraph* later described Cobb's attorney's performance as "brilliant," but the jury was unmoved and brought in a guilty verdict against Cobb with a sentence of life imprisonment. Cobb eventually was released after seven years on death row, although Hollowell's role as chief counsel was assumed by Howard Moore.[7]

§§§

The Atlanta Bar Association had high hopes in 1961 of persuading Dean Rusk, the Secretary of State, to address its annual gathering. It would be a coup to bring this high-ranking member of the new Cabinet to Atlanta. Rusk, a native Georgian, was willing, but there was a problem. The Kennedy administration had a policy that its representatives would not appear before racially segregated audiences, and the Atlanta Bar was a lily-white organization.

E. Smythe Gambrell was president of the local bar that year. He was not prepared to let what he considered his association's obsolete policy stand in the way of a successful event. Reportedly, when Rusk asked him about its racial makeup, he replied, "It may be segregated now, but it won't be by the time you get here." Gambrell then arranged for Atlanta's leading Negro attorneys and their spouses to be the guests of bar association members, who would personally escort them to the banquet. On the appointed evening, DeJongh Franklin and his wife, Phoebe, pulled up in their car at the home of Cassandra Maxwell Birnie and her husband on Chappell Street to pick up them and the Hollowells. The three couples then proceeded to the banquet at the Biltmore Hotel. This breaking of the color line was an important — and, for the time, even somewhat daring — first step. Nonetheless, it took several more years for the Atlanta Bar Association to desegregate itself officially. Even then, as a matter of principle, it took many more years before Hollowell would join it. He contended that lawyers, as officers of the court, should always have been in the lead of the battle for a racially integrated society.

§§§

That same year, Atlanta was preparing for a major transition in leadership. William B. Hartsfield, after many years of service as the city's mayor, was reluctantly leaving public life. The major contenders to succeed him included Lester Maddox, a local restaurant owner and vocal segregationist. Maddox, who had sought political office before, was already becoming Georgia's poster child of "red-neck" resistance to racial integration.

The seeming front-runner was Ivan Allen, Jr., a respected office supply company executive. He had been adopting an increasingly progressive attitude about the need for fundamental changes in Atlanta's race relations. Allen's opinions had undergone a remarkable sea change within three short years. While considering a run for the governorship of Georgia in 1958, he had voiced support for such concepts as sending Negroes to Africa or establishing all-black counties. He enjoyed the strong endorsement of the downtown white business community, and he was slowly building a bloc of Negro supporters. They recognized his vote-getting ability and had no wish to see Maddox elected.

However, a third candidate threatened to cut into that support. M. M. "Mugsy" Smith, a State Representative from Fulton County, had demonstrated an even more moderate posture on racial issues than Allen. He, for example, had sponsored a bill to outlaw the wearing of masks in public by members of the Ku Klux Klan. Both Smith and Allen knew that they would need Negro support to win.

During the final three weeks before the primary, Hollowell made public his support of Smith, and became an active campaigner for him. In what may have been a mass media "first" for Atlanta, he even delivered a fifteen-minute speech during prime time that Smith's campaign purchased on a local television station. Hollowell's prestige attracted support for Smith from many of the Movement leaders, especially those associated with the Atlanta University Center.

Allen's campaign was well organized and certainly had the best financing. As Allen tells the story, the morning of the primary election his polls showed–quite accurately, in fact –that he would receive thirty-eight per cent of the vote. Maddox would get twenty-one per cent, thereby pitting the two of them against each other in a runoff.

Allen reasoned that he could capture all of the Negro support and maybe as much as half of the white votes in the general election. As he mulled over these figures, his thoughts turned to Hollowell, who had in a very short period assembled about ten thousand Negro votes for Mugsy Smith, primarily on the strength of his own popularity.

He placed a call to Hollowell and asked for the lawyer's support. Hollowell smoothly replied that he was, in case Allen had not noticed, active in Smith's campaign. Allen explained that he wanted his help after the primary. Hollowell parried with the observation that he expected Smith to be in the general election against Lester Maddox; they would appreciate Allen's help when that time came.

With that verbal jousting out of the way, though, Allen laid out the results of his poll. Confronted with the likelihood that Smith would finish well behind the other two candidates, Hollowell promised, "If you're right, I'll be the first person in [your campaign office] tomorrow morning." The next day Allen and Maddox were indeed the top vote-getters, and Hollowell threw his support and influence in the Negro community behind Allen.[8]

Before doing so, however, he received another telephone call the morning after the primary election. To his amazement, the caller was Lester Maddox. In his high-pitched, raspy voice, the normally strident Maddox said politely, "Mr. Hollowell, you made a right good showing last night. I don't suppose there'd be much chance of you sending some of those votes my way, would there?" Hollowell was taken aback, but he recovered sufficiently to reply, "I'm afraid there's not much I can do for you, Mr. Maddox. I've asked my people to support Mr. Allen." There was a pause, and then Maddox simply said, "I figured that probably would be the case." He thanked Hollowell, and the conversation came to an end.

Allen became the next mayor. From that position and with relatively few missteps[9] he began to lead the city toward full racial desegregation and Atlanta's emergence as the unofficial capital of a New South. He and Hollowell remained good friends and allies during those critical years of transition.

ENDNOTES

[1] Georgia law at the time of Preston Cobb's conviction could be interpreted as permitting the execution of children as young as ten years old.

[2] Marshall Funderburg (the father of I. Owen Funderburg, who later would become President of Atlanta's Citizens Trust Bank until 1992). Dr. Funderburg, in another one of the anomalies of the times, maintained a practice that included a large white clientele.

[3] State law required that a prisoner whose case was being appealed had to be returned to his home county.

[4] In the previous legislative session, during which the General Assembly's attention was focused primarily upon the desegregation of the University of Georgia, there had been attempts to change the law. M. M. "Mugsy" Smith from Fulton County had introduced a bill to set the minimum age for capital punishment at eighteen, and Thomas B. Murphy from Haralson (who became Speaker of the House in 1973 and still holds that position) had sponsored legislation to abolish capital punishment. Smith's bill was defeated, and Murphy's never got out of committee.

[5] Moore had graduated from Morehouse College in 1954 and went directly into the Army for two years. After completing his military service, he enrolled in Boston University Law School, where he and F. Lee Bailey were classmates. He graduated in 1960 and passed the Massachusetts bar examination the following year. While still in Boston, Moore visited with Hollowell to explore the possibility of working with him. Moore, whose home was Atlanta, was not a complete stranger to Hollowell, and Hollowell also knew the younger man's aunt as a fellow parishioner at the Butler Street C. M. E. Church. He was impressed not just by Moore's intellect and preparation but also by his passion for the civil rights struggle. For the next several years, these two members of the Hollowell, Ward & Moore law firm constituted a formidable pair of advocates. Moore, like Hollowell, was a highly effective trial lawyer, a strength that was bolstered by his exceptional writing skills. In later years he would achieve even greater fame for his successful appeal of Julian Bond's case to the U.S. Supreme Court after the Georgia General Assembly denied Bond the seat he had won by election and for his successful defense of Angela Davis, who was charged with complicity in a shootout in a San Rafael, California, courtroom that killed the presiding judge and three other people.

[6] The authorities, asserted the attorneys, had obtained Cobb's confession under duress.

[7] Cobb's attorneys appealed the decision to the Georgia Supreme Court, and when that body affirmed the lower court decision, they carried an appeal to the U.S. Supreme Court. Those justices reversed the ruling of the state courts, but Lawrence was relentless. He had Cobb indicted for a third time. Cobb, who by now had been in prison for seven years, had during that time acquired some knowledge of the law. He filed his own writ of *habeas corpus*. At long last, a settlement was negotiated in the U. S. Court of Appeals which ruled that Cobb should be released on the basis of receiving full credit for all of the time he had spent in jail and prison since he was first arrested.

[8] Sadly, the experience embittered Smith, who felt he had been betrayed by the Negro community. Samuel D. Cook recalls that some time thereafter, when several of Smith's former supporters from the Atlanta University Center community approached him publicly for help with some legislation, his response was, "Leave me alone. You're embarrassing me in front of my friends."

[9] See Chapter 11.

10
"I NEVER THOUGHT I WOULD LIVE THAT LONG"

White resistance to the spreading Civil Rights Movement in the rural South intensified during 1961. Front page stories in the newspapers and lead stories on the nightly national newscasts made it painfully clear — both to Americans and the rest of the world — that a monumental struggle was underway between tyranny and freedom.

The treatment of Negroes in southwest Georgia had not yet attracted the attention of the mass media. Yet, conditions there were easily the match of more publicized events in other states. That section of Georgia was a malignantly racist region in which whites for many years had controlled thousands of Negroes by stark intimidation.

Jim Crow practices ranged from petty harassment to humiliation to physical brutality. Unofficial curfew laws restricted Negroes to particular areas after dark. All Negroes were addressed by their first names. In some communities Negroes dared not sit on their front porches unless they wore long trousers or dresses. Speed traps to catch unwary Negro drivers on back county roads were a form of sport for sheriff's deputies; attempts at voter registration by people of color provided county registrars with the opportunity to demand that the registrants interpret sections of the federal or state Constitution. The slightest provocation — a "smart" word or look directed to a white person — could trigger a tongue lashing or a beating.

This corner of the state seemed to have a particular inclination to add injury to insult. In the small town of Dawson, for example, black residents recall the odious practice of "greasing niggers." If a Negro male forgot his place — which could mean simply looking at a white person the "wrong" way — he would be dragged from his house and hauled to an isolated clearing in the woods. There his white captors would strap him to the feared "greasy log" and whip him. If he slid around the log or fell off this peeled and oiled section of tree trunk, they would continue beating him until he clambered back atop it. The sand particles from the soil that clung to his skin served to intensify the pain of the flogging. Once satisfied that they had meted out sufficient punishment, the vigilantes would return their victim to town and dump him on his front porch.[1]

Often the principal agents of suppression in southwest Georgia were the county sheriffs. Their legendary predisposition to violence helped to spawn grim nicknames — like "Bad" Baker County and "Terrible" Terrell County[2] — for the jurisdictions over which they held sway. These white-dominated counties, then, operated like autonomous fiefdoms. As far as they were concerned, Supreme Court rulings and social changes elsewhere in the country often might just as well have been occurring on another planet.

Before change could begin to come to this intimidating kingdom, someone had to penetrate the blanket of fear that smothered every Negro who lived within its borders. C. B. King, the only Negro attorney in the region, was one of the first to take a stand. Many people, both Negro and white, were convinced he was crazy, but he had the courage to begin representing those few brave souls who were willing to seek their civil rights under the law.

Hollowell and King had known each other for nearly thirteen years. Their first meeting was a chance encounter in the Jim Crow car of a northward bound train in early 1949. Hollowell was returning to law school in Chicago after a Christmas vacation with his wife in Atlanta. Seated in the same railroad car was King, on his way back from Albany to school at Fisk University in Nashville.

Hollowell was at first oblivious to the younger man. He was focusing all of his attention upon a set of large and heavy law texts as he attempted to cram in some studying that had gone by the boards during the holiday season. King's curiosity got the better of him, and he asked Hollowell what he was reading. When he discovered that Hollowell was a law student, he then confessed his own desire to prepare for a career as an attorney.

He told Hollowell about his life in Albany. His mother was an alumna of Fisk. His father, C. W. King, a retired railway mail clerk, now owned three stores and dabbled in real estate. The couple had seven sons.

The two students talked at length about the plight of Negroes in the South, and Hollowell shared with King his passion to be a part of the social change that was certain to be coming. He wasn't sure where he would practice, he said, and he further confessed that he wasn't even sure his temperament would supply him with the patience that might be required to practice in the South. Nonetheless, he was determined to be part of the legal challenge to segregation. King, who was fascinated by Hollowell's background and his stories about law school, had no such misgivings. If he were able to finish Fisk and then his professional training, he fully intended to hang up his shingle in Albany.[3]

They didn't see each other again until 1954, when Hollowell traveled to Albany to assist King with a voting rights suit in which they successfully forced the desegregation of polling places in the city. During the next several years, as the Hollowells would travel to Louise's family homestead near the Florida border, it became their practice to stop for visits with C. B. and Carol King.[4] They would spend evenings in the backyard, where King liked to grill steaks. The two men also saw each other regularly at state and regional NAACP conferences and later at training institutes sponsored by the Inc. Fund.

By the early 1960s, they were spending so much time together they might as well have been law partners. As such, they found themselves dealing with a singularly nasty case in nearby Early County. Their client was James Fair, a Negro man charged with the rape and killing of an eight-year old Negro girl.

Hollowell and King may have had their personal doubts about Fair's innocence, but they were more concerned with a broader Constitutional issue. Fair had been arrested early on a Sunday morning, May 15, 1960. Soon thereafter he asked the sheriff's officers to call his mother in New Jersey. She informed them and the solicitor general for the court circuit that she would come to Georgia as quickly as possible to engage an attorney for her son. They assured her that nothing would happen until May 23. Yet, the next day, encouraged by the information that Fair allegedly had confessed to the crime, a grand jury indicted Fair for murder. His mother called the Early County authorities again on Tuesday morning to confirm that she was on her way.

Late that afternoon, however, the Superior Court judge had deputies bring the indicted man to his court for arraignment. He asked him whether he wished to have court-appointed counsel. When Fair declined the offer, presumably because he was awaiting his mother's assistance with finding a private attorney, the judge demanded a plea from him. No sooner had the man pleaded guilty than the court pronounced the death sentence upon him. By the time his mother arrived in Early County late that same day, her son was on the way to the state prison in Reidsville. Called upon by the Inc. Fund, Hollowell and King rushed in to protest the rough, judicial processes that were intent on railroading Fair toward execution.

Their first step was to file a writ of *habeas corpus* in the city court of Reidsville, citing the denial of due process to their client. Then they began their appeal of the Superior Court decision. It finally reached the Georgia Supreme Court on March 13, 1961. On April 6 the justices upheld the appeal. They ruled that the rush to judgment against Fair, who had received no counsel before or during a trial, had occurred with a swiftness that may have set a Georgia judicial record and that it constituted a clear denial of his Constitutional rights. Noting that it was not in a position to rule on Fair's guilt or innocence, they sent the case back to the Early County Superior Court.

Judge W. I. Geer had presided over the original trial. He already enjoyed a measure of notoriety for having included in his election campaign platform the declaration that he didn't want the support of Negroes. Trezzvant W. Anderson, whose column, "The Traveling Reporter," appeared regularly in the *Pittsburgh Courier*, was fond of referring to the judge as W. I. ("I Don't Want No Nigger Votes") Geer. Evidence of the judge's intense bigotry was his apparent determination not to have Negro attorneys appear before him in a formal courtroom setting. Thus, even after Hollowell and King were successful in having the first judgment against Fair set aside[5] and forcing a new arraignment and trial, Geer managed to avoid hearing the case. No matter how hard Hollowell and King pushed for a trial, there was always a "reason" for delay. On one occasion, Geer took leave of the bench because his wife was ill. Other delays followed, despite the attorneys' motions to get the case back into court.

Eventually Geer simply dismissed the case on the grounds that several key witnesses no longer were living in Early County. Hollowell recalls with patent disgust, "To this day I don't even know where the courtroom is in Early County. One may certainly wonder to what extent the outcome of this case may have been affected by the racial tone which surrounded it."

Cementing the close, brother-like relationship of Hollowell and King was a love of the law, a delight in intellectual discourse and a fascination with the vocabulary and cadence of the English language. Hollowell himself was no slouch when it came to eloquence, but it is questionable whether he could ever match — or would choose to match — King's verbal convolutions.[6] They enjoyed teasing each other. King gleefully referred to Hollowell as "Reduc." It was a reminder of a case they had tried together in which a city court judge described one of Hollowell's lines of defense as a *"reductio ad absurdum"* argument. Hollowell, in turn, enjoyed calling his colleague "Bull," a testimony to King's sometimes headlong charges into the fray of controversy. For all of the differences in their styles, though, Hollowell cannot recall a single time when they had an argument that strained the relationship.

C. B. King was the most visibly defiant Negro in that region of Georgia, but slowly, as the ripples of protest began to touch its borders, other leaders were becoming bolder. Dr. William G. Anderson, the handsome and well-spoken osteopath who had moved to Albany from Americus a few years earlier, and other Negro citizens who belonged to the Criterion Club in Albany were quietly looking for a way to change the established order. The membership included Thomas Chatmon, a local businessman who had returned to his hometown in 1953 from Atlanta, where he had attended Morehouse College, and Slater King, C. B. King's brother.[7] They began holding increasingly frequent strategy sessions in their residences to discuss how they might begin the process of desegregating the city.

It is questionable, though, whether these middle-class leaders who had struggled hard for a measure of status and financial stability could ever have mustered the collective will to put everything on the line and engage in direct protest. The Movement did not really seep into the region until a small band of brave SNCC workers arrived in 1961 and began to turn up the heat. It was they in the final analysis who set in motion the sometimes chaotic chain reaction of events that would follow.

Charles Sherrod was one of the first young activists to venture into this frightening area. Sherrod in those days, as Hollowell recalls, was a bright and cheerful young man, in love with life and people of all ages. He laughed a lot, and his smile, says Hollowell, was so winsome that when police officers who later would arrest him frequently saw it, they must have said to themselves, "We can't bring ourselves to bash in this nigger's head; we'll just take him to jail again." There was absolutely nothing physically threatening about Sherrod's only average height and weight. Yet behind the smile and the unprepossessing stature was a fearlessness and fierce determination to bring about radical change.

Their arrival posed a problem for the established Negro leadership. Chatmon, for example, had been successful in establishing an NAACP Youth Council with more than a hundred members who were discussing ways to challenge segregation in the city.[8] However, when Sherrod, as well as Cordell Reagon and Charles Jones, two other activists, determined that they stood little chance of mobilizing Albany's Negro adults for protest, they turned their attention to the young people in the community. The SNCC workers were impatient to precipitate some activity. Much to the dismay of these teenagers' other adult mentors like Chatmon during the summer of 1961, the younger men insinuated themselves into the lives of the city's Negro high schoolers and began preaching the message of resistance.

By the end of October, they had built sufficient trust and put in place enough of a rudimentary organization to consider direct action. On November 1, the desegregation ruling of the Interstate Commerce Commission was scheduled to go into effect. The two young SNCC workers proposed that the young people test the ICC ruling by entering the "whites only" section of the bus station. Word of their plans leaked to the police, who were waiting when nine of them tried to purchase tickets. The officers turned them away, but there were no arrests.

However, those young people had thrown down the gauntlet, and adult leaders from the city's Negro organizations realized that events might soon slip from their control. On November 17 they organized what they called the Albany Movement and named William Anderson, a Morehouse classmate of Martin Luther King, Jr., to be its president. The stated goal was to bring an end to segregation in Albany, preferably through negotiation rather than "positive action."

Meanwhile the young people mobilized and trained by the SNCC workers were determined to provoke a response from the authorities. On Wednesday, November 22, the day before Thanksgiving, three high schoolers again entered the bus station. Police Chief Laurie Pritchett was waiting for them. When they refused to leave, he ordered their arrest.

That afternoon Thanksgiving vacation began for students from the city's historically black Albany State College. Hundreds of them on their way home for the holidays made their way to the bus station, intent upon joining the protest. A college official succeeded in turning most of them away, but two refused his orders. They too were taken to jail. Under pressure from the white authorities, President Dennis of Albany State on Saturday suspended them from college.

That evening there was a mass rally of the Negro community at Mount Zion Baptist Church — the first of its kind in the history of Albany. The Movement had reached southwest Georgia. Sherrod's analysis of what happened is straightforward: "people were afraid," he says, "but when you started messin' with their children they got mad."

On Monday, November 27, a crowd of some five hundred Negro spectators packed into the courtroom for the trial and sentencing of the young people. There were more mass meetings. Then, on December 10, another "test" of segregated facilities at the train station produced additional arrests. Several of the most respected adult Negro leaders — including C. B. King's sister-in-law, Marion, participated in a pray-in at City Hall. They, too, went to jail, and their incarceration precipitated new marches and demonstrations. On December 12, the police arrested nearly three hundred young people. Chief Pritchett had to negotiate arrangements with the surrounding counties to find jail space for all of them. Albany was now lead story material, and the media representatives began pouring into town. C. B. King simply couldn't respond to all of the demands for legal representation. He called Hollowell for help, and the Atlanta attorney headed south.[9]

The Albany Movement leaders also felt the need for reinforcements. As the situation became increasingly complex, many of them felt they might have bitten off more than they could chew The decision was not unanimous, but they decided to call upon Martin Luther King, Jr. for help. They felt that his high profile, coupled with the organization and funding of the Southern Christian Leadership Conference, might help to introduce a semblance of order.

Meanwhile other Civil Rights groups and hundreds of committed individuals — black and white, celebrities and ordinary folk — were not waiting for invitations to join the Albany crusade. By car, bus, train and plane they converged on the city. In the throng were brave white women like Frances Pauley from Atlanta, who directed the Georgia Council on Human Relations. Once-sleepy Albany began to resemble a convention center for the Movement and the alphabet soup of its organizations — SNCC, SCLC, CORE and the NAACP. This welter of constituencies was too confusing for most white Southerners. Thus James Gray, the conservative publisher of the *Albany Herald*, directed his newspaper's editorial attacks against the NAACP, which actually played a relatively limited role in many of the events that occurred.

Contributing to the confusion was the Albany Movement's early decision to call for the city to grant Negroes their "constitutionally guaranteed rights." Everything in Albany was thoroughly segregated — the schools, the libraries, the buses. Only the community's public pool was not; the city's officials had filled it with dirt, thereby denying its use to Negroes and whites alike. However, the Albany Movement's leaders initially did not target any single bastion of segregation. Rather than concentrate upon education or transportation, the leaders declared war on the entire gestalt of racial discrimination. This lack of focus often made it difficult to measure progress.

The professional reporters and analysts tended to direct their attention to the leaders with name recognition and to "results." They, and even Martin King himself, were later wont to view the events of Albany as a failure. Hollowell, however, insists that too many people overlooked the new and critical character of a deeper and more sustaining process that was taking place. Long-intimidated Negroes were on the rise.

One of the first responsibilities that Hollowell assumed upon joining forces with C. B. King was to find a way for literally hundreds of the arrested demonstrators to post bond. Cash for bail was in short supply. The authorities were also beginning to feel a financial pinch from the cost of caring for more prisoners than they had ever seen, and the police station was choking on the paperwork. Working with Chief Pritchett, Hollowell and C. B. King negotiated a series of procedures to reduce the confusion. One of the most important efficiencies was an arrangement under which many of those who were detained could qualify for release under their own recognizance by demonstrating their ownership of almost any kind of personal property. They further devised a procedure to relieve the crowded conditions as people were being moved from their jail cells to the courtroom and instituted a system under which the attorneys and their associates would help to interrogate new prisoners and, by their presence, both relieve anxiety and monitor police behavior.

Hollowell observes, "I understood that the chief had a job he was going to do, and I wanted him to exercise his job in as civil a way as possible. When people have confidence in your common sense, you can get a lot done." Pritchett quickly came to respect the thoughtful and deliberate attorney from Atlanta. The relationship that evolved between them was a curiously close one for two men who were clearly adversaries in the struggle. Before long, it was not uncommon at the end of a long day of arrests and arraignments for the two men to adjourn to Pritchett's office. There they would smoke the chief's cigars and discuss their mutual and separate responsibilities as well as the broader issues of race relations. (After the events in Albany abated, Pritchett one year sent the Hollowells a package of stick candy as a Christmas present.)

About two-thirty one morning as the attorneys were assisting Chief Pritchett and his staff with the processing of a new wave of demonstrators, Hollowell began to interview an older man in the group. When he asked the man his name and age, the elderly gentleman responded quickly and cheerfully, "My name is Jefferson, and I am seventy-two years old."

"How do you feel?" asked Hollowell.

"I feel fine, Mr. Hollowell," said Jefferson. "I am just so happy that I have lived long enough to be able to see Negroes in Albany stand up for their rights. *I never thought I would live that long.* So you see, I feel good!"

It was this kind of spirit that was beginning to pervade the Negro community on Friday, December 16, when the word arrived that Martin Luther King, Jr. had agreed to come to Albany. The SNCC workers opposed his arrival, but many of the older leaders believed that King's sheer presence would force a settlement. Others saw his impending arrival as a way to breathe fresh spirit into the movement. The crowds, diminished somewhat by the large numbers of protesters still in jail, gathered early, first at Shiloh Baptist Church and then at Mount Zion Baptist Church. There was glorious singing, interspersed with rapturous praying and fervid preaching. Hollowell, like others who were part of the dramatic events in Albany, remembers the powerful role that singing played throughout the struggle. It was far more than background music. "The songs and hymns like 'Over My Head I See Freedom in the Air' that had helped to bring people through slavery now were bonding them to each other and to the struggle. They stimulated and renewed a commitment to keep the faith."

King stepped into the pulpit at Shiloh and, as expected, inspired a crescendo of enthusiasm. When he concluded his remarks, Anderson spontaneously issued him a public invitation to march with the people of Albany. While King and his advisors retreated to the pastor's study to huddle and ponder that offer, Anderson called the emerging heroes of the swelling protest to the podium. When he introduced the attorney from Atlanta, the congregation applauded wildly for the man who had become a familiar figure. Hollowell's fearless manner in the city's courtrooms and his apparent ease with the white authorities ("that man's even smokin' Chief Pritchett's see-gars!") had been an important brace to everyone's spirits.

Hollowell spoke briefly and then concluded with words that others would later receive credit for having uttered first. He began by reminding his listeners that he was just one of the Movement's attorneys. Then he added, "But if I were you, I'd plan to show up here again tomorrow morning early and wear your walking shoes." No one had to spell things out any further. There would be another big march the next day.

There was, and leading the protesters to a prayer vigil at city hall were William Anderson, Martin Luther King, Jr., Ralph Abernathy and Bernard Lee. By nightfall they were locked up in the Sumter County jail in Americus, under the watchful and disdainful eye of Sheriff Fred

Chappell, whom King would later describe as the "meanest man in America."

Appeals for help to the White House produced only very cautious and tentative responses. Behind the scenes, Hollowell and C. B. King met with the city's elected leaders and other public officials, pushing for the most modest of written commitments to change. They were unsuccessful in obtaining any promises in writing, but the authorities made an offer to Marion Page, the Albany Movement's secretary. If his organization would stop the demonstrations, Albany would desegregate the bus and train terminals and the city's commissioners would meet with the local Negro leadership to discuss other demands.

Tension was high. Police and state agents, as well as members of the FBI, were everywhere. A week before Christmas, the Albany Movement leadership agreed to the proposal. Their decision initiated an uneasy truce between the two sides. Martin Luther King left jail and — after his trial was postponed — also left the city. It soon became transparently clear that the city had no intention of living up to its side of the agreement. The train and bus stations were still segregated and the commissioners now refused to meet with the Movement's leadership. As the Albany officials gloated, the press began to label the Negro insurgency as a failure.

The protests, as well as a series of attempts to register Negro voters continued, nonetheless, and soon a successful SNCC-organized bus boycott was underway. The arrests also continued, keeping Hollowell (now almost a commuter between Atlanta and Albany) and C. B. King running from jailhouse to courthouse, even as they tried to negotiate some improved relations in the community. Martin Luther King, Jr. returned to the city to stand trial. Judge Abner Israel, unmoved by the efforts of Hollowell and C. B. King to defend him, quickly found the civil rights leader guilty of marching without a permit. However, he delayed sentencing until July.

Martin Luther King, Jr. and the other SCLC leaders left town, but Charles Sherrod courageously continued to find ways to challenge the system personally and to keep Hollowell and C. B. King busy. Earlier in the year the charge was loitering after he took a seat in the white section of the cafeteria in the Trailways terminal. When he took a seat at the front of the courtroom during the trial of the Freedom Riders who had come to Albany in December, police officers knocked him to the floor and dragged him to the back of the room.

Sherrod insists that Hollowell's presence on the scene helped to infuse him and his fellow demonstrators with courage. "I knew I didn't have to worry," he says. "If they put me in jail, it would be just a matter of time before Don would be coming to get me out."

There was another group whose members drew inspiration from Hollowell. They were the young attorneys and law students who swarmed into Albany, hoping to throw their training and conviction into the battle for desegregation. It was an eye-opening experience for Dennis Roberts, Elizabeth Holtzmann,[10] Frank Parker, Jeff Haas and their colleagues — most of them white (and all of whom would go on to distinguished careers) — to see a brand of justice for which law school had not prepared them. Hollowell became their mentor, and he and C. B. King in turn were grateful for the availability of this pick-up staff to do research, negotiate releases on bond, write briefs and otherwise help to cope with the never-ending flood of paper work and court appearances.[11]

Martin Luther King, Jr. and Ralph David Abernathy returned to Albany for sentencing in July. Given the choice between paying the court-imposed fines or serving forty-five days in jail, they opted for incarceration. Their presence behind bars refocused the attention of the media upon Albany and brought the White House, which still was reluctant to provide direct federal intervention, back into the negotiations that continued behind the scenes.

The Negro community was restive. As many of the citizens gathered in churches for mass meetings, others vented their anger in violence. Then mysteriously, three days after their jailing, King and Abernathy were out of jail. Chief Pritchett would say only that an anonymous Negro had paid their fines.[12] Albany's white leaders fondly hoped that they had broken the back of the protest.

Struggling to reorganize and beset by conflicts between SNCC, SCLC and the NAACP, the Albany Movement responded by issuing a "Manifesto." The document recited a litany of bad faith and broken promises by the city and set in motion a new wave of attempts to integrate public facilities. Still, the officials of Albany refused to negotiate and responded only with more arrests. King, who had gone North to raise money for his organization and to address the National Press Club, now sought to give some focus to the protests. During a large church rally on July 20 he called for a mass march the following Saturday.

The federal government did finally intervene in Albany but not in the way the Movement leaders had hoped. J. Robert Elliott, the U.S. District Court Judge recently appointed by President Kennedy, was a thorough-going segregationist. In response to the pleas of the city authorities, he issued an injunction against the leaders who were organizing the march. Over the objections of Hollowell and C. B. King, Elliott's bizarre ruling claimed that Negro protests constituted a denial of white people's rights to equal protection; the demonstrations, he ruled, were making police and other resources unavailable to the white citizenry. He waited until late on Friday, the day before the proposed march, to sign the injunction, and then he quickly left town. It seemed clear to Hollowell that the judge's timing was calculated to make it impossible for him and his colleagues to file an appeal until after the weekend.

Nonetheless, he and C. B. King went to work. Assisting them was Constance Baker Motley, who, like Hollowell, had also become a virtual commuter to Southwest Georgia. Even as they began drafting their motion to the U. S. Fifth Circuit Court of Appeals, the march began, followed by the predictable arrests. Martin Luther King, Jr. stayed on the sidelines, realizing that to defy a federal order could have a disastrous public relations effect upon his position.

By Monday, Hollowell and his colleagues had reached Judge Elbert P. Tuttle in Atlanta with their appeal, and Tuttle had swiftly vacated Elliott's injunction. It should have been cause for at least modest rejoicing, but other events of the preceding weekend were inflaming Negro anger. Marion King, C. B. King's sister-in-law, and one of the most respected members in the community, had driven out from Albany to the Mitchell County jail in Camilla, where Charlie Ware also was imprisoned. Pregnant and accompanied by her two small children, she was planning to visit her maid's daughter, who had been arrested during the Saturday march, and to take her some food.

When sheriff's deputies became impatient with the singing crowd of Negroes who had gathered in anticipation of visiting hours, they tried to push them back from the fence around the jail. Marion King did not move fast enough to suit the sheriff, who slapped her face, causing her to drop the three-year old daughter in her arms. He slapped her again and another officer tripped her to the ground and began kicking her. She lost consciousness and later miscarried the unborn child.

A near-riot ensued in Albany, as some two thousand Negroes took to the streets, hurling bricks and bottles at the police who tried to contain them. Martin Luther King, Jr., who was trying to use Judge Tuttle's order as leverage to try again for negotiations with city officials, was caught between a rock and a hard place. Citing the principles of non-violence, he called for a Day of Penance.

Two days later King went to jail for the third time in Southwest Georgia when he began to lead a prayer meeting in front of city hall. Police also arrested a small group of other protesters, including William Hansen, a white SNCC worker, whom they placed in the white section of the Dougherty County jail. There other white prisoners, when they learned from the deputies that Hansen was one of those Yankee agitators, beat him unconscious and broke his jaw.

Hollowell returned to Atlanta to take care of other business, but C. B. King, accompanied by the Rev. James C. Harris, drove out to Dougherty County to check on his newest client and to demand medical treatment for him. King grew impatient at waiting, as ordered, outside the office of Sheriff D. C. "Cull" Campbell, and boldly walked into the room. The sheriff's response was to call him a "nigger" and smash a walking stick across King's head so fiercely that the cane broke. Fearing for their lives, the injured King and Harris fled the jail.

Hollowell had just arrived home. Louise was visiting her mother in Iron City. He was in the process of fixing himself a snack in the kitchen when a telephone call brought the news of the assault on his colleague. The southbound train was running late, so he chartered a small plane. He flew to Albany, found a cab at the airport and made his way to the hospital where King was being treated. Then, satisfied that there was nothing else he could do for the time being, he made his way to Iron City.

The unexpected break in his schedule provided the opportunity for a few hours of relaxation, and he decided to go fishing in Spring Creek several miles east of town. Soon after he left, two white men in work clothes with holstered pistols showed up at his mother-in-law's house and told the women that they needed to find Hollowell. Thinking them to be GBI agents, his wife described the car he had taken and a general idea of the direction in which he had gone. However, concerned for her husband's safety, she also called one of her cousins as soon as they left and told him to warn Hollowell.

Before he could find him, though, Hollowell, who had found a deserted area by the stream, heard someone crashing toward him through the brush. He remained where he was. A few minutes later he saw the two men approaching and immediately noticed their weapons. As he mentally calculated his chances as a single unarmed man, one of them called out, "Hey, Hollowell." He immediately felt better, theorizing that if they were simply a couple of locals who intended to harm him, they would have called him "boy." They turned out to be FBI agents, looking for information about C. B. King's situation. When he made it clear that he didn't know any of the facts of the case, they thanked him and left.

Through all the years that Hollowell traveled through the dangerous terrain of rural Georgia, he never carried a weapon. As he notes, "I always figured that if somebody wanted to get me, they would." In his Atlanta home there was a nine-millimeter pistol and a loaded shotgun. The only time he fired the handgun was when he tried to show Louise how to use it. At a time when Collier Heights still had relatively few homes and much of the land remained undeveloped, he took her down to the creek behind their house for a shooting lesson. However, after watching her try to discharge the weapon with the safety on and then discovering that she didn't have the strength to pull the trigger, he decided that a better form of protection would be a guard dog. A friend in North Carolina gave them "Ted," and the boxer, named for Louise's uncle, functioned as their security system until someone stole the animal.

C. B. King, Hollowell and Constance Baker Motley began drawing up charges against Sheriff Campbell and resumed the legal task of dealing with the presence of Martin Luther King, Jr. and the other protesters who still were in jail. They had not asked for his assistance, but they also had the "help" of William Kunstler. The flamboyant defense attorney with a national reputation was not publicity-shy. When the press turned its spotlight on Albany, he had seen an opportunity to contribute to the cause of civil rights while attracting some attention to himself. Hollowell and King welcomed all the legal assistance they could get, but they were annoyed to discover that Kunstler also was regularly sending press releases to the Northern newspapers in which his role tended to dominate the story.

After insinuating himself onto Martin Luther King, Jr.'s defense team, he filed a *habeas corpus* writ demanding King's release from jail. At one point during the proceedings, as he was dramatically presenting his arguments before the judge, and interrupting the flow of the other attorneys' arguments, Constance Baker Motley had heard enough of Kunstler's showboating. In an audible whisper, she turned to the egostic attorney and said, "Goddam it, sit down."

King and Abernathy appeared in court on August 10. Judge Israel gave them suspended sentences, and they left town. Several days later they returned for one last time. The SCLC leaders paid a brief visit to Lee County where night riders had firebombed the Shady Grove Baptist Church, and they managed at last to have a face-to-face meeting with Albany's Mayor Kelly. It produced no concrete results. The city still had no real interest in negotiating. Instead, it was trying to get Judge Elliott to issue a permanent restraining order against all demonstrations.

National interest gradually was shifting to other parts of the South. Martin Luther King, Jr. made one last attempt to refocus the attention of the media and the public upon the struggles in Albany. In a national appeal to the clergy, he begged them to come to southwest Georgia. A large contingent arrived during August and through that Labor Day weekend to demonstrate. John Middleton, the pastor of Allen Temple A. M. E. Church in Atlanta,[13] to which Louise Hollowell belonged, was among the first to arrive. Police Chief Pritchett's deputies seized them all and dispersed them to the network of surrounding county jails he had been using for many months. Middleton later would recall with repugnance the miserable conditions in the Leesburg jail which supplied no mattresses for the iron cots in the filthy cells.

During the many months of chaos in Albany, both sides of the conflict had come to rely upon the presence of Hollowell. His cool, unflappable demeanor won the respect of the white community and became the stuff of legend among Albany's Negroes as he moved from strategy sessions to courtroom appearances to negotiation meetings. Thomas Chatmon years later declared, "He was the chief...the Thurgood Marshall of Georgia. Without taking anything away from C. B. King and his importance, Chatmon noted, "Hollowell's stature inspired a level of confidence and hope that wouldn't have been present without him."

Frances Pauley put it another way. "Don never showed any fear of the judges; in fact, he mystified them. When he went into a courtroom, you would have thought he was the judge." Hollowell, continued Chatmon, had that down-to-earth quality that encouraged people to settle down. People didn't just respect Hollowell for his legal abilities. They also were inspired by his commitment and his common sense. "He could get along with everyone."

Hollowell seemed never to exhibit surprise or anger. Years later U. S. Supreme Court Justice Warren E. Burger, in his foreword to *The Profession of Law*,[14] wrote:

> Chief Justice Hughes and Justice Holmes were agreed that one of the most important qualities of the lawyer is tact in the performance of his function. Put in another way, manners and decorum, especially in the courtroom, are the indispensable lubricant to the inherently contentious adversary process. At every stage of the administration of justice good manners contribute enormously....Civility is not merely a necessity, it is indispensable to the adversary process.

The arrival of the ministers from around the country, however, provided one occasion when Hollowell could finally treat himself to a mild relaxation of his normally courteous behavior.

One bi-racial group of ministers was locked up in the Baker County jail. On a Sunday afternoon that August, Hollowell drove out for a visit, hoping to provide them with a few amenities. Sheriff "Gator" Johnson was in the office. Even though a broken leg limited his mobility, his huge bulk behind the desk was still intimidating. Hollowell first requested permission from the sheriff to bring in some cigarettes to the prisoners.

"Ain't gonna be no smokin' in my jail," replied Johnson.

When Hollowell suggested candy, the sheriff curtly said that his men would give the prisoners something to eat. Hollowell next mentioned the possibility of soap, and again the sheriff made it clear that he would take care of the inmates.

"Okay," replied Hollowell nonchalantly. He lighted his pipe and turned to leave. "Hey," yelled the sheriff, grabbing his crutches and hobbling after Hollowell. "Don't you ever just say 'okay" to me again. I'm the high sheriff here, and you ain't nothin' but a goddam nigger."

Hollowell turned and, as he did so, lightly blew a billow of smoke out of the side of his mouth. The sheriff howled loudly, "Don't blow that goddam smoke in my face."

As Hollowell moved swiftly toward the exit, he couldn't resist one last comment. "Okay," he repeated breezily. The sheriff crutched his way back to his desk, grabbed a pistol and began screaming that he was going to work Hollowell over if he didn't leave. Hollowell realized he had pushed "Gator" Johnson as far as he dared and quickly departed the jail.

Albany's white leaders continued adroitly to seek new ways to circumvent the law of the land and the Albany Movement continued, but in a more sporadic fashion and without the glare of publicity upon it. Martin Luther King, Jr. was responding to the call for help from Birmingham, and other hot spots in Alabama and Mississippi were of more interest to the press.

Even as Hollowell and C. B. King had been seeking to bring some legal order to the swirling events in Albany, they also were still engaged in the defense of Charlie Ware — the man charged with "assaulting" Sheriff Johnson of Baker County.[16] Ware's refusal to plead guilty to assault against the public official who had nearly killed him was yet another portent that change was coming to South Georgia. The two attorneys also were preparing to file a case against Johnson in federal court for his violation of Ware's civil rights.

Their client remained hospitalized from the injuries inflicted on him by the sheriff, and one afternoon during the Albany protests they slipped away to pay him a visit. Ware had recovered sufficiently from his injuries to be able to walk around, and the authorities permitted him to stroll to a small park about a block away. King parked his car next to the grassy area, opened the doors to catch what little breeze was available and the three held a brief conference in the vehicle, after which the attorneys drove Ware back to the front door of the hospital. A day or so later they learned that Sheriff Johnson had picked up Ware soon thereafter and had locked him up in the Mitchell County jail. There he remained for almost another year, since they were unable to have Ware's bail lowered.

Hollowell and King had strongly suspected since taking the case that the criminal charge against Ware was not the initial crime for which he had been arrested. In the register of the county clerk's office, the page that preceded the notation of the assault charge had been completely and meticulously inked out. There was not sufficient evidence to prove it, but Hollowell, as he puts it, is satisfied in his mind that Sheriff Johnson, after arresting Ware, originally booked him on a misdemeanor like being drunk and disorderly and then altered the record after shooting his prisoner.

One of their greatest impediments to building a defense for Ware was finding witnesses who would talk with them. Many of the men and women from whom they sought testimony were terrified of the reprisals that might follow if they were seen in the company of the attorneys. Often Hollowell and King would have to track them down in the country and meet with them late at night.

The case finally reached the court calendar a year later. The evening before the trial began, Hollowell and C. B. King drove out into the country to meet with several more witnesses. When they completed their work, Ware's brother, who had assembled the witnesses, pulled Hollowell and King aside. This uneducated man then produced a good luck potion he wanted the attorneys to deliver to his jailed brother. The vial he handed them contained a foul-looking reddish-brown liquid in which floated a glob of white substance, known colloquially as "goofer dust."

He next offered some further instructions. "After you give this to Charlie, tell him to rub it all over his head and body, and everything will be all right." He paused and then added thoughtfully, "It might not hurt you lawyers to use a little bit of it too."

The attorneys appeared the next morning before Judge Carl Crow (referred to sardonically in the Negro community as "Jim Crow"). It was a scene that reinforced some of the worst stereotypes about white justice in the rural South. The courtroom was hot, crowded and racially segregated, with Negroes relegated to benches in the balcony. As he presided, the judge made frequent and generous use of the brass spittoon beside his desk.

Hollowell and C. B. King, as always, presented their case forcefully. They were convinced that even an all-white jury could not overlook the obvious ridiculousness of the charges against Ware. The defendant's brother, though, may have been right. Perhaps they could have used some of that "goofer dust." Within ninety minutes, the jurors returned from their deliberations and declared Ware guilty.

Even before the trial began, Hollowell and King had filed several pleas of abatement, including a challenge to the absence of Negroes on the jury. Now they quickly presented a motion for a new trial. Judge Crow ignored the request for several weeks. Then, aware of the prosecution's reluctance to continue, he quietly ordered Ware's jailers to turn him loose.

§§§

The civil trial of Sheriff Johnson before Judge Elliott in Columbus, Georgia, attracted a throng of Negro observers and further solidified Hollowell's increasingly legendary image. The spectators were witnessing something that most would never have dreamed to be possible — a white sheriff on trial being challenged by a Negro attorney. Before the trial began, Hollowell had taken Johnson's deposition and learned a great deal about him.

Using that information, his examination of the sheriff on the witness stand helped him to present the picture of a bully with limited education who had been feeding and enriching himself at the public trough for the past fifteen years. Johnson did not take well to the way in which the attorney skillfully led him to this admission of a most unflattering self-portrait. When Hollowell asked him about the size of his Black Angus herd, he resisted. "What's that got to do with anything?" Johnson demanded. Hollowell responded, "I'd just like to get some idea of what you have?"

"I ain't going to tell you," the sheriff replied smugly. However, to his surprise, when Hollowell asked Johnson's attorney to instruct the witness to reply, B. C. Gardner told Johnson to answer the question. "I got eighty head," he muttered truculently. Nonetheless, despite the unflattering picture of the sheriff that emerged during the trial, the jury could not bring itself to equate Johnson's reckless violence against Ware with a violation of Ware's civil rights. It found Johnson not guilty. Although he maintained his calm composure, Hollowell was furious at Johnson, at this latest evidence of blatant racism, and at the charade that passed for justice in this part of the world. However, he and C. B. King had one last card to play from their legal deck. Mindful of the fact that the courtroom audience included a contingent of Negroes from Albany, he quietly requested a polling of the jury. He wanted the onlookers to know exactly who had voted for acquittal. One of the jurors was Carl Smith, the owner of a grocery store in the Negro section of Albany called Harlem.

The Albany Movement demonstrators had picketed Smith's establishment in the past, demanding that he hire Negro clerks and cashiers to serve his all-Negro clientele. A week after the public polling of the jury, the picketing resumed with new fervor. It triggered not only arrests, but a new kind of reaction from the white community. B. C. Gardner, the same attorney who had anonymously bailed Martin Luther King, Jr. out of jail months before and represented Sheriff Johnson, now filed a civil suit on behalf of Carl Smith against William Anderson and Willie Ricks, one of the picketers, charging them with illegally destroying Smith's business. Smith, contended Gardner, was the victim of retaliation for his vote on a jury, and that constituted an obstruction of justice.

Somewhat surprisingly, the trial in federal court produced a hung jury. Even before the case might have been scheduled for retrial, the decision was made not to continue. William Anderson was exhausted and in failing emotional health. He was anxious to leave Albany and to move to Detroit. The court authorized the transfer of the case to the Sixth District, which accepted jurisdiction over it. Once in Michigan, Anderson pleaded *nolo contendere* to the obstruction of justice charge and was placed on probation.

§§§

Hollowell joined C. B. King for one more case before pulling back from legal work in southwest Georgia. It was the challenge to the fully segregated public school system of Dougherty County. Constance Baker Motley joined them again and brought with her Norman Amaker, a colleague from the Inc. Fund. On July 12, 1963 — more than nine years after the original Supreme Court ruling against segregated public education — U. S. District Judge Elliott reluctantly conceded that the Dougherty County Board of Education was in violation of national law. He gave the board thirty days to produce a desegregation plan.

The board members and superintendent of schools complied with the letter of the law, choosing to place themselves within the sheltering protection of the "deliberate speed" phrase in the Supreme Court ruling. Their plan recommended a gradual desegregation, one that would begin with the first grade in September, 1964, and continue at a crawl of one more grade per year thereafter.

Hollowell and the other attorneys for the plaintiffs sought more immediate relief, asking that integration begin the following month. Elliott, however, ruled against them, employing defensive language that bordered on maudlin self-pity:

> The people of all races residing in Albany and Dougherty County, Georgia, have been abused by agitators, castigated by commentators and larruped by litigators to a degree unprecedented....the last thing that is needed is a precipitate rake of the judicial claw over racial wounds only partially healed....

The topsy-turvy logic of the case against the Albany Movement for picketing Carl Smith's store and the court-supported resistance to federal intent made it clear that even-handed justice in Albany would be a long time in arriving. Still and all, Hollowell contends that what happened in Albany was not a failure. Charles Sherrod (who would become a city commissioner) returned and kept the "home-grown" protests alive. C. B. King and other leaders kept challenging the system, and gradually Negroes began to assume a more equitable role in the life and even administration of civic affairs.

However, the principal victory of Albany, says Hollowell, was that an entire population overcame the debilitating terror that had subjugated them as much as the white intimidation that produced it. The day they crossed the line from fear to fortitude, everything became possible. There are many people in Albany who insist that Donald Hollowell's courageous presence through those early difficult days was one of the key catalysts in helping them to cross that line.

ENDNOTES

[1] Since those dreadful days, Dawson and other small towns of Southwest Georgia have greatly improved race relations, the most obvious symbol of which has been the election of black officials like Dawson's mayor.

[2] See Chapter 7 for account of Brazier case.

[3] C. B. King subsequently completed his education at Fisk and then earned his law degree from Case Western Reserve University in Cleveland. While in Ohio he met his wife-to-be, Carol, a native of the state who was attending Kent State College. The two returned to Albany where he established his law practice, she taught school and they together raised five children.

[4] In 1963, in a note to Martin Lehfeldt, Hollowell wrote, "No book about the Albany Movement should be written without mentioning Carol R. King. [She] was the mother of five children and taught grade school when the Movement started. But she became so engrossed in the activities of the Movement that she found it necessary to quit teaching. As a matter of fact, she did not have time to teach, for the King household, even with one or more of the children away in school, kept her tremendously busy. Moreover, she often found herself making pallets and extra meals for a new arrival who was to work in the Movement or assisting her husband in entertaining lawyers who [were] in the city to work on one of the multiple cases that existed either in Albany or in some nearby county. Ultimately, she became the director of Head Start under the Community Action Program...while serving as a member of the Board of Education."

[5] The legal significance of the case was the ability of Hollowell and King to establish, in effect, that the 5th and 6th Amendments were applicable to the State of Georgia, just as they were to other states. This was the first time that the State of Georgia had come completely in line with the U. S. Constitution on these issues.

[6] To illustrate this "verbophilia," here is a brief sample from an interview with C. B. King conducted by Louise Hollowell not long before his death in which he talked about the growing impatience of younger blacks in Albany to demand change:

> Antecedent to Martin [Luther King, Jr.]'s presence being expressed in the Albany context, there needs to be given recognition to the dynamics of SNCC representatives in Albany, because they contribute rather significantly to a divestment of

gross inertia, the character of which I've spoken to in terms of the kind of conservatism within the Criterion Club, the oldsters representing an attitude of conservatism, whereas the youngsters expressed a greater concern....[the sentence continues for several more lines] ...to the likes of Emmanuel "Bo" Jackson who quit his job with the *Albany Herald* to work with the Movement [for which] his wife, Goldie, served as the very efficienct secretary....Indeed, there were many other men, women and students, besides those named, who made sacrifices of their time, gave money, board and/or provided rooms for students, marched, went to jail, or served in some other capacity. Would that all of them could have their names on a beautiful plaque that would be placed in an...appropriate place. The list would be surprisingly long.

[7] Slater King died of injuries received in an automobile accident during the time of the Albany Movement.

[8] Chatmon, in an interview with Louise Hollowell, described how a group of students came to him after being denied seating in a local movie theatre. The balcony to which Negroes were restricted had been full and they tried to find space in the "whites only" section downstairs. The management refused to seat them and instead refunded their money. Chatmon asked the young people what they wanted to do. When they said they wanted to organize a protest, he agreed to help them form the NAACP Youth Council and to serve as their advisor.

[9] Tom Jackson also came to work with C. B. King for a year during this period. As the first Negro to establish a practice in Macon, Jackson felt he could learn a great deal from the experience of the pioneering Albany lawyer.

[10] Ms. Holtzmann would later become a prosecutor and then U. S. Representative, representing the distrist that included Brooklyn, New York.

[11] Space simply does not permit reference to all the many individuals who contributed to the work of the Albany Movement. In the letter to Lehfeldt (see Endnote #4), Hollowell also wrote, "My mind also runs to the likes of Emanuel "Bo" Jackson who quit his job with the *Albany Herald* to work with the Movement [for which] his wife, Goldie, served as the very efficient secretary... Indeed, there were many other men, women and students, besides those named, who made sacrifices of their time, gave money, board and/or provided rooms for students, marched, went to jail, or served in some other capacity. Would that all of them could have their names on a beautiful plaque that would be placed in an... appropriate place. The list would be surprisingly long."

[12] Years later, further investigation would uncover the likelihood that B. C. Gardner, a law partner of Mayor Asa Kelley, as part of a strategem to get King out of Albany, had appeared at the jail early one morning, handed over the cash and disappeared.

[13] Middleton later became the President of Morris Brown College.

[14] *The Profession of Law*, L. Ray Patterson, Elliott E. Cheatham, The Foundation Press, Inc., 1971.

[15] Also see Chapter 9 for an account of the events that led to this case.

11

THE COMING OF CHANGE

Change was coming to Georgia. The so-called "Southern way of life" was losing its stamina. Slowly but inexorably, like the small cloud which once appeared to be only the size of a person's hand and now was filling the sky, the movement toward a racially integrated society was reaching into every corner of the state. And hastening that change was Donald Hollowell.

During the 1960s, Muhammed Ali, the flashy young heavyweight fighter, popularized an expression that he used to characterize his boxing style: "Float like a butterfly, sting like a bee." He could just as well have been describing the brave attorney from Atlanta.

Over the next three years, from 1962 until 1965 and beyond, Hollowell and his associates seemed to be everywhere. They were in constant motion, from city and superior courts in communities across the state to the Georgia Supreme Court or the U.S. Court of Appeals and back again. Thus, even while he was embroiled in the Albany whirlwind, another case in Atlanta also demanded a portion of his attention.

For nearly a decade the city's Negro citizens had been pushing for more living space. Yet virtually all of Atlanta's residential sections remained racially restricted. Exacerbating the situation was the presence of large tracts of unused land that the city had improperly zoned for commercial use, essentially to establish buffer zones between white and Negro neighborhoods.

Now, though, middle-class professionals who had the money to purchase homes were putting increased pressure on the old system. Something had to give, and it did. Sometimes with the calculated use of block-busting techniques by real estate companies, more than fifty Atlanta neighborhoods underwent racial transition during 1962. Most were on the south and west sides of the city.

The steadily westward settlement of Negroes along the Gordon Road[1] corridor reached a critical impasse. To the north, Hightower Road led into Collier Heights, the Negro suburb in which the Hollowells and some of their friends lived.[2] To the south, Peyton Road ran into Peyton Forest, a relatively new and lovely all-white subdivision that spread across hilly acres of wooded land. It seemed only a matter of time until Negroes became candidates for home ownership on the south side of the dividing line.

The first breach in the dam — the purchase of a house in Peyton Forest by Hollowell's physician, Dr. Clinton Warner, unleashed a wave of hysteria by most of the white residents. Mayor Allen, by his own later admission, completely misread the situation. In his search for a balanced solution, he decided to address the obvious need for space[3] by having eight hundred acres of "commercial" property rezoned for Negro residential use.

No reasonable people seemed to have a quarrel with that move, but Allen almost completely exhausted his large reservoir of good will in the Negro community with his next step. Intending to calm white alarm, on December 17 he persuaded the Board of Aldermen to enact a city ordinance that permitted construction of barricades across the access points to Peyton Forest on Peyton and Harlan Roads. Now short vertical sections of railroad track imbedded in concrete made it impossible for automobiles to enter or leave the neighborhood.

The outrage of Negroes and liberal whites was strong enough to catch the attention of the national media. Within days the network newscasts were reporting on the *cause celebre* and describing Atlanta's "Berlin Wall." A new, bi-racial group, the All-Citizens Committee for Better City Planning, retained Hollowell to file suit for an injunction against the barricades.

Superior Court Judge George P. Whitman seemed to be in no rush to arrive at a solution, and the case dragged on for two months, while the offensive blockades remained in place. Allen sought to negotiate behind the scenes but could find no representative Negro group that would even talk until the "wall" came down. The gradual improvements in racial dynamics that had occurred during his new administration were in serious jeopardy.

Despite the growing racial tension, even as the case lurched laboriously forward, Hollowell and Allen had maintained a cordial and even friendly relationship. As both sides waited for the judge's ruling, the two met one day for an off-the-record discussion of the situation. Settled into the Kennedy-style rocking chairs in Allen's office at City Hall, it was clear that each from his own perspective was deeply committed to Atlanta's emergence as a model city. Neither was happy about the damage that this confrontation was doing to its image.

As Hollowell recalls, the mayor finally said, "Don, what do you think I ought to do?" Hollowell's response was, "Mayor Allen, when you're stuck in the mire, if you just try to crawl out, you get even muddier. Sometimes you just have to leap out all at once to the high ground. Then you can get some solid footing and move ahead."

"Maybe you're right," Allen replied.

On March 3, Whitman finally ruled that the city's actions were unconstitutional. Within minutes of the court's order that the city remove the barricades, Allen had dispatched a crew to open Peyton and Harlan Roads. A few hours later they were gone forever. Allen never again seriously fumbled the ball of race relations.[4]

As soon as the barricades were down, Allen went to the aldermanic council. He asked it to establish a special real estate committee to review housing patterns in Atlanta, to direct him to meet with both sides in the dispute during a cooling-off period and to intensify efforts to utilize undeveloped land for Negro housing. Change was coming in Atlanta.

§§§

In the fall of 1963, William H. Alexander returned to Georgia and joined the Hollowell legal team.[5] The firm, which enjoyed a widespread reputation throughout Georgia, now was Hollowell, Ward, Moore and Alexander. Hollowell and his colleagues — often assisted by Constance Baker Motley and other Inc. Fund attorneys — burned up the highways as they handled cases from Rome to Brunswick, from Augusta to Macon, from Savannah back to Atlanta.

By then, the Movement was beginning to make itself felt one hundred and fifty miles east of Atlanta, in the somnolent city of Augusta on the banks of the Savannah River. Students, primarily from Paine College, the historically Negro institution established by the Christian Methodist Episcopal Church, began sit-ins on the city's buses and in local drug stores and other businesses. In a now familiar pattern, racial tensions quickly escalated. Police arrested the protesters, often using excessive force, and additional students and local Negro citizens marched and demonstrated. During one of those demonstrations, a white man cut a Paine student in the stomach, and in short order Negroes organized a boycott of the white-owned stores which had depended heavily upon their trade.

Vernon Jordan, now the Field Secretary for Georgia's NAACP, arrived to meet with both Negro leaders and white businessmen in an effort to restore a measure of calm to the city. Together they tried to work out a plan that would physically separate the two sides to avoid face-to-face conflicts. However, the plan did not prevent a group of rowdy young white men from finding a way to provoke more trouble. They took it upon themselves to pile into their cars and drive by the Delta Manor apartment complex to throw rocks at the Negro males who were gathered in the yard outside the apartments. That pattern continued for several evenings until the night that the Negro men retaliated. They charged the automobiles and began fighting with the whites. In the course of the fight, someone shot and killed one of the whites who had provoked the attack.

White Augustans lost all patience with the notion of negotiation. They wanted swift revenge. In short order they arrested eight young Negroes between the ages of fourteen and twenty-one, picked up two more the following week and then found four additional suspects and threw them in jail to complete the round-up. After questioning all of them, they indicted nine of them for murder.

The city leaders were determined that someone would go to the electric chair and they gave George Hains, the local solicitor, permission to hire a special prosecutor. The defense retained John Ruffin and John Watkins, two young black attorneys who had been in practice for little more than a year. After they conferred with Frank Reeves, a private attorney from Washington, D.C., whom the NAACP sent in to review the case, the decision was made to summon Hollowell.

When the case of the "Delta Manor Nine," as the press called them, came to trial, the atmosphere in the courtroom was highly charged.

Keeping it that way was Randall Evans, the bombastic "hired gun" from Thompson, Georgia, a tall, heavy-set man. Possessed of a quick mind and plenty of legal savoir-faire, he relied heavily upon his booming voice both to impress the jury and intimidate the witnesses. As he stalked the courtroom, invariably he would make his way to the rear of the spectators, from which spot he would bellow his questions or offer the judge his responses to motions on behalf of the defendants.

The defense had determined that Hollowell would present the opening argument for its clients and Reeves would offer the closing statement. In contrast to the special prosecutor, they chose to offer a quiet, tightly-reasoned case for why their clients should not be convicted of murder. Carefully they explained that the charge of murder required malice aforethought, a motivation that they did not believe had been established. They noted that the young white men had provoked the fight, and they further observed that the city itself was at fault for not having taken steps to defuse a situation that had for several days been moving toward a confrontation.

The all-white jury then listened to the judge's charge and instructions and retired to deliberate. They remained in session for many hours. When they returned to deliver their verdict, the white observers were in shock. All of the defendants were acquitted of the murder charge. No one would be executed. No one received life imprisonment. After the sentencing, during which the young black man who had fired the gun during the fight was sent to prison for twenty years, the Augusta solicitor quietly approached the defense attorney from Atlanta. "Mr. Hollowell," he said courteously. "You did a great job. After I heard your opening argument, I knew we'd never be able to give anyone the chair." Change was coming in Augusta.

§§§

Martin Luther King, Jr. had observed in a nationally publicized remark that the eleven o'clock hour on a Sunday morning was the most racially segregated period of the week. The sit-in demonstrators agreed and accordingly began targeting white churches for attention early in the Movement. Kneel-in demonstrations by black and white students started in Atlanta during August, 1960, and had continued for several years.

On June 30, 1963, a small band of protesters sought admission to the worship services of First Baptist Church, a large white congregation with an enormous sanctuary on Peachtree Street. In the group was the Rev. Ashton B. Jones, the sixty-seven year old pastor of the non-denominational Neighborhood Community Church of Los Angeles. A veteran of the Movement, he already had been arrested before for his part in other demonstrations. No sooner had they entered the the building than they were greeted by the all-male, so-called hospitality committee. These ecclesiastical bouncers summarily blocked their passage.

The Rev. Mr. Jones had a bull voice, and when the church representatives sought to restrain him from entering the sanctuary with his young black friends, he began to trumpet, "Isn't this a church? How are you going to save people if you don't let them in?" When he refused to lower his voice, they escorted him outside. Then, despite his efforts to grab the brass hand rail, they dragged him down the monumental front steps toward the street.

The trial of Jones was an especially contentious one. Judge Durwood Pye, as had so often been the case before, presided from the bench. To the thinking of Hollowell and Moore, who were representing Jones, the judge operated in what they considered, even for him, to be an inordinately high-handed manner. He, of course, repeatedly shot down their motions and objections, a response with which they were thoroughly familiar. To their greatest dismay, however, he permitted the introduction of evidence about Jones' previous arrests for civil rights activities and took what they thought to be extra-legal liberties in his instructions to the jury.

After the dust cleared, Pye sentenced Jones to eighteen months in prison and fined him one thousand dollars for interfering with religious worship. The Hollowell team filed a lengthy and unsuccessful appeal for a new trial, to which Pye took his time in responding. Meanwhile Jones remained locked up for one hundred and eighty-eight days, a portion of the time under a twenty thousand dollars appeal bond.

The case finally reached the Georgia Supreme Court nine months after Jones' arrest at First Baptist Church. That bench reduced the elderly minister's bond to five thousand dollars — quickly posted by a white Atlanta citizen — and then Chief Justice W. H. Duckworth heard oral arguments. On the basis of that hearing, Duckworth announced his intention to throw out Jones' conviction.

Central to his decision was a technicality raised during the original trial by Hollowell and Moore. The attorneys had successfully convinced the prosecution to delete a key phrase from the indictment on the grounds that it was too vague. The initial indictment charged Jones with the misdemeanor of disturbing worshippers by using profanity or obscenity or being intoxicated or *otherwise behaving in an indecent manner*. However, although that last phrase was deleted, Judge Pye included it in his charge to the jury. Moore and Hollowell had contended that without its inclusion, the remaining charges against Jones were spurious. "I don't think this court will sanction that sort of thing for a second," said Duckworth.

By that time some social change was evolving faster than legal relief. An assistant pastor and some of the First Baptist members, thoroughly embarrassed by what had transpired, had added their voices to the requests for Jones' release from jail, and the church had voted to admit Negroes to worship.

§§§

The frantic pace refused to stop...
- in Americus, several young people who conducted a desegregation demonstration were thrown in jail by Sumter County Sheriff Fred Chappell, whose notoriety included being called the "meanest man in America" by Martin Luther King, Jr. They were charged, predictably, with unlawful assembly, but also with violation of the so-called Georgia "insurrection statute." Hollowell, who represented Donald Harris, and Morris Abram, the attorney for Zev Aelony, could not secure their release on bail, because violation of the insurrection law carried with it a possible death penalty. After the Georgia Supreme Court also denied the right of bail, the lawyers took their case to federal district court. There Elbert Tuttle and Frank Morgan ruled both statutes to be unconstitutional and void and issued an injunction against any further prosecution of the demonstrators. (Robert Elliott, the third judge on the panel, not surprisingly "respectfully" dissented from his colleagues' opinion.)...

• In Savannah, the owner of the Tropical Market beat a young Negro boy for allegedly stealing from his store. When the local branch of the NAACP launched a protest boycott of the market, it was slapped with an injunction. Hollowell was called in to assist the local attorneys....

• Hollowell and Moore were quickly on the scene in Macon when two white Macon policemen fatally shot a 15-year old Negro boy in the back — the third killing of Negroes by white policemen in fourteen months —and convinced a coroner's jury to indict the officers for murder. Although a Bibb County grand jury refused to indict the policemen, more than a thousand Negroes donned black arm bands and conducted a silent protest march on City Hall....

• In Milledgeville, after a Negro prisoner at the Baldwin County Prison Work Camp was killed by guards, Hollowell arrived to charge them with murder....

• As they represented sit-in demonstrators in Rome or students seeking to integrate the school system of Brunswick or a black man indicted for rape by an all-white jury in Muscogee County, Hollowell and his partners were changing the social landscape of an entire state.

And as these challenges to an entrenched system of segregation and suppression unfolded, a new spirit of determination to bring about even more change began to sweep across Georgia. The courage of Hollowell and his associates in turn emboldened the victims of discrimination and oppression. Knowing that capable attorneys were willing to represent them, increasing numbers of them were willing to demand their day in court.

§§§

In February, 1964, Hollowell and Horace Ward were before the U.S. District Court. Assisted by Jack Greenberg, James M. Nabrit, III and Michael Meltsner of the Legal Defense Fund, they sought an affirmation from the justices that the all-white Northern District Dental Society (and its parent Georgia Dental Association) could not bar blacks from membership. The original suit was brought by Dr. Roy C. Bell, who had unsuccessfully applied for membership and had subsequently picketed against both the Dental Society during its Atlanta convention and Grady

Hospital. He and the plaintiffs who joined him in the suit contended that the society was indeed subject to the Fourteenth Amendment. The defendants in turn stated that the society and others like it were simply voluntary and private associations of professional men.

Carrying the day for the plaintiffs was the attorneys' demonstration that state law called for the Georgia Dental Association to appoint members to the Board of Dental Examiners, the State Board of Health and the Hospital Advisory Council. Judge Hooper thus ruled that the society's discriminatory membership practices made it impossible for black dentists to have a voice in the election of state-ordered officials, including those who certified them. The Society, said Hooper, was in clear violation of the Equal Protection Clause of the U.S. Constitution.

§§§

The courtroom battles between Hollowell and Judge Pye continued into early 1964. That January 13, Miss Mardon R. Walker, an exchange student from Connecticut College who was attending Spelman College, had been arrested and charged with trespass during a sit-in demonstration at a downtown Krystal restaurant.

Miss Walker's father was a full colonel in the U.S. Air Force, stationed at the Pentagon. He arrived as quickly as possible and began searching for the best possible lawyers to represent his daughter. He may have thought initially that he would be directed to white attorneys, but his quest had led him to Hollowell and Moore. Having retained their services, he sought an appointment with Judge Pye. Colonel Walker later reported —both in anger and ruefully — that never during his military years had he received as severe a dressing down as he got from the judge.

Hollowell and Moore had filed a plea of abatement which Pye denied. The Superior Court judge apparently was still on the warpath against all white supporters of the Civil Rights movement, especially students. He chose to throw the book at Miss Walker. Scheduling her trial first among all of the sixteen students who had been arrested as part of the protest, he sentenced her to twelve months on the public works and six months in jail (the maximum allowable for a misdemeanor in Georgia), imposed a fine of five thousand dollars and then set an exorbitant bond.

(Mrs. Louise Bradley, a widow of color, unwilling to have the young exchange student remain behind bars, used her own house as collateral to post a property bond.)

Complicating the defense attorneys' case when they appealed Pye's sentence was the fact that twelve days after her arrest at the Krystal sit-in, the persistent Miss Walker had participated in a demonstration at the nearby Leb's Restaurant.

The police had locked some forty protesters inside the restaurant, but she had remained outside close to the window. From that position she was able to read the notes they held up, relay messages to the demonstration's leadership and then pass information back to the students on the inside. Her participation in that event had been introduced as evidence during Miss Walker's first trial. The Solicitor General argued that her behavior at Leb's made it clear that she was an agitator. He contended that it contradicted her testimony to the grand jury that she and her friends from Spelman had not gone to the Krystal to be arrested but were just students who wanted something to eat.

Hollowell's attempt to have this evidence ruled inadmissible failed, as did all of the other motions. The Georgia Supreme Court upheld the conviction that November, but the case eventually reached the U.S. Supreme Court, which overturned it. The ruling reportedly so enraged Judge Pye that for a time he considered finding a way to retry Miss Walker, but nothing ever came of that quixotic desire. Colonel Walker, who was proud of his daughter, was also deeply impressed by her two attorneys. He sent both Hollowell and Moore a set of Air Force wings.

§§§

The morning on which Judge Pye denied the plea of abatement brought by Hollowell and Moore on behalf of Mardon Walker was to be a busy one for the overworked attorney and a highly frustrating one for his contentious adversary. Having enjoyed the opportunity to blunt the defense attorneys' efforts on behalf of Miss Walker, Pye next turned his attention to Miss Debbie Amis.

Miss Amis was a black student from the North who had been arrested for participating in the Leb's Restaurant sit-in demonstration with her friends. Hollowell had represented her during her first court appearance. At the time, William Boyd, the Solicitor General, with Judge Pye's full encouragement, was seeking to introduce as evidence the fact that the young woman had belonged to a so-called Communist organization in Philadelphia. Hollowell and Moore were able to marshal enough legal technicalities to defeat that attempt. Nonetheless, they subsequently had removed themselves from her case. Their feeling was that her political leanings might eventually jeopardize their representation of other clients like SCLC. As Pye put Miss Amis on the witness stand and began to harangue her, Hollowell sought to get the judge's attention. Pye, knowing that Hollowell was no longer her attorney, refused to recognize him.

What the judge did not realize was that Hollowell had something else in mind. Thoroughly weary of Pye's shenanigans and use of the bench as a bully pulpit, he and Howard Moore had been seeking a new strategy. Their mining of the law had unearthed a valuable nugget. A century-old federal law, in effect, permitted defendants involved in state court proceedings to have their cases transferred to a federal trial court if the state law under which they were charged was in violation of federal civil rights law prohibiting racial discrimination. Coupling this precedent with the new Civil Rights bill, they secured an order from the U. S. District Court that removed a collection of sit-in cases involving Thomas Rachel and nineteen other defendants from Pye's jurisdiction.

At nine o'clock that morning, before going to Pye's courtroom, Moore and Hollowell had filed the order with the clerk of the state court. Armed with this certified order, which took immediate effect, they had proceeded to Fulton County Superior Court.

When Hollowell continued to seek the judge's attention, Pye simply declared with exaggerated politeness, "Have a seat, Mr. Hollowell," and proceeded with his interrogation of Miss Amis. He had just determined that the young woman before him did not have legal representation when Hollowell politely interrupted, "Your honor, may I speak?" Pye again told him to take his seat..

At last Hollowell was able to get the judge's full attention. "Is it appropriate to ask the court a question?"

When Pye at last grudgingly acknowledged the attorney, Hollowell said, "Would the court be interested in knowing that none of these cases is any longer before this court."

Pye looked stunned, and became even more flabbergasted when Hollowell announced that the disposition of the demonstrators' trials now was a matter for the federal court. As proof, he exhibited the copy of the order stamped by the clerk. "You mean to tell me," Pye ranted, "that there is a procedure in which the U.S. District court can take jurisdiction over cases that have been properly lodged in a state court."

Hollowell assured him that such was indeed the case.

Pye demanded to see the law. Hollowell proceeded to show him the citations, but the judge was not satisfied. "I want to see the law," he insisted. He gave Hollowell permission to go the courthouse library and track down the actual legal reference. While Hollowell searched for the volume, Pye grew impatient and sent a bailiff to hurry him along. Several minutes later Hollowell reappeared in the courtroom with the correct tome and placed it before the judge. He began reading aloud, muttering from time to time that he didn't see any reference to Hollowell's claim. Finally he came to the paragraph that concluded, "once having been filed in the state court, the case shall stand removed."

Pye's face, already creased with frown lines, assumed an ugly scowl. In a loud and belligerent tone, he asked Hollowell whether the attorney was playing "fast and loose" with the law. Hollowell, in more calm but equally audible tones, fired back, "I resent the insinuation."

Next Pye instructed William Spence, the Assistant Solicitor General, to contact U.S. Judge Boyd Sloan to determine whether that justice had signed Hollowell's petition. Tracked down in Gainesville, Georgia, Judge Sloan indicated his knowledge of the petition and assured Spence of its validity.

Pye's first response was to declare petulantly, "This court wants it fully understood that if the United States court passes an order taking charge of these cases, they are welcome to them.... I'll be glad to get rid of them." But then, stretching out his arms and beginning the now-famous Pye-Pye Twist, he launched into a tirade. "This is a striking illustration of the deplorable position in which the judicial processes of this country now find themselves." He concluded with a loud indictment of "the aggrandizement of power on the part of all the departments of the federal government," but there was nothing else he could do. Moore's and Hollowell's strategy had carried the day, and when the decision was upheld in federal district court after an appeal by the state, it set important precedents for cases throughout the South.

§§§

Most of the time, Hollowell represented others who sought to overthrow the strictures of a segregated society. Every now and then, though, there were opportunities for the Hollowells to participate directly in the challenge. Their friend, State Senator Johnson, provided one such chance not too long after he became a member of the Georgia legislature.

His account of what happened begins with Jimmy Bentley, the Commissioner of Insurance, deciding to sponsor a luncheon for his wife at the Commerce Club. This private downtown establishment, directly across Broad Street from the headquarters of C&S Bank, had been founded by Mills B. Lane, the bank's president, whose power and authority in Atlanta were formidable. Of course, the only Negroes permitted inside the club were kitchen, custodial and dining room employees. Nonetheless, Mrs. Johnson received an invitation to be part of the festivities and was encouraged to bring some of her friends. She in turn invited Louise Hollowell, who delayed her trip back to the University of Pennsylvania to attend this moderately historic event, and Jesse Hill's wife, Azira. Somehow Mills Lane learned about the proposed breach of racial etiquette and affront to his sense of the proper social order. He angrily sent the demand to Bentley to withdraw the invitations that had been issued to the black women. Bentley called Johnson, and they both agreed to stand firm. Word of the growing brouhaha reached Mayor Ivan Allen, who, as Johnson remembers, "got to Mills and calmed him down." Mrs. Johnson, Mrs. Hollowell and Mrs. Hill attended the party for Mrs. Bentley, and there were no incidents.

§§§

Not long after Hollowell entered the political arena in 1964 (see Chapter 12), another major case that was to involve his law firm once again made Atlanta's race relations the lead story in the mass media. On July 2, 1964, after helping to overcome a lengthy Senate filibuster, President Johnson signed the Civil Rights Act. It outlawed discrimination in public accommodations, provided injunctive relief against such discrimination and further authorized the Attorney General to institute legal action to protect the right of all individuals seeking access to those accommodations. Charles Weltner, the Congressman representing the district that included Atlanta, had been the only U. S. Representative from Georgia to vote for its passage.

One day later, three students from Turner Theological Seminary, the African Methodist Episcopal constituent of the Interdenominational Theological Center, decided to test the law. Alfred Dunn, Charles Wells and George Willis[6] drove to the Pickrick restaurant near the campus of Georgia Tech. The Pickrick was owned by Lester Maddox, the vocally ardent segregationist who had unsuccessfully sought to become the mayor of Atlanta four years earlier. Although other restaurants in Atlanta had quietly desegregated their facilities, Maddox had made public his determination to hold the line. To dramatize his position, he ran weekly advertisements in the *Atlanta Constitution* in which he proclaimed his allegiance to the gospel of apartheid.

No sooner had the three theological students driven their car into the parking lot and prepared to enter the Pickrick than Maddox and his son stormed out of the restaurant. Although later exonerated of threatening his would-be customers, pictures of the occasion make it clear that Maddox was holding a pistol. The segregationist soulmates who frequented his establishment grabbed pick handles that Maddox kept inside the door and prepared to repel the invaders. Maddox ranted at the young men who had dared to challenge his citadel, demanding that they leave, and smashed a pick handle across the top of their car as they drove from the scene.

The students quickly made their way to the office of the Hollowell firm to seek help, and it was agreed that William Alexander would take the case. Alexander brought suit against Maddox in criminal court for pointing a pistol at his clients, but the case quickly took on landmark proportions. Attorneys from the U. S. Department of Justice and Jack Greenberg and

Constance Baker Motley from the Inc. Fund arrived to assist the Hollowell firm. They took Maddox and the owners of the Heart of Atlanta Motel in the downtown area, which also had refused to serve Negroes, to federal court.

As the Pickrick case was unfolding, student demonstrators also were attempting to force the integration of this rather nondescript motel, which included a small restaurant.[7] Its owner, Moreton Rolleston, on the very day that the new Civil Rights bill was signed into law, had filed suit against the federal government in U. S. District Court, challenging the constitutionality of legislation that infringed on his private property rights.

Justices Tuttle, Hooper and Morgan of the U.S. Fifth Circuit Court of Appeals showed little patience with the defendants' contentions that their rights as business people were being violated and that their trade did not qualify as interstate commerce under the Civil Rights bill. The three judges took only a few days to issue the ruling that forced the integration of both establishments. Maddox attempted to circumvent the law by closing the Pickrick and re-opening it as the Lester Maddox Cafeteria — for which he was found in contempt. Then he and Rolleston, an attorney who represented himself, mounted several legal appeals. However, these actions were only rear guard skirmishes. On December 14, 1964, the U. S. Supreme Court, in a landmark decision, denied the appeal from the Heart of Atlanta Motel. The back of segregation in public establishments was broken.

§§§

In the spring of 1965 the white leadership of sparsely populated Taliaferro County, midway between Atlanta and Augusta, recognized that it had a problem on its hands. Negroes, who constituted more than sixty per cent of the county's sparse population of 3,400 citizens and had for decades been subjected to massive discrimination, were seeking to enroll their children in Alexander Stephens Institute, the white high school. After a period of stonewalling their enrollment, the all-white Board of Education devised a creative way to circumvent the desegregation of its school system. That summer it secretly made arrangements to use the Taliaferro County school buses to transport white students to schools in several of the adjoining counties the next September. Then it simply closed Alexander Stephens Institute.

The Negro parents were still not well organized, but they were angry. Even before learning of the school board's plans, many of them had pulled their children from the all-Negro school. Instead they enrolled them in a Freedom School that the field staff of the Southern Christian Leadership Conference organized under the leadership of Hosea Williams. Many of the Negro teachers walked out of their classrooms and joined the boycott.

As the Negro community began to organize the Taliaferro Voters League and elect its own leadership, there began a series of confrontations and subsequent arrests of the protesters. The confused situation attracted a growing amount of media attention, and the potential for violence steadily increased.

The white power structure was not above stretching the law to quell the unrest. On August 22 a group of about one hundred and twenty-five students and parents marched in double file from the Tabernacle Baptist Church to the county courthouse in Crawfordsville. There they sang "God Bless America," prayed, listened to a brief statement from one of the leaders and then returned to the church. While they were conducting this peaceful demonstration, an itinerant preacher had set up shop at another corner of the courthouse square, where he was playing religious music and preaching over a portable loudspeaker. His audience included a lackluster collection of perhaps fifteen people on the sidewalk or sitting on the fenders of parked automobiles. The local authorities arrested nine of the demonstrators and, in a remarkable stretch of interpretation, charged them with disturbing a congregation gathered for divine worship.

After the closing of the white high school, Calvin Turner, one of the teachers in the Negro school, had filed transfer applications for three of his students to enable them to attend the schools to which white students were to be bused. Despite the fact that the applications, as later determined by the court, were illegally designed to require their notarization, the county indicted and imprisoned Turner on twelve counts of forgery for his actions.

Negroes also began attempting to block the buses that were transporting the white students out of the county, and the Voters League applied for federal funding to organize a Head Start program.

Complicating the situation was a parallel request for federal education funds from the Taliaferro Board of Education.

Hollowell and Moore were soon on the scene to represent Turner and the other Negro leaders and students who had been charged. With the assistance of Jack Greenberg and Derrick Bell from the Inc. Fund they filed a series of counter-suits in the U.S. District Court before a three-judge panel headed by Griffin Bell, who only a few years earlier had been one of Hollowell's adversaries in the battle over the integration of the state university.

Judge Bell's written opinion showed his disdain for the county leaders' attempts at subterfuge and his dismay over the shallowness of the attempts to provide a legal justification for their actions. By the end of October that year he had placed the Board of Education in what amounted to receivership under the authority of the court and made it clear that he was going to monitor the situation closely until the county brought itself into compliance with federal law.[8] The success of Calvin Turner and his colleagues in this case helped to energize a spirit of empowerment within the Negro community. They then filed another suit, which went to the U. S. Supreme Court,[9] in which they successfully challenged the constitutionality of the way in which both juries and school boards were selected in Taliaferro County.[10] Many years later, as he reflected on the changes that have come to this rural area of Georgia, Hollowell remarked, "You know, this case was another illustration of two amazing phenomena. The first is the incredible lengths to which white people used to go to avoid assimilation with black people. The other is the remarkable amount of power that the court can find upon which to act when people are brave enough to bring their claims and demand attention." Characteristically, Hollowell neglected to note the role he had played in using the law to bring the claims of black people before the bar of justice and thereby to bring white and black people into more equitable dialogue with each other.

§§§

It was still far too early to declare total victory, but in the State of Georgia the momentum in the combat was shifting to favor the forces of freedom. Donald Hollowell, Horace Ward, Howard Moore, and William

Alexander — interestingly, all veterans of military service — had within the space of less than a decade conducted an incredible series of successful engagements on the battlefield of the legal system against the entrenched forces of racial apartheid. They had important allies like the federal bench, their colleagues from the Inc. Fund, co-counsels like C. B. King and a corps of brave clients. Nonetheless, it is doubtful whether any other small cadre of attorneys can lay claim to having secured as much legal ground on America's expedition toward equality as did the Hollowell firm.

ENDNOTES

[1] Now Martin Luther King, Jr. Drive.

[2] See Chapter 6.

[3] The generally accepted statistics of the time showed that Negroes represented one-third of Atlanta's population, but were confined to sixteen per cent of the land.

[4] In 1963, Mayor Allen, at the request of President John F. Kennedy, was the only elected official from the South to testify before Congress in support of the proposed civil rights legislation that would extend equal access to all public accommodations.

[5] Alexander, a native of Macon, had served in the Army after graduation from Booker T. Washington High School and then completed his undergraduate education at Georgia's Ft. Valley State College. He earned his J.D. degree from the University of Michigan and a master's degree in law from Georgetown University and then became a legal assistant with the national headquarters of the Social Security Administration's Payment Center in Baltimore. Alexander returned to Georgia and won election to the Georgia House of Representatives. His tenure with Hollowell's firm was brief. In 1975 he began a judicial career, progressing from the bench of Atlanta's City Court to Fulton County's Criminal Court and then, in 1985, to the Fulton County Superior Court, a position he continues to hold today.

[6] Dr. Charles E. Wells is now pastor of Allen Temple A. M. E. Church in Atlanta. The Rev. Mr. Dunn and the Rev. Mr. Willis are pastors in Texas. Dr. Wells shared his recollections in a taped interview with Louise Hollowell, and all three ministers reminisced about their experiences in the Fall, 1994, issue of *The Lantern,* a newsletter of the Interdenominational Theological Center.

[7] William Jackson, then the Dean of the Atlanta University School of Social Work, during an interview with Louise Hollowell many years after the event offered a wonderful account of one demonstration that helped to lead to the emergence of the Heart of Atlanta case as a legal landmark.

His recollections especially serve to reveal the way in which the student demonstrators pulled their elders into the struggle and thereby helped to speed the course of change. As he told the story, during a Saturday meeting of the Atlanta Summit Leadership Conference (a group of black and white leaders committed to the achievement of civil rights), chaired by Clarence Coleman, Head of the Southern Regional office for the National Urban League, several SNCC workers, led by James Foreman, suddenly appeared. Although most of them were dressed in the Movement "uniforms" of overalls and blue jeans, Foreman, quite uncharacteristically, was wearing a coat and tie. They reported on their hereto unsuccessful attempts to integrate the motel and then informed the leadership group that "it was about time" for it to provide some assistance.

After some discussion, the older leaders agreed to help. However, they asked the students, in effect, to let them, all dressed in suits and ties, test the motel's willingness to provide service. Then some forty of them, including Foreman, jumped into their automobiles and drove to the motel on Courtland Street. They arrived late in the afternoon and divided themselves into two groups — one headed for the cafeteria and the other for the room registration desk.

Jackson, who was in the restaurant group, remembers that they seated themselves at tables for four, careful not to sit too close to the handful of white patrons who already were eating. After a Negro waiter approached and informed them that he wasn't sure whether he could serve them, they asked him to summon somebody in charge.

When the manager appeared, he informed them that he had no intention of serving them and left the room. Foreman, whom Hollowell later would represent when the case came to trial, took it upon himself to begin walking around the restaurant, informing the other patrons that were witnessing a sit-in and what the issues were. His colleagues, however, wanting to maintain decorum, pulled him back into the group, and they all continued to sit at their tables. As they sat, they slowly realized that they had the restaurant to themselves. The earlier white patrons had left, and the staff was turning away other would-be customers.

The manager reappeared and unsuccessfully demanded that the protesters leave. When they refused, he announced his intention to call the police — a step they encouraged him to take. Then he locked them in the restaurant and began brandishing a pistol. When Lee Shelton, one of the group, went to the telephone to call his wife and inform her why he wasn't home for dinner, the manager ripped the instrument from the wall.

Some thirty minutes later, when a single white police officer who was a veteran of civil rights demonstrations entered the restaurant, the manager demanded that he arrest the group on anti-trespass charges. The officer calmly studied the group and then said, "I don't see any problem here. They're all well dressed, they look like reputable people, they're not causing a disturbance, and we have orders not to file charges against anyone who is acting in a law-abiding fashion." The manager turned and left, announcing his intention to find a judge who would issue an injunction against the group.

When he returned an hour later, apparently having been successful in finding a friendly judge, he told them the police would soon return to force their removal. However, no sooner had he issued that pronouncement than he was called to deal with a problem that seemed to be developing outside. A female SNCC worker had stretched herself across the driveway leading into the motel parking lot, where she was blocking traffic and attracting a crowd of curious onlookers. In his haste to respond to this emergency, the manager had neglected to lock the door behind him, so all the sit-in demonstrators followed him outside.

Lee Shelton and Albert Davis, both physicians, immediately ran to the young woman and knelt beside her. Davis quietly asked her, "Are you hurt?" After she had assured him that she was in perfect health, he whispered, "Just lie there," and then called out, "Quick, I need something to cover this young woman before she goes into shock." She soon was buried beneath a pile of coats. In the meantime, an ambulance from Grady Memorial, the public charity hospital, had arrived, but the two doctors insisted that their patient be taken to the segregated Georgia Baptist Hospital.

The other adults, who by now were almost in a party mood, followed the doctors and the young woman in their automobiles. They arrived to find their physician colleagues in debate with a staff physician. When neither he nor the admitting nurse would admit her, despite the contention of Davis and Shelton that they were dealing with a medical emergency, an Egyptian doctor in residence volunteered to sign her in, and she was installed in isolated and segregated splendor on the unused top floor of the facility.

It was now nearly nine-thirty in the evening, and as the group considered its next step, the members remembered that they were still hungry and promptly returned to the Heart of Atlanta Motel. The cashier almost fell from her stool and the manager seemed in a state of disbelief when they reappeared at his establishment, but he still refused to let the Negro wait staff serve the group. Their response finally was to move to the counter, where they were permitted to order. However, Foreman and two colleagues refused to leave their table. The protest finally petered out around two o'clock the next morning, but the Movement had gained a new corps of protest veterans.

[8] This judicial action later served as a precedent for similar court rulings around the country, including a highly publicized case involving the schools in the Roxbury section of Boston.

[9] Argued by Michael Meltsner, Jack Greenberg and Howard Moore, Jr.

[10] Black citizens still constitute somewhat more than 62% of the people in Taliaferro County, but the population has shrunk to 1,900, as both blacks and

whites have emigrated from this economically depressed area. There is no high school, and all high school students, 95% of whom are black, now are bused to adjoining Greene County at taxpayer expense. (Most of the white students attend private academies in other counties.) Yet there has been positive change as a result of the dogged pursuit of equity by Calvin Turner and his fellow black citizens. The principal of the single elementary school in Crawfordsville is black, as is the school superintendent. The county has a black sheriff and deputy, and the Crawfordsville police force is racially integrated. Both the Board of Commissioners and the school board have black majorities, and black men and women regularly serve on petit and grand juries.

12

A POLITICAL DETOUR

In 1964, Durwood T. Pye, Hollowell's untiring judicial nemesis, had declared his intent to run for re-election to the Superior Court bench of Fulton County. Even though the idea at first seemed preposterous, Hollowell began to entertain thoughts about challenging him. It was a heady thought to envision ending the all-white judiciary tradition.[1] The fact that his success also would engineer the removal of a man who was a persistently embarrassing obstacle to change made the notion even more enjoyable.

Hollowell was not the only one with ambitions for Pye's seat on the bench. Among those who felt the time might be right to defeat him was Paul Webb, Jr., a white, Harvard-educated and decidedly moderate attorney.[2]

All in all, it was proving to be an exciting election year as dramatic political races began to shape up from the national down to the state assembly levels. Lyndon B. Johnson was seeking his first full term as President of the United States, opposed by the unswervingly conservative Senator Barry Goldwater from Arizona. The progressive Charles L. Weltner of Atlanta, whom the press enjoyed touting as a symbol of the New South, was campaigning for re-election to his Fifth District seat in the U.S. House of Representatives. Leroy Johnson, Georgia's first Negro State Senator since Reconstruction, also hoped to keep his place in the legislature, and Horace Ward, Hollowell's own law partner, was making a run for office too. It was his ambition to join Johnson in the Georgia Senate by representing the 39th District.

Hollowell was not naive. Racial attitudes were changing, but he still knew that his chances would be slim. Nevertheless, after a great deal of careful deliberation, he at last decided to enter the race against Pye. He also believed that his well known name on the ballot might help to stimulate a greater Negro turnout than usual for other candidates. Late in the afternoon on the last day for qualifying, Leroy Johnson picked him up at Tibbs Soda Fountain on Hunter Street, and the two drove to the courthouse.

For most Negroes in Atlanta, with the exception of a small cadre of Lincoln Republicans who unswervingly voted the party ticket, the choices in most of the political races seemed obvious. Only in the case of this Superior Court judgeship was there sharp division of opinion. Hollowell quickly discovered that he could count upon the support of a strong contingent from the Atlanta University Center institutions. All of the city's younger leaders who had been in the forefront of the civil rights struggles during the previous four years were solidly behind him. For this assertive group, Hollowell was a hero behind whose banner they were only too pleased to rally.

Across town, though, the entrenched Negro establishment from the Fourth Ward dug in its heels. A. T. Walden, Warren Cochrane from the Butler Street YMCA, John Calhoun of the Atlanta NAACP, C.A. Scott, publisher of the *Atlanta Daily World*, and other civic and religious leaders represented the old guard. They were opposed to Hollowell's candidacy, and some of them had already pledged their support to Webb.

"Daddy" King belonged to that group. In a meeting at the Butler Street Y during the early days of the campaign, he told Hollowell, "Don, I'm sorry, but I can't go along with you this time. I've given my word to Paul Webb, and my word is my bond." Although the older men also wanted to oust Pye from office, they simply didn't believe that Hollowell had a chance. They feared he might draw votes away from the one man whom they believed could beat the incumbent.

Wiley Branton, the brave attorney who had been the key Negro civil rights attorney in Little Rock, was in town and came to the same meeting. After others had explained why they couldn't support Hollowell, he took the floor. "Don," he began, "I'm sorry that I can't go along with you this time." He paused dramatically, as everyone present stared in astonishment at the man whom they expected to speak on Hollowell's behalf. Then he continued, "The reason that I can't go along with you this time is that I am registered to vote in Arkansas. But if I could vote, you can rest assured that I would cast my ballot for you." He then proceeded to deliver a strong and compelling endorsement of his friend and legal counterpart from Georgia.

Branton's persuasive appeal notwithstanding, most of the old Negro leadership held its ground as the campaign picked up speed and intensity. This non-support from these highly public figures presented a major impediment to Hollowell's chances. The young Turks intensified their efforts. Samuel DuBois Cook,[3] who became a member of the leadership team for Hollowell's campaign, wrote a strong letter of endorsement to the *Atlanta Constitution*. Offsetting that kind of support, however, was an editorial in the same newspaper by Eugene Patterson that supported the position of the established Negro leadership. Hollowell, wrote Patterson, was playing the role of a spoiler.

Cook remembers that as hard as Hollowell's supporters worked, the candidate himself worked even harder. Regular sleep disappeared from his regimen as he continued to fight against the political odds. Often the only break from the strain would be a quick catnap on the sofa in his office.

Though exhausting, the campaign also could be heady. There were gala fund raising parties for Hollowell throughout the city. Jondelle Johnson, society editor of the *Atlanta Inquirer* and active NAACP volunteer, sponsored one of these events at the Royal Peacock club on Auburn Avenue, where Little Richard performed for a crowd of more than six hundred people. More modest functions, like the one hosted by Ben Brown at his home on Napoleon Avenue, attracted some of the younger, less affluent activists in the community.

The precedent-setting nature of Hollowell's campaign even attracted the attention of the Negro/liberal white coalition in New York. There Arthur and Marian Bruce Logan hosted a party in their swank uptown apartment to raise funds for Hollowell's effort. Duke Ellington was there, as was Charles Merrill, the white Chairman of the Morehouse College board. Cleveland Robinson, the New York labor leader showed up, as did Coretta Scott King and Jack Greenberg from the Legal Defense Fund. So did Charlayne Hunter and her husband, Walter Stovall.

Chauncey Waddell, the philanthropist and member of the Inc. Fund board, made it a special point to attend. He had met Hollowell when the attorney delivered a speech at the Harvard Club in New York, and he wanted to renew the acquaintanceship. Waddell had just arrived home from an overseas trip and didn't have his checkbook with him. After the fund raising pitch to the assembled guests, he found a scrap of paper and on it scribbled, "I owe Don Hollowell $1,000" — a pledge he later fulfilled.

Meanwhile, back on the home front, Hollowell was cutting into the lead of Webb, who seemed to be the initial front-runner against Pye. "Daddy" King, after his son counseled with him privately, went against his own conscience and switched his support from Webb to Hollowell. Q. V. Williamson, the politician and realtor, declared publicly, "I'm a Republican, but I'm a Negro first and will vote in the Democratic Primary for Don Hollowell. Hollowell is qualified... and made more headway than any of the other candidates involved, and he can win if Negroes stick together." Williamson, who had lost his Aldermanic seat in a previous election, went on to note that Negroes still had not learned to support candidates of their own race.

However, even these endorsements were not sufficient to bridge the division in the Negro community that had surfaced early during the campaign. At times the conflict became hot and even acrimonious. On August 29, Judge Walden,[4] Hollowell's former colleague, sent an open letter to Negro voters strongly endorsing Webb. Another letter followed — this one signed by, among others, the Rev. William Holmes Borders, the powerful pastor of the Wheat Street Baptist Church, and Dr. Frank Cunningham, President of Morris Brown College. Walden, as well as Warren Cochrane and Walter "Chief" Aiken, another prominent Auburn Avenue businessman, presided over many political rallies in the Negro community that summer. At one of them in Southeast Atlanta, Cochrane exhorted his audience, "Follow your tried, respected leaders." During an executive committee session of the Fulton County Democratic Club, which had voted its overwhelming support for Hollowell, Walden stormed from the meeting.

Charles Black, Managing Editor of the *Inquirer*,[5] wrote:

> Opposition to Hollowell's candidacy is thought by many observers to be based on a fear that Hollowell's

election would lead to a major shift in leadership in the Negro community wherein conservative community leaders based on Auburn Avenue and Butler Street will lose their bargaining power with the city's white 'power structure' as being able to promise the delivery of the Negro vote in exchange for business and personal favors.

In its regular issue of September 6 as well as a special "Election Extra" on September 8, the *Inquirer* pulled out all of the editorial stops. The former's banner headline on the front page proclaimed, "FIRST BALLOT VICTORY SEEN FOR HOLLOWELL." It supported that contention with the statistical research of Cook, whose previous political analyses had earned respect.

Both editions also carried a less-than-subtle political cartoon, one that the gracious Hollowell never would have approved had he been given the opportunity. The setting for the drawing was the front step of a home through whose front door a white woman peers. Standing before her is a stooped Negro man (who bears a striking resemblance to Walden) with a cane and hat in his right hand. In his right hand he holds the end of a chain which is attached to the nose of another Negro man whose hands are shackled. The caption reads, "MA'AM, WOULD YOU PLEASE TELL MISTER WEBB THAT I'M HERE TO DELIVER THE NEGRO VOTE."

The *Inquirer*, despite its pro-Hollowell stance, had, of course, to carry other political advertisements, and there were seven paid display ads for Webb in the "Election Extra" edition. Nevertheless, the paper devoted the entire back page to a listing of three hundred and sixteen names under the declaration, "WE ARE BEHIND HOLLOWELL ONE HUNDRED PERCENT." The "signatures" included the names of Benjamin E. Mays, Albert E. Manley, and Harry V. Richardson, the presidents of, respectively, Morehouse and Spelman Colleges and the Interdenominational Theological Center. Many faculty members from the Atlanta University Center added their names as did Martin Luther King, Sr., A. M. E. Bishop H. I. Bearden, C. M. E. Bishop P. Randolph Shy and other pastors.

In the primary election on September 9, Pye beat both Webb and Hollowell decisively. As predicted by some critics, the Negro vote did split. The moderate white vote for which the Hollowell camp had hoped never materialized. Hollowell carried twenty precincts and did receive two-thirds of the Negro vote, but it was not enough. A post-election analysis by Wiley Branton sought valiantly to put some positive spin on the results. He observed that between five and seven thousand Negro voters who might not otherwise have cast their ballots went to the polls to support Hollowell.

The *Inquirer* was less charitable in its account of the primary results. It cited:

> ...reports of Atlantans here in the city and across the country who generally term the failure of Negroes to strongly support Atty. Hollowell as 'tragic' in this day of the freedom struggle.... Perhaps the real tragedy in the whole election falls at the feet of voter apathy. There were 31,000 Negroes who failed to cast their votes.

Hollowell issued a prepared statement, urging a greater Negro turnout in the runoff election on September 23. "Eight more years is a long time to await another opportunity to express ourselves," he warned. The numbers did increase about four per cent as fifty-five per cent of the Negro registered voters — some thirty-three thousand people — cast ballots. Webb lost anyway, though, receiving even fewer white votes than he obtained in the primary. All told, Pye received some forty-five thousand votes to Webb's forty-three thousand, and, in the process, garnered eighty-two per cent of the white vote.

The race for the Superior Court judgeship was to be Hollowell's only foray into political candidacy. From the benefit of hindsight it seems clear that he was several years ahead of his time. By the end of the decade he probably would have handily won election. However, his challenge emboldened others to present themselves as candidates for public office. From his campaign they learned important political lessons. Hollowell's loss still managed to be another victory for the Negro struggle in Atlanta.

ENDNOTES

[1] Negroes who held elected office in Atlanta — as elsewhere in the South — were still a distinct novelty in the early 1960s and had been for many decades. In 1870, during the Reconstruction era, the Rev. William Finch, a tailor, and George Graham, a carpenter, won races to serve on the city council. After one term, though, white backlash set in, and Jim Crow laws soon assured Atlanta of having a lily-white government for nearly another century. In 1952, Dr. Rufus E. Clement, the distinguished and internationally respected President of Atlanta University, won election to the Atlanta Board of Education. Several years later Q. V. Williamson became the first Negro elected on a city-wide basis to Atlanta's Board of Aldermen.

[2] Webb's father, Paul Webb, Sr., had been the County Solicitor when Hollowell successfully defended Willie Nash ten years earlier.

[3] Cook was a professor of political science at Atlanta University. A classmate of Martin Luther King, Jr., he graduated from Morehouse and then earned his master's and doctorate degrees from Ohio State University. He would, in later years, go on to become a professor at Duke University and a program officer of The Ford Foundation before assuming the presidency of Dillard University in New Orleans.

[4] His relatively new title derived from an *ad hoc* position on the Municipal Court bench to which he had been appointed late in his professional career.

[5] The *Atlanta Inquirer* was an early journalistic product of the Civil Rights Movement, established both to provide a voice for its emerging leaders as well as in reaction to the relatively conservative editorial policies of the *Atlanta Daily World*.

13

CLOSING THE DOCKET

The first half of the 1960s had been an exhausting time for both Hollowells. Even as he raced from courtroom to courtroom across the state and then campaigned for the Superior Court bench, his wife had been maintaining her own grueling schedule. For nearly fifteen years she had carried a full teaching load at Morris Brown College. She also had found time along the way to serve for one year as acting chair of the English department and to travel to Boston University for studies in human relations. In 1963 she determined to continue the progress toward the doctorate that she had started at the University of Pennsylvania in 1958. For the next two years she spent a great deal of time in Philadelphia completing her course work and foreign language requirements.

Then the need to care for her beloved mother who was very sick and nearly blind brought her back to Atlanta. She herself was in weakened health. The burden of her mother's illness, academic demands, and the strain of being married to a man who was daily on the public firing line all took their toll. Yet, she managed to continue work on her dissertation and to teach.[1]

Throughout those hectic days of the 1960s, the Hollowells were blessed with one escape route from the pressure chamber. It was the drive to the family homestead in Iron City, Georgia. At sporadic intervals the couple — usually at Louise's urging — would leave the turmoil and travel to this peaceful pocket of southwest Georgia for a few days of rest and recuperation.

During the Christmas holidays of 1965 they departed for a weekend visit to their retreat haven. Along the way they stopped at a service station in Albany, Georgia, where Hollowell had fought many legal battles.[2] Departing from his usual pattern of challenging the segregated restrooms, this time he simply used the "Colored" facilities. When he finished, however, he immediately reported to the attendant that they were filthy and had no paper or soap. He further noted that he had also checked the white-only restrooms and found them to be both clean and fully equipped. The attendant simply stared at him with seeming indifference.

On the return trip to Atlanta that Monday, although his wife felt he might be exerting too much pressure, Hollowell made a special point of stopping at the same gas station again. To their amazement, the "Colored" facilities now were thoroughly cleaned and had been supplied with adequate soap and paper. When they thanked the operator for his service, he in turn seemed pleased that they had returned and noticed his efforts. This modest moment of civility offered at least a hint that change could occur.

For more than a decade Donald Hollowell had been in the vanguard of the battle for civil rights. In case after case he had fought to bring local government into compliance with national law. Years later, when Emory University's law school established a professorship in Hollowell's name, Elbert P. Tuttle, Senior Judge of the U. S. Court of Appeals' new 11th Circuit, said of his friend and colleague in social change, "He was the most successful advocate for civil rights cases that I participated in."

The passage of the Civil Rights Act on July 2, 1964, radically altered the legal landscape of America, and Hollowell now began to reflect upon what his future might hold. The first answer was to come from an unexpected source. Title VII of the new bill addressed the issue of employment discrimination and thereby focused on the heart of the struggle for equality. The right to enter a restaurant was, after all, an empty opportunity for someone who couldn't earn enough money to buy a meal.

Because Title VII prohibited discrimination in private industry, many business and corporate leaders saw and feared what they rightly perceived as the coming of a new era that would be marked by government intervention in their affairs. However, this section of the Civil Rights law raised as many questions as it answered. Would the new law punish only intentional discrimination? Would it be retroactive? What effect would it have on seniority and merit systems? Would there now be reverse discrimination? What did it mean that gender discrimination too was forbidden by the bill's language?[3]

The responsibility for finding and sorting out the answers to these and many other problematic questions fell to the newly created Equal Employment Opportunity Commission — the EEOC. Modeled after the National Labor Relations Board, it was scheduled to come into existence on July 1, 1965, one year after President Johnson signed the Civil Rights bill.

Johnson appointed Franklin Delano Roosevelt, Jr., an Assistant Secretary in the Department of Commerce, as its first chairman. To him fell the challenge of building an organization from the ground up. The magnitude of this undertaking quickly made it clear that his success would depend upon the recruitment of regional directors to carry the EEOC message to every section of the nation.

Samuel Jackson, a long-time friend of Hollowell and also a native of Kansas, was one of the five commissioners of the new agency. He enlisted Hollowell's help in trying to find a director for the Southern region. After lengthy conversations, Jackson became convinced that he didn't want Hollowell's help with the recruitment of candidates; he wanted Hollowell.

His friend demurred. He was, as he explained, exhausted. Having spent nearly fifteen years building a busy law practice on the foundation of clients who, in the main, could not pay well, he was ready to slow down a bit and accept more cases that were better financially rewarding. He felt he had earned the right to cash in on some of his unsought but hard-won popularity; to draw upon the experience gained along the way; to practice in areas that went beyond the boundaries of civil rights.

Hollowell's arguments failed to move Jackson. From his perspective, no one was better suited to establish what would be EEOC's first regional office. He began lobbying for his choice with Roosevelt even as he stepped up his efforts to sell Hollowell on the importance and opportunities of the job.

In response to a formal letter of invitation from Roosevelt himself, Hollowell at last agreed to travel to Washington for a meeting with Roosevelt and all of the commissioners. They too quickly concluded that Jackson had indeed found the right person for the new position and urged Hollowell to accept. Honored as he was by their interest in him, he expressed doubt. As he told them, the agency wasn't as far along as

Jackson, a good salesman, had led him to believe. Their response was that he could help to speed up the process.

Louise Hollowell's reaction was that her husband should accept the position. Concerned about his health, she was in favor of anything that would liberate him from the whirlwind of activity that had dominated their lives. Besides, she observed, "You don't have to stay for a long time."

Hollowell agreed to let the government's nomination and confirmation process move forward, although he demanded and received guarantees of a salary well above the flat G-16 scale called for by the job description. For the first time in his life he was assured of fair if not overly generous compensation for his work.

In the course of the background investigation, the incident that had propelled him into a legal career surfaced. After the FBI had concluded a full field check on him, Roosevelt called and laughingly reported, "I know all about your involvement with the Southern Negro Youth Congress."

A front page story of the *Atlanta Inquirer*'s February 5, 1966, edition described the administration of the oath of office by Roosevelt, to "the first Negro to be appointed as a regional director for a major federal agency." It was a happy day, graced by the presence of many dignitaries from both Washington and Atlanta.

During the next month, Hollowell worked half-time on agency matters. The rest of his schedule was taken up with making arrangements to dissolve his relationship with the law firm he had so carefully assembled. On March 3, the new EEOC office opened for business in the same building as the General Services Administration offices at 1776 Peachtree Street. Hollowell, Willie King (who came from the Southern Christian Leadership Conference) and Mary Ellen James constituted the entire staff that greeted people at a small reception to commemorate the occasion.

What was intended to be a relatively short-term assignment became a nineteen-year tour of duty. In retrospect, it also proved to be perhaps one of the most important — and the most thankless — challenges of his career. Gone was the opportunity to confront the power structure. He now belonged to it. Gone too was the drama of the courtroom. He still had a righteous cause, but he would have to advance it from a federal administrator's desk, using only the tools of "investigation, conciliation and persuasion."

Actually, he didn't even have a desk. Aside from the space allotted to him, the new regional director had nothing. The job began literally with the selection of furniture and then proceeded to the assembling of a full staff. Happily, he could call upon the leadership experience he had gained from military service and managing a law firm. Further assistance came from Walter Davis, EEOC's assistant executive director, and Mary Valentine, the agency's personnel director, whom the Washington office dispatched to help.

It was axiomatic that the new staff would be an interracial group. However, finding the right people was not a simple task, despite the fact that new professional positions carried relatively high grade classifications. Atlanta was a regional center for federal government operations, but there were hardly any black employees who had been able to climb to the minimum G-9 level required of the agency's new investigators.

White candidates were far easier to locate. Veteran federal employees, trapped in the glacial promotion system of the government, were anxious to move to a new agency where the opportunities for advancement might be greater. A good number of them had experience in contract compliance work with the Department of Labor, the Civil Service Commission and the National Labor Relations Board.

However, the challenge of building the right kind of staff went beyond simply ensuring that it was bi-racial. The people Hollowell was trying to find would require a unique blend of skills. It went almost without saying that they would need to have experience in or at least deep sensitivity to civil rights issues. In addition, they would have to possess the ability to work with claimants who often had limited educational backgrounds. Yet, even personal sensitivity and a commitment to equal rights were not enough. Since most of the new employees would be investigators, they would also would have to be able to write clear and cogent reports to be sent to Washington.

Washington wanted everything on a fast track, so somehow, within a month, Hollowell managed to assemble his initial team. They came from government and the nonprofit sector. When he accepted this new assignment, it was with the assurance that his life would be less hectic. On the job for barely two months, he was already finding it difficult to distinguish between its pace and that of the one he had left behind.

Hollowell, without clear direction from Washington, took the initiative of organizing a structure for the new office. When his provisional operation generated no complaints from the national office, it quickly became standard operating procedure. The new staff met for its first training session during the first week of April, 1966. Again, Hollowell had to take charge. The training materials prepared in Washington turned out to be far more limited than he had been led to believe, so he and his staff designed many of their own.

Complicating the start-up process was the fact that the EEOC headquarters began routing cases to Hollowell's people even before all of the furniture was in place at the regional office. There was no need to drum up trade. The flow of claims quickly swelled to a flood, and soon the packets of mail from Washington were supplemented by claimants walking directly through the doors of the still-organizing Atlanta unit. One early staff member of the national office notes that EEOC within six months of beginning operations had 10,000 cases to investigate.

Despite the pressure, the job was not without its amusing interludes, like one that occurred the day an insistent claimant, a white female, demanded to speak with the Regional Director to make clear how important her case was. Having finally overcome the resistance both of the first person who first interviewed her and then the supervisor, she at last gained entrance to Hollowell's outer office. As his secretary rose and began slowly to open the door to his chamber, the claimant saw the black man behind his desk and cried out in shock, "Is that the Regional Director? Oh Lord, let me get out of here."

And there were also touching moments, as occurred the day another white woman came into the office to pick up a three thousand dollar check she had been awarded after a successful claim of discrimination against her employer. "Well, well," she said in quiet astonishment. "I never knew we'd come to the day when ordinary working people like us would get this kind of response from the government."

For that first year or so there still were no field offices. As a result, the regional office had to function as both an administrative and operational center. From it the newly trained investigators — usually a two-person team composed of an experienced veteran and a newcomer

— fanned out across a region that initially included Alabama, Florida, Georgia, Louisiana, Mississippi, North Carolina, South Carolina, Virginia and Puerto Rico. John Rayburn, a staffer from those days recalls, "Once we were relatively satisfied that [the investigators] were competent, we would hand them eight cases and a book of airline ticket requests...and tell them to be back in a month with complete investigative reports."

The investigators were, of course, not welcome guests, and the corporations and other institutions on whom they called were often less than cooperative. Thus, the field work was seldom routine. Harry Boyte, who was looking into employee complaints at a major corporation, found himself intentionally locked up in the office when it closed at five o'clock in the afternoon. Another investigator at a mill in Rock Hill, South Carolina, who had pulled into a fast-food restaurant parking lot at the end of a long morning of taking depositions and fallen asleep in his car after consuming a quick lunch, was arrested and jailed for loitering and had his automobile confiscated. The EEOC, which got the charges dropped, later learned that the secretary of the plant manager was the wife of the police chief.

Since the new agency had no litigation powers, for the first six years the field staff's activism was limited to investigation. Its members would file their reports, which then went to Washington and became the responsibility of the Justice Department to litigate or negotiate. It was a frustrating process for both the claimants and Hollowell's own team which was trying to promote more rapid change.

§§§

That first year on the new job again saw the Hollowells on the road to Southwest Georgia. Louise's uncle in Philadelphia had died, and they were driving to his funeral in Iron City. Traveling with them were Louise's mother and one of her friends.

The foursome had decided to take a back route along secondary roads. As evening approached, and needing gas and the use of a restroom, they stopped at a Standard Oil station in Buena Vista, just east of Columbus. The station still had the customary three separate facilities for white men, white women and "Colored." While Hollowell watched the teenaged attendant service the car, the women obtained the key to the restroom for Negroes. After they returned, Hollowell then requested the key to the men's restroom. The attendant in response simply pointed to the key that the women had placed beside the cash register. Hollowell made it clear that he had no intention of using the segregated facility. When the young man pleaded that he was only operating under orders from his boss, Hollowell didn't push the matter further. Stepping outside, he simply began recording the name and address of the station on a notepad and then returned to the car.

Several miles outside Buena Vista, as they continued on their way, a pickup truck roared up behind them, flashing its bright lights. In a clear attempt to intimidate, the white driver, accompanied by a young woman and a very small girl, passed their vehicle and then abruptly reduced his speed. He clearly intended to force them to stop or turn off the road. Hollowell's response, though, was to ease the hood of his Buick to within inches of the truck's tailgate and to keep it there with his bright lights on. Realizing that the black man he was trying to frighten showed no fear, the driver of the pickup finally pulled off the highway into an abandoned gas station.

Hollowell's three passengers were not so calm as he. The incident had shaken them, and they were concerned that other vehicles might try to intercept them. Nonetheless, Hollowell's mother-in-law cried out bravely, "Just keep going, Don. The Lord will take care of us." The trip continued without further incident.

Upon his return to Atlanta, Hollowell again wrote to the oil company, as he had in 1954,[4] reminding it that the Buena Vista station was operating illegally. This letter elicited a personal visit from a company representative who repeated the contention that Standard Oil had no authority over the operations of the stations that it leased to others. However, he promised to pay a visit to Buena Vista.

Not long afterwards, he reported to Hollowell that the manager, not without reluctance, had agreed to be the first in the area to desegregate his gas station. He had asked the Standard Oil representative to pass on that message to the Hollowells and other black travelers. Several months later they made it a point to stop in Buena Vista again. To their surprise, they received a courteous greeting and discovered that all racial restrictions had been removed from the restroom facilities. During the coming years the Hollowells became regular and welcome patrons of the establishment. Change, however small, was coming.

§§§

Among the more pleasant interludes during the years at the EEOC were the three-day federal judicial conferences, to which Elbert Tuttle and his wife, "Ms. Sarah," began inviting the Hollowells while Tuttle was chief justice of the Fifth Circuit. Their first participation in these events in 1967 with several other black couples marked the racial integration of the proceedings. Away from the protocol of the courtroom, judges and their guests were on a first-name basis. Mornings were given over to speeches and seminars, but the afternoons and evenings provided ample opportunity for social activities. At evening sing-alongs Hollowell's strong voice attracted applause (Judge William Bootle's wife was a special fan), and for years people who witnessed it enjoyed retelling the story of an evening revue that several of the participants staged during the meeting in Hollywood, Florida. After receiving initial instructions from the entertainment coordinator, Hollowell and some of the other men had costumed themselves to perform the hula. Seeing the tall muscular attorney outfitted with a blonde wig and swiveling his hips beneath a grass skirt was funny enough, but the sight of Hollowell awkwardly gesticulating with his enormous hands as his large feet slid back and forth brought down the house.

§§§

Without prosecutorial power of their own, Hollowell and his peers around the country were left with the less forceful tool of persuasion. Much of his schedule was filled with public relations and peacemaking missions to the offices of reluctant corporate and government executives and personnel managers whose support he sought.

Even as Hollowell valiantly tried to make the new system work, his name surfaced again in connection with the possibility of a judicial appointment. The front page of the July 20, 1968, *Atlanta Inquirer* featured his picture and reported, "Atlanta Attorney Donald L. Hollowell, director of the six-state Southeastern Region of the U.S. Equal Employment Opportunity Commission for the past two and one-half years, is reportedly under presidential consideration for appointment as judge in the 5th Circuit Court of Appeals."

The story was accurate. It looked as if there would be an opening on that bench. President Johnson apparently was looking for someone from the Fifth Circuit to take the place of Abe Fortas, whom he had hoped to name as Chief Justice of the Supreme Court before Fortas was forced to step down for ethical improprieties. Hollowell had the approval of the American Bar Association, and there were indications that Senators Herman Talmadge and even Richard Russell would not block the appointment. However, soon thereafter, the President announced that he would not seek reelection, and the chance of a judicial appointment for Hollowell by Johnson slipped away.

Meanwhile, although decentralization and the clustering of cases were beginning to take some of the pressure off the EEOC regional office, the expanded network and enhanced efficiencies did not stop the arrival of new cases. So great was the pileup that EEOC staffers started referring to the backlog as the "saglog." All realized that they were barely making a dent in the mountain of charges calling for investigation. The major bottleneck in the system remained in Washington, through which all cases from every region had to be funneled.

The claimants and advocacy groups were not interested in the location of the problem within this new federal system. They just wanted action, especially those who had already waited several years since first filing their claims. Many of them had marched and sued for the changes that had contributed to the creation of the Title VII legislation. The law, as they understood it, said that they were entitled to relief from employment discrimination. Why weren't they getting it? Unfamiliar with the complexities of both legal and bureaucratic procedures, they grew increasingly angry.

It was painful for Hollowell and those of his colleagues who had been directly involved in the civil rights struggle to discover that old friends now considered them to be part of the enemy camp. Although they begged Washington to give them increased powers to approve cases for litigation and increased funding to cope with the ever-increasing workload, their pleas went unanswered.

The very backlog of cases, which should have been an argument for more money to process them, backfired, because critics could in turn point to the small number of actual suits being filed and question why it cost so much to produce so little. Furthermore, foremost in the mind of the national administration was the winning of the war in Vietnam and controlling the building wave of domestic protest against it. There was little time, interest or energy left over to nurture a new agency that was concerned about the rights of minorities and women.

Early during his tenure as regional director, Hollowell began to receive regular complaints from women in the South that EEOC was not doing enough to respond to their charges of employment discrimination. Hollowell, in whose region easily ninety per cent of the cases hinged on charges of racial bias against black people, patiently pointed out to them that the major obstacle confronting them was their lack of organization — that their access to legal rights needed to be undergirded by political pressure. As he notes, they were quick to understand the message. In the South and throughout the country women began to "get it together," and associations like the National Organization of Women became increasingly sophisticated about championing the fight against gender discrimination.

The morale of the EEOC field staff during the early days of the agency had been high and energized by the excitement of implementing changes for which the Movement had fought. Now, however, it was in jeopardy. Hollowell, as leader of the regional operation and also Chairman of the national Regional Directors' Council, was especially frustrated that he could not indulge himself in the luxury of publicly expressing his personal anger about the lack of help he was getting from Washington, despite his pleas for greater latitude within which to promote positive change.

This frustration contributed to his desire once again to be part of an activity that might produce quicker results. In 1971 he accepted the presidency of the Voter Education Project's Board of Directors. Known most commonly by its initials, VEP was essentially about the business of registering black voters and promoting the use of the ballot to effect the changes made possible by new laws. Spun off from its founding parent, the

Southern Regional Council, VEP had first selected Wiley A. Branton, Sr., Hollowell's friend and colleague from Arkansas to be its Executive Director and later named Vernon E. Jordan, Jr., Hollowell's former law clerk, to the position. When Jordan left for New York to direct the affairs of the United Negro College Fund, he was succeeded by John Lewis, the courageous veteran of the Civil Rights Movement. Hollowell remained as VEP's board president until 1986. During that period black voter registration in the 11 Southern states escalated from 3,000,000 to 5,500,000.

During these years Hollowell also found time to serve as President of UNCF's National Alumni Council, to remain active in the affairs of the Christian Methodist Episcopal Church at the local, district and national levels, to lecture and teach, and to be a trustee and director of many educational and civic organizations.

Looking back on those early years at EEOC, Hollowell has offered two perspectives. The first is that change, although generally unpublicized, did occur. Some companies and government agencies were quietly instituting non-discriminatory employment practices. Minorities were beginning to appear on some payrolls for the first time and, even more important, beginning to enjoy the benefits of promotion. Finally, there was a slowly emerging consciousness that the law of the land prohibited discrimination in the work place.

However, as he has also noted, one of the greatest impediments to change had nothing to do with government policy or practices. Rather, it stemmed from the collective weight and power of special interest groups — the "fourth branch of government not described in the Constitution" — that were not sympathetic to the new law. In that number were major industries with many thousands of employees and millions of dollars available to their representatives in Washington to support legal delaying tactics, lobbying and other forms of political pressure.

Nonetheless, the cumbersome EEOC process began to see some improvements. By 1972, every region had some district offices, including Southeast offices in Atlanta, Birmingham, Charlotte, Jackson, Miami and Memphis. The advocates of Title VII, both within and outside the agency, were able, despite strong opposition, to muster enough pressure of their own to extract amendments to the bill from Congress. As Eleanor Holmes

Norton took over the leadership of the EEOC, it gained some new clout.

One important change was that the agency's staff now could shift from the passive stance of simply processing claims. Instead, investigators also could provide technical assistance to individuals and groups who were organizing legal challenges to employment discrimination. The most significant element of the amended law, though, was that it handed the agency some of the prosecutorial power that until then had been the sole responsibility of the Justice Department. Instead of collecting evidence and submitting it to Washington with the hope that federal attorneys might consider it sufficient to bring suit, EEOC lawyers now could bypass that filtering process.

Even this new power constituted a compromise in the eyes of some who had fought hard for changes in Title VII. Many of them had prodded, unsuccessfully, for the agency's right to issue "cease and desist" orders to employers who were shown to be discriminating.

Hollowell, however, was a realist. He was relatively satisfied simply with the new right to institute legal action. After all, he had the hard-won wisdom gained from years of trying to force compliance with Supreme Court rulings that ostensibly had eliminated segregation in education and public accommodations. In short, he had his doubts about the value of "cease and desist" orders if there was no way to enforce them.

As he saw it, it could have been counter-productive for the bark of cease-and-desist language to be greater than its bite. He also knew that the enforcement procedure — which by law would have included the right of defendants to appeal — might simply have shifted the logjam of cases to the federal courts. For the time being, Hollowell, although some of his friends thought he had sold out, was satisfied that the agency's new prosecuting power gave it the teeth needed to speed up change. Just being able to bare those teeth and growl, he observed, could in some cases encourage compliance with Title VII directives.

The assembling of a legal staff brought with it its own difficulties. The new attorneys had to learn to operate within a system that was subject to intense political pressure. They also did not have the complete discretion they might have envisioned being available to them when they joined the agency. Accustomed to being the sole authority on legal matters, they learned that other staff members had a lot to say about which cases could and should be carried to court. Yet another discovery was that they were in many cases being asked to take on some of the duties that had been the responsibility of compliance officers — seeking out-of-court settlements.

In 1976 Hollowell had the opportunity to leave administration and to become the regional attorney. It was a welcome change of pace, and it coincided with one of the happier periods in the agency's history as President Carter sought to broaden the responsibilities of EEOC.

During that period, taking advantage of his access to an administration that included many Atlanta figures whom Hollowell knew well, he scheduled an appointment with Attorney General Griffin Bell. Only fifteen years earlier Bell had been one of his legal adversaries as Hollowell sought to dismantle the barriers of segregation at the University of Georgia. Now they were both federal officials.

Bell received him graciously, and listened as Hollowell made a strong appeal for the Carter administration to appoint black federal judges in Georgia. Hollowell noted that Georgia was lagging behind states like North Carolina, Tennessee and even South Carolina in taking this step. He made it clear to Bell that he himself was not looking for an appointment to a federal bench. At the conclusion of the forty-five minute conversation, Bell assured Hollowell that he would make those concerns known to President Carter.

On December 7, 1978, the *Atlanta Journal* reported that the Carter administration wanted Senators Herman Talmadge and Sam Nunn to reconsider the list of five individuals they had submitted as possible appointees to the U. S. District Court's Northern District of Georgia bench. Noting that the list included only one black nominee, Fulton Superior Court Judge Horace T. Ward, the Carter people expressed a desire to see the names of more blacks and women.

Hollowell paid a visit to Herman Talmadge. He told Georgia's senior senator that he would appreciate Talmadge's endorsement, unless Talmadge was prepared to support "one of my men." Recalling that time, Hollowell notes, "After all, I was already sixty-one years old. By the time I would have settled into that job, it would have been time for me to be 'settling out.'" The Federal Merits Review Council appointed by Talmadge and Senator Sam Nunn, which was headed by former Atlanta

City Attorney Henry Bowden, subsequently reviewed the credentials of four other black and five women attorneys. Hollowell's name was on that list, but the appointment went to Ward.

Two years later, Hollowell's name surfaced again within the context of judicial appointments. Noting that Governor George Busbee was about to appoint someone to fill a vacancy on the Georgia Supreme Court, *Atlanta Journal* Columnist Jim Wooten wrote a piece entitled, "The Best Lawyers I Know." After citing George Lawrence's prosecutorial skills, Denmark Groover's political savvy and Bobby Lee Cook's legal adroitness, he continued:

> And the fourth is Donald L. Hollowell of Atlanta, a man I have seen in court only once — 15 years ago when he defended Preston Cobb, Jr. ...
>
> ... In the heyday of the civil rights movement, Donald Hollowell was the best legal mind around.
>
> ... the man who should be appointed is Donald Hollowell. There is truly no man or woman in the state more qualified or more deserving.
>
> Sooner or later, a governor is going to acknowledge that blacks ought to be represented on the state's high courts. If a white man in the profession was regarded as highly as Hollowell is, he would already have been there, or would at least have had the position offered.
>
> There are plenty of competent black lawyers available; several are among those being mentioned for consideration. In due time, they will wind up on the bench.
>
> Hollowell is now past 60; appointment to the Supreme Court would be fitting recognition of the contribution he has already made and would afford the citizens of Georgia to draw on his experience and wisdom before it is too late.

Charles Weltner, who would himself be named to the state's highest bench in 1981, was among the group of Hollowell's long-time friends who encouraged him to be a candidate for the position. Weltner, who had been one of the few Southern Congressmen to support federal civil rights legislation, had also been one of the individuals who had supported his campaign for the Superior Court in 1964. Nonetheless, despite these encouragements, Hollowell was not really interested. For all of the honor that would come with an appointment of that kind, he also realized that it would require a lot of work, and he, frankly, was tired. He decided to finish his career by continuing the tough task of holding the middle ground between extreme positions on either side in the fight over employment discrimination.

The prevailing mood of the country after the activism of the Lyndon Johnson years steadily assumed an ever more conservative cast. As manifested in presidential politics, that shift began with the election of Richard Nixon and reached its zenith in 1980 with Ronald Reagan's landslide victory. (The four-year term of President Carter, who sought to expand the agency's authority, proved to be an aberration, as it became clear that EEOC did not enjoy strong support from the national administration.)

Complicating everything by the early 1980s was a shift in the battle lines. Although the hiring of blacks and other minorities continued to be an issue, its importance started to diminish. Now the emphasis increasingly was upon promotion, a much more complex matter. While it had been relatively easy to document racial discrimination as a barrier to employment, it was necessary to take into account other factors like skills and performance when trying to determine why someone had not advanced in the work force.

President Reagan spoke a language that those most opposed to affirmative action had been waiting to hear for a long time. The laws against discrimination remained on the books, to be sure, but the new president and his commitment to safeguarding the interests of his wealthy and conservative corporate backers made it clear that pro-active enforcement had a decidedly low priority.

Perhaps the most disturbing symbol of the dramatic sea change was his appointment of Clarence Thomas to the chairmanship of EEOC. Although black himself and a clear beneficiary of affirmative action, Thomas made no secret of his conviction that minorities needed no special considerations. He was publicly vocal in his opposition to remedies like goals, timetables and quotas.

In 1984 the Equal Employment Opportunity Commission established a new enforcement policy that basically reduced the volume of selective litigation. The emphasis now was to focus more upon conciliation. Increasingly, the determination of which cases would go to court returned to Washington. For several years it had been customary for the agency's general counsel to sign off on recommendations from the field and for the commissioners virtually to rubber stamp their executive attorney's authorizations. Now, although the process was cumbersome and eventually stopped, the politically appointed commissioners started to take a more active role in reviewing each case. One of the net effects of this change was a whittling away of the regional attorneys' authority.

By 1985, after nineteen years of government service, Hollowell was more than ready to retire. For many years, through times that sorely tested his unfailing courtesy and decorum, he had done his part to keep a fledgling agency on track. His first love had been the practice of law. His finest hours had been in courtrooms where his keen mind, rhetorical skills and dramatic presence instilled hope in the black community and earned the respect of his white adversaries. Those trials and appeals had justifiably earned him lasting fame and honor.

Yet, during the years of EEOC the applause had died. Their personal admiration of the man who had fought for civil rights continued, but many of his former colleagues-in-arms suspended that high regard when they dealt with him as a government representative. It had not been an easy road for Hollowell to walk.

Nevertheless, he had no regrets. As he reflected on nearly two decades of implementing the programs that his battles in the courtroom had helped to make possible, he could see progress. Whatever the critics of EEOC might say, he knew that the program had never sought to advance unqualified people. Furthermore, it had led to the important promotion of men and women whose career tracks would otherwise have prematurely come to an end. Finally, the much-maligned emphasis upon affirmative action had been remedial and corrective; it did not come into play until the government had demonstrated conclusively that discrimination had governed an organization's hiring policies.

In 1935, Charles Houston, who as Dean of Howard University's Law School transformed that institution into the nation's premier civil rights legal training academy, declared that any attorney who was not a social engineer was a parasite on society. Donald Hollowell was never a parasite.

§§§

There remained one more career shift. Marvin Arrington, the President of Atlanta's City Council, had been steadily building a strong law practice. Starting after graduation from Emory Law School, he first established a reputation as a criminal defense attorney and then moved on to capture a significant list of corporate and municipal clients. His firm consisted of a first-rate, biracial team of young attorneys. Missing from the equation, though, was a seasoned veteran who would bring both experience and prestige to the partnership.

Arrington had been in awe of Hollowell since the first time he saw him in a courtroom, defending Atlanta University Center students who had been arrested during the sit-ins. Hollowell's legal skills, his political influence behind the scenes and his civic leadership made him an almost larger-than-life role model. The younger attorney credits Hollowell with inspiring him to become a lawyer. He also has a keen appreciation of the way in which Hollowell's accomplishments, as well as his personal and financial sacrifices, laid the foundation for the success that Arrington and other younger black attorneys have enjoyed.

To honor his legal hero, Arrington named the conference room in his Mitchell Street offices after Hollowell and repeated the practice when the firm relocated to the twenty-second floor of the First Atlanta Tower and then to its current suite of offices in the 191 Peachtree Street Tower. Soon thereafter, the opportunity to expand upon those tributes presented itself. Arrington encountered Hollowell on the street one day as the semi-retired attorney was on his way to the courthouse library to do some research on behalf of a client. As they talked he became increasingly disturbed that the man he revered did not have an institutional base. Arrington would later say, "If a white attorney of Don's stature had retired from public service, a major law partnership would immediately have made arrangements to bring him into the firm." He subsequently invited Hollowell to become counsel to the firm and gave the partnership a new name — Arrington & Hollowell. The law firm, aided by Hollowell's involvement, grew and prospered.

§§§

The telling of the Hollowell story cannot conclude without one final mention of his fifty-five year marriage. It is a remarkable union — marked by mutual love, admiration and respect — that had to survive decades of pressure that might have crushed other relationships. During the first nine years of their marriage the Hollowells were able to see each other only sporadically. Even after they established a home in Atlanta, his travels and her studies also separated them for long stretches of time. However, they have validated that old truism about absence encouraging fondness. The courageous legal pioneer and his fully liberated wife, whether together or apart, draw great strength from each other.

In a letter to her on the occasion of their forty-seventh wedding anniversary, Hollowell wrote:

> ...*you were always a source of pride for me as we moved together in many varied societies...in church, academe, with the politicians, among our respective peers, with the poor and the affluent. Yes, whether it was the Johnsons or Carters, governors, other politicos, bishops, university presidents' families or run-of-the-mill [folk], you were able to be yourself and be a source of pride to me. As time has passed, you have had to suffer because you were the wife of this so-called civil rights lawyer. Yet you bore up like the solid woman of strength you are. As we look back, I am pleased to say I have been wonderfully blessed by having you as my wonderful wife....*

ENDNOTES

[1] Morris Brown College in 1966 promoted her to the status of full professor. She remained in that position until her retirement in 1982, after thirty-five years of service to the institution. Today she is a Professor Emeritus and a Trustee of the college.

[2] See Chapter 10.

[3] House Rules Committee Chairman Howard Smith had added "sex" to the list of prohibited bases of discrimination in an attempt to kill the legislation.

[4] See Chapter 7.

EPILOGUE

Donald Hollowell is officially retired. Nonetheless, his telephone at home rings steadily, and people continue to seek his advice and counsel. He is in frequent demand as a speaker—so much so that his wife each February jokingly expresses her longing for the end of Black History Month. He is an authentic icon—someone who, as model and mentor, has profoundly affected both the lives of thousands of individuals and the course of the American struggle to make democracy a reality.

Langston Hughes, in one of his most famous poems, asked:

> What happens to a dream deferred?
> Does it dry up
> like a raisin in the sun?
> Or fester like a sore—
> And then run?
> Does it stink like rotten meat?
> Or crust and sugar over—
> like a syrupy sweet?
> Maybe it just sags
> like a heavy load.
> Or does it explode?[1]

Forty-five years after Donald Hollowell began to practice law in Georgia, it is sometimes difficult to remember how thoroughly the virus of racial segregation had spread through society. Discrimination and psychological abuse were a daily reality for virtually every black person, and physical brutality was a constant threat. This wholesale intimidation had succeeded in creating a stifling climate of fear. Black people, as the principal targets of racism, lived in constant dread of what could happen to them, but sympathetic whites also knew the danger of aligning themselves too closely with the oppressed. And deep down, the oppressors were also frightened. Even if they could not admit it, they knew in their hearts that dreams deferred might not just shrivel up; they might even explode.

The only cure that could transform this sick situation was courage. Donald Hollowell's courage revived hope. It inspired bravery and daring in others and, gradually, it helped to bring healing. Dreams no longer had to fester and rot. They could ripen into reality. They could help to create the world that Langston Hughes further described in another poem:

> A world I dream where black or white,
> Whatever race you be,
> Will share the bounties of the earth
> And every man is free,
> Where wretchedness will hang its head,
> And joy, like a pearl,
> Attend the needs of all mankind,
> Of such I dream—
> Our world.[2]

The realization of that dream — the same dream of which Martin Luther King, Jr. spoke — remains in the future. Yet, on Hollowell's now infrequent trips to his office at the Arrington & Hollowell law firm in downtown Atlanta, he has the opportunity to reflect upon the changes he has witnessed. The partnership is far removed by more than geography from the small towns of Kansas in which he grew to adolescence. It bears little resemblance to the modest space in the Cannolene Building on Hunter Street from which he once set out daily to challenge the established order or to his federal offices where he struggled to translate legal victories into practical opportunity for minorities and women.

One ascends to the handsomely appointed suite on the thirty-fifth floor of 191 Peachtree Street in elevators whose walls are lined with brass-rimmed panels of polished European marble. The soaring granite tower, connected to a deluxe hotel, is headquarters for prestigious corporations and law firms. Business and community leaders regularly huddle over power lunches in the private club on the fourth floor. Symbols of success abound.

However, Hollowell, who still lives in the modest home to which he and his wife moved more than forty years ago, prefers to measure his accomplishments by different standards. He would prefer to point to desegregated institutions of higher education, increased voter registration rolls of African-American citizens, the rise in the number of black judges at all levels of the judiciary and a steadily growing corps of black elected officials. The list of positive social changes and transformed attitudes that he helped to bring about is a long one.

Fifty years ago, this champion of justice heard what Paul Robeson described as a sacred call. He responded to the call. Choosing public good over private gain and risk over reward, he selected the road that most of his peers did not travel. In the words of Robert Frost, "that decision made all the difference..." for him and for his fellow citizens.

ENDNOTES

[1] American Negro Poetry, edited and an Introduction by Arna Bontemps, New York, Hill and Wang, p. 67.

[2] *Ibid.*, p. 75.

LIST OF CASES CITED

CITATIONS OF MAJOR CASES DESCRIBED IN THE NARRATIVE

Chapter 1

Holmes v. Danner
        Case No. 450; 191 F. Supp. 394 (M.D. Ga. 1961)

Chapter 6

(Also Chapter 7)

Ward v. Board of Regents of Georgia
        191 F. Supp 491, (N.D. Ga. 1957)

State v. Nash (1953-1954)
        Fulton County Superior Ct. - December term (1953
        Indictments #70024 - Not guilty - March term; #70025 & #70026 - dead docketed.

Chapter 7

NAACP, et al. v. T. V. Williams
        98 Ga. App. 74, 104 S.E.2d 243
        98 Ga. App. 753, 107 S.E.2d 243 (1958)

Hunt et al. v. Arnold, et al (Georgia Board of Regents)
        Civil Action No. 5781; 172 F. Supp. 847 (1959)

H.D. Coke v. City of Atlanta, Dobbs House, et al.
        Civil Action No. 6733 (N.D. Ga.) 184 F. Supp. 579

Brazier v. Cherry No. 18620
        U.S. Court of Appeals Fifth Circuit
        293 F.2d 404 (1961)
   also   Civil Action 475, (M.D. Ga.)

Calhoun et al. v. A.O. Latimer
        C. A. No. 6298, (N.D. Ga. 1962)
        623 S. Ct. (1964)
        377 U.S. 263, 84 Supreme Court 1235
        Argued March 31, 1964, decided May 25, 1964

Chapter 8

King v. The State (two cases) 38648, 38718
    Court of Appeals of Georgia; 119 S.E.2d 77, 103 Ga. App. 272 (1961)

Chapter 9

(Also Chapter 10)

State v. Ware   Superior Court of Baker County
    Pataula Judicial Circuit (1963)
    Indictments #933 - Albany Circuit, #934, #935, #987

Ware v. Warren Johnson   USDC Middle Dist. (1961)
    (Records unavailable at court or archives)

Cobb v. The State No. 21578, Supreme Court of Georgia
    218 Ga. 10, 126 S.E.2d, 231
    Argued March 12, 1962, Decided May 14, 1962

Cobb v. The State No. 22166, Supreme Court of Georgia
    219 Ga. 388, 133 S.E.2d 596.

Chapter 10

Fair v. Balkcom   1184 Supreme Court of Georgia
    216 Ga. 721, 119 S.E.691
    Argued March 13, 1961, decided April 6, 1961
    MLK case when he was arrested in Albany (1961)

Shirley Gaines v. Dougherty Board of Education
    Case No. 764; 222 F. Supp. 166 (M.D. Ga. 1963)

Chapter 11

Peyton Road and Harlan Road case - Superior Court of Fulton County
    (1962-63/64?)

State v. Frank Doomus   (The Augusta Story - same as Delta Nine case)
    Richmond County Superior Court - March term (1962)
    Augusta, Georgia - Indictments #22, #23, #24, #25

Ashton B. Jones v. The State
    219 Ga. 848, 136 S.E.2d 358 (1964)

Cases Cited

Harris v. Chappell
Aelony v. Pace
Harris et al v. Pace
      RRR (Race Relations Reporter) Vol. 8, p. 1355
      (M. D. Ga. Americus Division)

      Georgia Supreme Court No. 22276, (1963)

Roy C. Bell v. Dental Associations
      Case No. 7966; 231 F. Supp. 299 (N.D. Ga. 1964)

Mardon Walker v. The State
      220 Ga. 415, 139 S.E.2d 278 (1964)
      381 U.S. 355, 85 S. Ct. 1557, 14 L.Ed.2d 681 (1965)
      221 Ga. 181, 144 S.E.2d 172

Georgia v. Rachel, et al.   No. 147
      U.S. S. Ct. (1953-56); 384 U.S. 780, 86 S. Ct. 1783, 16 L. Ed. 2d 925
      Decided June 20, 1966

Turner, et al. v. Goolsby, et al.
      Civil Action No. 1226; 255 F. Supp. 724 (1965)
      (S.D. Ga., Augusta Division
      Supplemental Opinion May 20, 1966

George F. Willis Jr., et al v. Pickrick Restaurant
      231 F. Supp. 396; (N.D. Ga. 1964), stay denied, 379 U.S. 241

George F. Willis Jr., et al. v. Pickrick Restaurant
      234 F. Supp. 179 (N.D. Ga. 1964); See also U.S. S. Ct. October term 1965.

Heart of Atlanta Motel, Inc. v. United States, et al.
      379 U.S. 241, 85 S. Ct. 348, 13 L.Ed.2d 258 (1964)

Haldred Overstreet v. Savannah Branch NAACP, et al.
      142 S.E.2d 816, 221 Ga. 16 (1965)

Credits and Permissions

We hereby give grateful acknowledgement to the National Broadcasting Company, Inc. (NBC) for the use of all photos on pages 5 and 6 of this "Book" pertaining to Martin Luther King, Jr. and his release from the Reidsville State Prison, Reidsville, Georgia in October, 1960. All rights are reserved by NBC.

We are grateful to the United Negro College Fund (UNCF) and Bud Smith, photographer, for the use of the photo on the cover of *The Sacred Call*, as well as the display of the cover design of the Summer/Fall, 1993 issue of *"A Mind Is"*, page P-36.

We are grateful to the Kappa Alpha Psi Fraternity, Inc. for their courtesy to allow us to display the cover design of the 1968 *Kappa Journal* of two Kappa Alpha Psi Laureates - C. Rodger Wilson and Donald L. Hollowell.

All other photos in this book are the property of Donald L. Hollowell and Louise T. Hollowell except the photos of the Buffalo Soldier Monument, Chief Warrant Officer 4 Harry H. Hollowell, (Ret.) and Joint Chiefs of Staff Colin Powell (Ret.).

All rights reserved. No part of this book may be reproduced or transmitted except for brief excerpts in any form or by any means, electronic or otherwise, without the permission in writing from the owners.

AWARDS AND HONORS

DOCTOR OF LAWS, 1961
(Honoris Causa)
Clark College

DISTINGUISHED SERVICE AWARD, 1961
College of Bishops and the Christian Methodist Episcopal Church

LEGAL EXCELLENCE IN THE CIVIL RIGHTS STRUGGLE, 1961
Zeta Phi Beta Sorority, Inc.
Epsilon Zeta Chapter

THE TWENTY SEVEN CLUB ACHIEVEMENT AWARD, 1961
The Twenty Seven Club

OUTSTANDING ACHIEVEMENT AWARD, 1963
Kappa Alpha Psi Fraternity, Inc.
Pi Chapter

OUTSTANDING ACHIEVEMENT AWARD, CIRCA 1964
Kappa Alpha Psi Fraternity, Inc.

ASSOCIATE OF ARTS, 1961
(Honoris Causa)
Massey Junior College

BROTHERHOOD AWARD, 1965
The National Conference of Christians and Jews

DEDICATED SERVICE AWARD, 1965
Christian Methodist Episcopal Church
Seventh Episcopal District

"LAWYER OF THE YEAR AWARD," 1965
NAACP Legal Defense and Educational Fund, Inc.

OUTSTANDING ALUMNUS AWARD, 1966
United Negro College Fund

SERVICE AWARD, 1966
Pine Acres Town and Country Club

APPRECIATION AWARD, 1967
Kappa Alpha Psi Fraternity, Inc.
Athens Alumni Chapter

Distinguished Service Award, 1967
Phi Alpha Delta Law Fraternity

OUTSTANDING INDIVIDUAL AWARD circa 1967
United Negro College Fund

CIVIL LIBERTIES AWARD, 1967
The American Civil Liberties Union of Georgia

CENTURY CLUB AWARD, 1968
Young Men's Christian Association

LAUREL WREATH AWARD, 1968
Kappa Alpha Psi Fraternity

LIFE MEMBERSHIP CERTIFICATE, 1968
Kappa Alpha Psi Fraternity, Inc.

OUTSTANDING SERVICE AWARD, 1968
Lane College

DISTINGUISHED MEMBER AWARD, 1969
Butler Street C. M. E. Church

EQUAL OPPORTUNITY DAY AWARD, 1969
The Atlanta Urban League, Inc.

OUTSTANDING CONTRIBUTION IN THE FIELD OF LAW, 1971
Human Relations and Civil Rights
Resurgens
City of Atlanta

OUTSTANDING SERVICE AWARD, 1973
Kappa Alpha Psi Fraternity, Inc.
Southern Province

SPECIAL ALUMNI AWARD, 1974
FOUNDERS DAY SPEAKER, 1974
Lane College

OUTSTANDING SERVICE AWARD, 1974
Kappa Alpha Psi Fraternity
Atlanta Alumni Chapter

UNSUNG HERO IN THE FIGHT FOR FREEDOM AWARD, 1974
National Association for the Advancement of Colored People
Southeast Region

CITIZENSHIP AWARD, 1975
Atlanta DeKalb Voters League

OUTSTANDING SERVICE IN GOVERNMENT AWARD, 1975
Board of Law Activities
Georgia Annual Conference, C. M. E. Church

A. T. WALDEN LIBERTY AWARD, 1976
Georgia Conference of Black Lawyers

ACHIEVEMENT IN CIVIL RIGHTS AWARD, 1976
The Atlanta Branch NAACP

DISTINGUISHED SERVICE AWARD, 1976
The Atlanta Branch NAACP

KAPPA ALPHA PSI AWARD, 1976
Kappa Alpha Psi Fraternity, Inc.
60th Grand Chapter Meeting

LIFE MEMBERSHIP CERTIFICATE, 1976
National Association for the Advancement of Colored People

SERVICE AWARD, 1976
Equal Employment Opportunity Commission, Atlanta Region Staff

DISTINGUISHED SERVICE AWARD, 1978
Kappa Alpha Psi Fraternity, Inc.
Gamma Kappa Chapter

PRESIDENT'S CLUB MEMBERSHIP, 1978
Lane College

SERVICE TO YOUTH AWARD, 1978-1984
YMCA of Metropolitan Atlanta
Board of Directors Legal Affairs Committee

ROY WILKINS "FREEDOM FIGHTER AWARD," 1979
The Atlanta Branch NAACP

ACHIEVEMENT AWARD, 1980
Kappa Alpha Psi Fraternity
Atlanta Alumni Chapter

ACHIEVEMENT AWARD, 1980
Kappa Alpha Psi Fraternity
Columbus (GA) Alumni Chapter

APPRECIATION AWARD, 1980
Interdenominational Theological Center and the Phillips School of Theology

SPECIAL RECOGNITION, 1981
Gate City Bar Association
and the Georgia Black Lawyers

CECELIA E. WASHINGTON MEMORIAL AWARD
FOR OUTSTANDING SERVICE, 1981
United Negro College Fund
National Alumni Council and the National Pre-Alumni Council

ALPHA KAPPA MU HONOR SOCIETY AWARD, 1982
Morris Brown College
Honor Society

Awards and Honors

COMMUNITY SERVICE AWARD, 1982
The Seventh Day Adventist Church

THURGOOD MARSHALL AWARD, 1983
Georgia State Chapter, NAACP

C. L. HARPER AWARD, 1984
Atlanta Branch NAACP

CHAMPION FOR CIVIL RIGHTS AWARD, 1984
Region V, NAACP

SERVICE AWARD, 1984
NAACP Diamond Jubilee Anniversary

SERVICE AWARD FOR OUTSTANDING PERFORMANCE AND COUNSEL, 1984
Decatur County Voters League

APPRECIATION AWARD, 1985
Kappa Alpha Psi Fraternity, Inc.
Atlanta Alumni Chapter

APPRECIATION AWARD, CIRCA 1985
193rd Year Church Anniversary Celebration, Butler Street Christian Methodist Episcopal Church

BLACK GEORGIAN OF THE YEAR AWARD, 1985
State Committee on the Life and History of Black Georgians

LIFE FELLOW, 1985
Southern Regional Council

JESSIE O. THOMAS COMMUNITY SERVICE AWARD, 1985
Atlanta Urban League, Inc.

DEDICATED CIVIL RIGHTS PATRIOT AWARD, 1985
United States EEOC Commission

DISTINGUISHED ACHIEVEMENT AWARD FOR FEDERAL SERVICE, 1985
Kappa Alpha Psi Fraternity
Atlanta Alumni Chapter

DEDICATED SERVICE AWARD, 1985
United States EEOC Commission'
Atlanta District Office

LAUREL WREATH LAUREATE, 1985
Kappa Alpha Psi Fraternity, Inc.
Atlanta Alumni Chapter

FOR LIBERTY AND JUSTICE UNDER THE LAW, LAW DAY, 1985
Gate City Bar Association

NATIONAL CONFERENCE OF CHRISTIANS AND JEWS AWARD, 1985
Georgia Region

OUTSTANDING SERVICE AWARD, 1985
LANE COLLEGE

LIFE FELLOW AWARD, 1985
Southern Regional Council

THURGOOD MARSHALL AWARD FOR DEDICATED SERVICE, 1985
Concerned Black Clergy of Metro Atlanta

DEVOTED AND DILIGENT SERVICE TO THE CAUSE OF CIVIL RIGHTS AWARD, 1986
Alpha Kappa Alpha Sorority, Inc.

DISTINGUISHED SERVICE TO THE CAUSE OF CIVIL RIGHTS AWARD, 1986
Alpha Kappa Alpha Sorority, Inc.
South Atlantic Region, 33rd Conference

OUTSTANDING SERVICE TO THE CIVIL RIGHTS STRUGGLE, 1986
The Atlanta Constitution Newspaper

APPRECIATION FOR EFFECTIVE PROFESSIONAL SERVICE AWARD, 1987
Phillips School of Theology (ITC)

GERTRUDE E. RUSH AWARD, 1987
National Bar Association

MERITORIOUS SERVICE AWARD, 1987
Interdenominational Theological Center

"WE THE PEOPLE" SERVICE AWARD, 1987
Cascade United Methodist Church

SERVICE AWARD, 1987
U. S. Equal Employment Commission

TRAILBLAZER AWARD, 1987
Antioch Baptist Church

TRADITION OF EXCELLENCE AWARD, 1989
State Bar of Georgia
General Practice and Trial Section

DISTINGUISHED LEADERSHIP AWARD, 1989
Kappa Alpha Psi Fraternity, Inc.
Atlanta Alumni Chapter

RESOLUTION FOR CONTRIBUTIONS TO THE ADVANCEMENT OF BLACKS AT THE UNIVERSITY OF GEORGIA, circa 1990
The University of Georgia
Black Faculty and Staff Organization

HUMAN RIGHTS AWARD, 1990
Clark Atlanta University

OUTSTANDING SUPPORT AWARD, 1990
Butler Street Y. M. C. A.

TIMELESS CONTRIBUTION AWARD, 1990
Gate City Bar Association

CERTIFICATE OF APPRECIATION, 1991
Phillips School of Theology (ITC)

AFRICAN AMERICAN HERITAGE AWARD, circa 1991
Federal Employees, Department of Justice
Citizens Trust Bank Building

SERVICE AWARD, 1990
"Donald L. Hollowell Day"
City of Atlanta

APPRECIATION AWARD, 1991
Health Resources Management, Inc.

NESTOR AWARD FOR CONTRIBUTIONS TO THE LEGAL PROFESSION, 1991
Georgia Legal History Foundation

OUTSTANDING SERVICE AWARD, 1991
Lane College Alumni Association

HONORABLE ACHIEVEMENT AND RECOGNITION AWARD, 1991
Kappa Alpha Psi Fraternity, Inc.
Zeta Iota Chapter

EVELYN HAWKINS HOOD DISTINGUISHED SERVICE AWARD, 1992
Sigma Gamma Rho Sorority, Inc.

PIONEER AWARD IN LAW, 1992
The Apex Museum

DISTINGUISHED SERVICE AWARD, 1993
Loyola University, Chicago
Black Law Students Association

CERTIFICATE OF RECOGNITION, 1994
Phillips School of Theology (ITC)

Awards and Honors

DISTINGUISHED SERVICE AWARD FOR EQUAL OPPORTUNITIES FOR ALL MANKIND, 1993
Arrington and Hollowell Staff

DOCTOR OF LAWS, 1994
(Honoris Causa)
Clark Atlanta University

HEROS, SAINTS AND LEGENDS AWARD, 1995
The Apex Museum

DISTINGUISHED SERVICE AWARD, 1994
The College of Bishops
The Christian Methodist Episcopal Church

LEADERSHIP AWARD, 1995
the Atlanta Bar Association

BEN JOHNSON PUBLIC SERVICES AWARD, 1995
College of Law
Georgia State University

LEADERSHIP AWARD, 1995
Atlanta Bar Association

"OUR WIND BENEATH OUR WINGS" AWARD, 1996
Benita Brown Bryant Award Fund, Inc.

CERTIFICATE FOR FAITHFUL SERVICE, 1996
Sixth Episcopal District, Lay Department
Christian Methodist Episcopal Church
University of Georgia

DOCTOR OF LAWS, 1996
(Honoris Causa)
University of the District of Columbia

NATIONAL BLACK COLLEGE ALUMNI HALL OF FAME Inductee, 1996
Lane College

OUTSTANDING GEORGIA CITIZEN RECOGNITION, 1996
State of Georgia
Secretary of State

THE SPIRIT OF EXCELLENCE INSPIRATION AWARD, 1996
American Bar Association

LENGTH OF SERVICE AWARD, 1996
U. S. Equal Employment Opportunity Commission

LIFETIME ACHIEVEMENT AWARD, 1997
Gate City Bar Association

CERTIFICATE OF APPRECIATION, 1997
Atlanta Public Schools

BLACK HERITAGE AWARD, 1997
Lane College

SCALES OF JUSTICE AWARD, 1997
Atlanta Association of Bench and Bar Spouses

About the Author:

Louise T. Hollowell

Louise Thornton Hollowell has been married to Donald Hollowell for fifty-five years. A native of Iron City, Georgia, she is a Magna Cum Laude graduate of Morris Brown College, from which she received a B.A. in English, and of Atlanta University, which awarded her a master's degree in English. She also did advanced studies and conducted Special Thesis Research at the University of Chicago. Further, she studied human relations at Boston University's Osgood Hill Laboratory and pursued the doctoral degree at the University of Pennsylvania.

Prior to beginning her higher education she was a successful businesswoman in New York and Atlanta, where she managed and was the head teacher at the Apex Beauty College and later owned the Modelle Beauty Salon.

Mrs. Hollowell was a member of the English department for thirty-five years at Morris Brown College, where she is now Professor of English (Emeritus) and a member of the Board of Trustees. She is also a charter member of the Alpha Kappa Mu and Omicron Delta Kappa honor societies of Morris Brown College and was a member of the National Council of Negro Women. She was honored by the Council in 1982.

A former Trustee and now a Steward of Allen Temple A.M.E. Church, she was honored by that congregation on Women's Day in 1983 for her "Outstanding Achievements in Education and Service." The Women for Morris Brown College presented her with "A Salute to Our First President" in 1986. In 1988 the Atlanta Barristers Wives dedicated its Founders Day to her for her contributions as the organization's first president; and in 1992 the Atlanta Association of Bar and Bench Spouses (AABBS) honored her for life member and founder, and for distinguished service, leadership and participation in the organization.

Mrs. Hollowell also is the recipient of numerous teaching awards and other recognitions of achievement from Morris Brown College and her former classes. In 1971-1972, the *Morris Brown College Yearbook,* which was dedicated to her, cited her as a "great teacher" during her tenure as a faculty member. She is a Life Member of the NAACP, and a member of the YWCA, Alpha Kappa Alpha Sorority, the AABBS, the Kappa Alpha Psi Fraternity Silhouettes, the President's Club of Morris Brown College, the President's Club of Clark Atlanta University, and the National and Georgia Democratic Clubs, as well as the Fort Benning Alumni Veterans Club and the Morris Brown College Visionary Club.

Upon her retirement in 1982 she established an English/Alpha Kappa Mu Scholarship at Morris Brown College.

About the Author:

Martin C. Lehfeldt

Martin C. Lehfeldt, as President of The Lehfeldt Company in Atlanta, has been providing planning, evaluation, fundraising, facilitation and editorial services to national, regional and local nonprofit organizations since 1979.

A native of New York City, he adopted Atlanta as his home in 1969, when he became Vice President for Development at Clark College. After seven years of service at that institution, he became Director of Development for the Atlanta University Center, where he directed the successful campaign for funds to construct the Robert W. Woodruff Library.

Mr. Lehfeldt received his B.A. in English from Haverford College and the Master of Divinity degree from Union Theological Seminary in

New York. He has been a reporter for the Youngstown(Ohio) *Vindicator* and the president of Academic Associates, Inc., a small service company. From 1965 until 1969 he was the Director of Internship Programs for the Woodrow Wilson National Fellowship Foundation in Princeton, New Jersey, where he recruited, placed and oversaw the work of young faculty members at more than sixty historically black colleges.

He is an Elder of Central Presbyterian Church, a member of Central Atlanta Progress, a trustee of Johnson C. Smith Theological Seminary, a board member and former chair of the Center for Positive Aging, a board member of The Sullivan Center, and a member of the Advisory Board of the Open Door Community. He also has served as board chairman of Literacy Action, Inc. and of the Academy Theatre.

Mr. Lehfeldt is a graduate of Leadership Atlanta and President of the Haverford College Class of 1961. His alma mater honored him with the Haverford Award in 1976. He is the author of professional articles, portions of *The Agile Servant*, a book about community foundations, and two produced plays, *Back to Bethlehem* and *Can You Hear Me in the Back Pew*. He is married to the former Linda Graham and has three children.